Allan Williams is Professor of Organizational and Occupational Psychology at the City University Business School. He is also Director of its Centre for Personnel Research and Enterprise Development, which he founded in 1978. He read psychology at Manchester University, and received his MA and PhD in Occupational Psychology at Birkbeck College. He is a Chartered Occupational Psychologist. Since entering the management education field in 1963, he has researched and consulted in many well-known organizations, and published widely in the human resource management and organization development literature. He has been particularly active in promoting the use of psychological theories and methods in the development of managerial and organizational effectiveness.

Paul Dobson is a Chartered Psychologist and lecturer in Organizational Behaviour at City University Business School. He read psychology at North East London Polytechnic and then undertook postgraduate research in Occupational Psychology at Birkbeck College. He obtained his PhD at the City University. He taught applied psychology at Middlesex Polytechnic before joining the Business School, where he teaches organizational behaviour on the MBA programmes. He has carried out research for many public and private sector organizations and has published widely in the field of assessment and selection.

Mike Walters was educated in Nottingham and at Queens' College, Cambridge. He completed a postgraduate Diploma in Personnel Management and then worked in personnel for Shell and the BBC. Between 1987 and 1989, he was Manager – Organization and Human Resource Planning with the Institute of Personnel Management. He is currently a Senior Consultant with ER Consultants. He is a corporate member of the IPM and the author of *What About the Workers? Making employee surveys work* (IPM, 1990).

CHANGING CULTURE

New organizational approaches

Second Edition

Allan Williams, Paul Dobson and Mike Walters

Institute of Personnel Management

© Institute of Personnel Management 1989, 1993

First published 1989
Reprinted 1990
Second edition 1993

Typeset by The Eastern Press (Typesetting Division), Frome, Somerset
and printed in Great Britain by the Cromwell Press, Broughton Gifford, Wiltshire.

British Library Cataloguing in Publication Data

Williams, Allan P. O.
  Changing Culture: New Organizational
  Approaches. — 2 Rev. ed. — (Developing
  Strategies Series)
  I. Title   II. Series
  658.3

  ISBN 0–85292–533–6

ipm

INSTITUTE OF PERSONNEL MANAGEMENT
IPM House, Camp Road, Wimbledon, London SW19 4UX
Tel: 081-946-9100   Fax: 081-946-2570
Registered office as above. Registered Charity No. 215797
A company limited by guarantee. Registered in England No. 198002

Contents

Acknowledgements

The authors wish to thank the following: first, the contributing organizations, without whose support this project would not have been possible, in particular Margaret Attwood (Mid-Essex Health Authority), Peter Cox (J Sainsbury plc), Alan Hepburn (Jaguar Cars Ltd), David Kitchen (Johnson Matthey plc), Bob Lisney (Hampshire County Council), Mike Mosson (Royal Bank of Scotland), Terry Murphy (formerly Abbey National Building Society), Mike Oram (Toshiba UK Ltd), J A Salt (Marley plc), M B Smaje (Unisys Ltd), Mike Williams (Rank Xerox UK Ltd), B B Wilson (National Freight Consortium), P Worden (BP Chemicals International); secondly, the members of the IPM working party on Organizational Culture Change for their ideas and support throughout the study: Mike Stanton, Chairman (Coopers & Lybrand), Tony Attew (Digital), Alan Cowling (Middlesex Polytechnic), David Dawson (independent consultant), Mike Martin (Texaco), Judith Mills (Marks & Spencer), Christina Vaughan Griffiths (independent consultant), Vivienne Walker (Northern Ireland Southern Health and Social Services Board).

Preface

The first edition of *Changing Culture* was written in the late 1980s. At the time, the concept of organizational culture was a highly fashionable topic in the UK, dominating both popular and academic management journals. Peters and Waterman's *In Search of Excellence* had been around since 1982, but its implications were still being widely discussed and debated by UK managers. Tom Peter's *Thriving on Chaos* had just emerged, and was stirring up further reactions. The work of other commentators in the field – Terrence Deal and Allan Kennedy, Roger Pascale, Roger Harrison, Edgar Schein and Charles Handy to mention only some of the most well known – was well established, but was still being assimilated by practising managers. Above all, managers across a whole range of industries were wrestling with what 'culture' meant for their particular organizations. And many of these – over half of our original survey sample – were actively engaged in culture change programmes aimed at improving organizational performance.

Against this background, the Institute of Personnel Management commissioned the research for *Changing Culture*, with the aim of shedding some light on the UK experience of culture change. In conducting the research, we uncovered some fascinating case studies of practical culture change. We highlighted some significant conclusions about the nature of culture, and about the processes required to change it. We identified an increasingly critical role for the human resource function as the 'culture managers' of the organization. And, above all, we hope that we succeeded in shedding some new light on the complex challenges facing organizations in a world of accelerating change.

Into the 1990s

In the years since our original research and the publication of the first edition of *Changing Culture*, the dust has settled to some degree. Organizational culture is now a well-established concept. It has been joined on the management agenda by a host of related topics – the management of discontinuous change, empowerment, the learning organization, business process re-engineering, performance management, competitive advantage, and countless others, many if not all of which have cultural implications. Quality tools such as total quality management which at the time of our original publication were still seen as relatively pioneering in the UK have now become an accepted and important part of life for organizations of all types and sizes.

At the same time, while interest in culture remains undiminished, it is possible in many organizations to discern a more thoughtful and focused approach to culture change. This reflects a variety of factors – greater management understanding of the determinants and components of culture, the lessons learned from successful or unsuccessful culture change initiatives elsewhere, and, particularly in difficult operating conditions, an increasing emphasis on business and performance outputs as key drivers of culture change. A widely reported article by R Schaffer and H Thomson in the *Harvard Business Review*,[1] for example, reinforces one of the central conclusions we drew from our original case studies, namely that culture change needs to be driven by a focus on business strategy and performance, as well as by programmes designed specifically to change culture, behaviour and values.

Revisiting culture

Against this background, it is fair to ask whether the concept of organizational culture is still an attractive and useful concept for managers. Over the next decade, will organizations really be able to achieve sustainable competitive advantage or performance improvement by addressing issues of corporate behaviours and beliefs? Or have we moved into an era when short-term commercial or operating targets are likely to be more relevant than the lengthy efforts involved in creating a culture in support of organizational strategy?

In revisiting our research for this new edition, our conclusion is that, if anything, the developments of the last few years have *increased* the relevance and importance of organizational culture. It is therefore worth reaffirming the conclusions we reached in our original research, as well as supplementing our original 15 case studies with three new cases. These new case studies provide the opportunity to highlight and elaborate some of the guidelines we put forward for changing organizational culture – for example, the need to adopt a revolutionary rather than an evolutionary approach in order to help 'unfreeze' the existing culture (see chapters 3 and 4), the need to recognize the strengths and weaknesses of the traditional 'top down' approach to change (see chapter 4), and the need to adopt a systems or holistic approach to culture change (see chapters 2 and 3).

Accelerating change

In the years since the original research, perhaps the most significant development has been the accelerating pace of change across all sectors of the economy. The effective management of change has long been a key element of corporate performance, and over the last decade the speed and unpredictability of such change has increased almost exponentially. Now, the impact of such change is so widely felt that few organizations or sectors have been left untouched. In the private sector, companies have been affected by the globalization of competition, by dramatically shortening production and development cycles, by quantum leaps in technology, by the often frantic intensification of competition, and most recently by the effects of economic recession. In the public sector, change has become endemic. Most of the public utilities have experienced some form of privatization, and the remainder expect to undergo significant commercialization in the near future. Local authorities have experienced a major expansion of compulsory competitive tendering, allied with growing pressures on spending. In the Civil Service, we have seen the creation of the Next Steps Agencies and the introduction of market testing. In the Health Service, we have seen the introduction of the internal market and the increasing shift to Trust status. In education, there have been significant structural changes at all levels. And in all parts of the public sector, the Citizens' Charter has focused new attention on issues of customer requirements and operational performance.

This intensification of change has driven many organizations to rethink and revisit issues of organizational culture. As we indicate in chapter 1, in this kind of environment, an inflexible and deeply internalized culture can actually undermine organizational performance. For example, the corporate cultures of many long-established organizations – including some 'blue chip' companies, as well as public sector bodies – have traditionally emphasized values such as safety, control, low risk-taking, and gradual evolution. Over the past few years, many of these organizations have faced the challenge of changing their culture, not to accommodate other steady-state values but to foster a climate that can handle continuous, potentially discontinuous change.

For organizations operating in such turbulent environments, an adaptive and innovative culture is likely to be a prerequisite for achieving high performance. This may, for example, involve the empowering of local-level managers so that they have the authority and ability to respond immediately to environmental or competitive shifts. It may require the building of analytical and problem-solving skills and processes, enabling managers to deal systematically and efficiently with unprecedented challenges. It may lead to the breaking down of traditional hierarchies and lines of authority, or the loosening of conventional job definitions. It may be underpinned by the promotion of cross-functional networking or teamworking, so that organizations can be rapidly reconfigured to meet changing circumstances. It may demand the redefinition of relationships between different parts of the organization, or a more precise focus on key business or operational processes. And, above all, it is likely to require a precise and universally understood definition of core organizational goals and values, so that local responsiveness is directed always towards the organization's best interests.

Many of these trends were already evident in many of our original case studies, although at the time some expected to be undertaking a once-and-for-all change rather than embarking on a process of continuous revolution. Now, attitudes to culture change are typified by the Royal Mail among our new case studies. The Royal Mail perceives its recent major restructuring as only one more step in a continuing process of change. One of its key objectives has been to develop the skills, attitudes and infrastructure to enable the organization to respond rapidly and effectively to external challenges. Specific goals have included the increasing empowerment of local managers, the promotion of team-working skills, the removal of management layers and the shortening of communication lines, the development of a strategic focus, and the development of more effective processes for market and product development. The aim has been to create a business which can handle not only the challenges of today and tomorrow, but also the as yet unknown developments of the day after.

The conclusion from this is that culture change is likely to become more, rather than less, significant over the coming decade. Increasingly, though, organizations will have to treat such change, not as a one-off, discrete phenomenon, but as a continuing process which constantly reviews, refines and improves the organization's overall capacity to respond to external developments.

Evolution and revolution

One of the core assumptions behind our original research was that culture change is inevitably a slow process. Deal and Kennedy, in their pioneering work, *Corporate Cultures*, estimated that it can take anything from five to eight years to have any real impact on the culture of a large organization.[2] The experiences of our case study organizations – most of whom saw themselves as only part of the way down the road when we interviewed them – gave us little reason to doubt this.

To a large degree, our views on this remain unchanged – and, indeed, as we suggest above, the experience of culture change will increasingly become a permanent aspect of organizational life. Nevertheless, many organizations have begun to express some cynicism about the long-term timescales against which many culture change exercises have been operating. All too commonly, the argument that 'you can't change culture overnight' becomes an excuse for not changing culture at all. Organizations become reluctant to apply explicit performance measures to the change process. Managers fail to change their behaviour today, because they are working towards some unspecified tomorrow. Employees learn to accommodate the language and artefacts of the new culture without fundamentally altering their beliefs and values. In short, the new culture is only superficially different from the old, and traditional behaviour patterns or ways of doing things soon reassert themselves.

It is this experience which underlies Shaffer and Thompson's rejection of 'programme driven change', or Roger Pascale's recent emphasis on the importance of conflict and revolutionary change in organizations like Ford in the United States.[3]

Countless organizations – from local authorities through public utilities to commercial companies – can testify to the difficulty of achieving lasting change through a long-term process. As a result, an increasing number of organizations are considering the possibility of applying revolutionary change as an impetus towards their longer-term goals. The aim is to create an environment where the old ways of thinking and acting are simply no longer tenable – where employees are compelled to develop new values and behaviours. The expectation is, not that the new culture will be created overnight, but that the 'unfreezing' of the old culture will be rapid and permanent, providing a strong foundation for the development of new values and behaviour. In our early chapters, we recognize the importance of this unfreezing process, and a more revolutionary approach is compatible with our theoretical framework.

Among our new case studies, both the Royal Mail and McVitie's are powerful examples of this trend – both organizations are embarked on long-term change processes designed to optimize their performance over the next decade. In both cases, however, the recent restructuring is seen as a major and dramatic step along this road. It has established systems and structures designed to underpin the new culture. It has provided extensive and successful experience of managing in the new style. And above all it has compelled the organization to relinquish its old ways and face a range of new challenges. As a result, both organizations believe that they have provided a major impetus to the longer-term process of culture change.

Top-down and bottom-up

Alongside this growing focus on revolutionary change, there has also been a growing debate about the process by which culture change is managed. The traditional assumption –

unquestioned by the majority of our original case study companies – is that culture change must be 'top-down'. Indeed, a number of the case study organizations commented on the importance of energetic and charismatic leadership in driving through the changes.

More recently, however, commentators such as Beer, Eisenstat and Spector[4] have questioned this assumption, arguing that top-down change programmes rarely produce significant or lasting changes at lower levels in the organization. Above all, it is argued, such change programmes do not take account of lower-level concerns and motivations, do not involve junior staff in the identification and development of their objectives, and so do not succeed in building universal commitment and ownership. The solution suggested by Beer and his colleagues is for senior managers to 'direct a non-directive process', by creating a climate for change, defining core objectives and values, disseminating examples of success and failure, and providing support for all parts of the organization to develop their own responses.

Much of this was implicit in our original conclusions, which emphasized the need both for clear leadership *and* for effective participation in the decision-making process (see, for example, chapter 4). Among our new case studies, this trend is even more clearly discernible. In James Cropper plc, for example, much of the detail of the change process was developed by performance improvement teams, dealing with specific problems and objectives, and developing solutions which suited their needs. The role of the senior management team, and of the consultants who supported the process, was to set the overall aims and benchmarks, to facilitate the process, and to coordinate and manage the outputs. In the Royal Mail, similarly, the detailed planning of the change exercise was devolved to an interlinked network of functional and divisional planning teams. In both cases, the result of this approach was to build a high level of commitment to and ownership of the change process and achievements.

Holistic change

Above all, over the last few years, there has been increasing confirmation of our conclusion that culture change cannot stand alone, and that it has to be part of an overall set of mutually reinforcing organizational improvement activities. This awareness was implicit in many of our original case study organizations. In a number of the organizations, for example, the process of culture change was introduced in response to some significant organizational or business imperative which simultaneously inspired parallel activities in other areas. Indeed, the culture change was sometimes consciously intended to reinforce or underpin changes in operational or business practice.

In recent years, this linkage has become even more explicit, with few organizations now seeing culture change as an isolated activity, but rather as one key element in a wider programme of change activities. Recent commentators such as Rummler and Brache[5] have identified the need for a coherent change programme which operates at various levels — organizational needs and goals, operational and management processes, and individual jobs and performance. Other writers, such as Charles Hampden-Turner,[6] have focused explicitly on the links between organizational culture and corporate performance. These commentators reinforce our original conclusion that the purpose of culture change is to provide a coherent set of attitudes and values to underwrite an overall programme of organizational change.

This explicitly holistic approach to culture change is clearly reflected in our new case studies. For McVitie's, the Royal Mail and James Cropper plc, culture change was firmly built into a broader drive towards total quality, improved business processes, more effective market development and exploitation, and better overall business performance. Moreover, in all these cases, the change process was managed against precise and explicit business performance measures, and subject to rigorous monitoring and evaluation.

Change and culture

In revisiting our research, we have left the main text unchanged but added three major new case studies. Our experience since the first edition has largely served to confirm and reinforce our original conclusions, although we recognize that many aspects of culture still need to be reliably researched, as Furnham and Gunter have argued in a recent critical review.[7] At the same time, some subtle developments are evident in the practical application of culture change activities in organizations. Our new case studies – McVitie's, the Royal Mail and James Cropper – have been selected to illustrate some of these developments. We believe that these three cases will enrich the learning material available to managers and others seeking to increase their insight into the advantages and disadvantages of different methods of changing organizational culture.

In conclusion, we believe that culture and the processes of culture change are even more important now than they were when we conducted our original research. Certainly, the concept of organizational culture has become less modish in the intervening years. However, this means simply that it has become assimilated into the mainstream of management thinking. Culture is no longer the magical panacea that some readers of *In Search of Excellence* thought they had discovered. Rather, it is one of a number of critical variables which organizations must manage effectively in order to optimize their performance, alongside variables such as strategy formulation, organizational structure, process effectiveness, and market and product development.

In case we ever thought otherwise, the last few years have confirmed that there are no performance 'quick fixes'. If we are genuinely to deliver 'excellence' – whatever that might mean for individual organizations – we need to define our organizational objectives, decide how we can best achieve them, and develop effective tools to evaluate our progress. Moreover, we will have to learn how to do this against a background of constant change. There are no short cuts, but the development of an adaptive and innovative culture is likely to be a critical part of the process. In this context, we hope that the second edition of *Changing Culture* will continue to be a source of ideas for clarifying understanding of organizational culture and how it can be managed and changed.

References

1 'Successful Change Programs Begin with Results', R Schaffer and H Thomson, *Harvard Business Review*, January–February 1992.
2 *Corporate Cultures: The Rites and Rituals of Corporate Life*, Terrence E Deal and Allan A Kennedy, Reading, Mass., Addison-Wesley, 1982.
3 *Managing on the Edge*, Roger Pascale, London, Penguin, 1991.
4 'Why Change Programs Don't Produce Change', M Beer, R Eisenstat, B Spector, *Harvard Business Review*, November–December 1990.
5 *Improving Performance*, G Rummler and A Brache, San Francisco, Jossey Bass, 1990.
6 *Corporate Culture: From Vicious to Virtuous Circles*, Charles Hampden-Turner, London, Random Century, 1990.
7 'Corporate Culture: definition, diagnosis and change', A Furnham and B Gunter, *International Review of Industrial and Organizational Psychology*, Vol. 8, C L Cooper and I T Robinson (eds), London, John Wiley, 1993.

Introduction

The research on which this book is based was commissioned by the Institute of Personnel Management. We are indebted to it for providing us with the opportunity to explore an exciting and important, but most certainly complex, aspect of organizational life.

Corporate culture has dominated much management thinking over the past decade. Countless books and articles have taken a cultural perspective on management and organizational issues. Some of the books – William Ouchi's *Theory Z*, Pascale and Athos's *Art of Japanese management*, Deal and Kennedy's *Corporate cultures* and, above all, Peters and Waterman's *In search of excellence* – have been extraordinarily influential among practising managers. The word 'culture', as many of our case studies indicate, has become part of everyday management language. Managers in organizations as diverse as the Abbey National Building Society, Hampshire County Council and Unisys have referred explicitly to corporate culture as a major contributor to business effectiveness.

Despite the growing awareness of cultural issues, comparatively little attention has been paid to the practical, day-to-day processes involved in creating, managing and changing organizational culture. This is particularly surprising given that most of the books mentioned above are presented, at least ostensibly, as practical handbooks for managers seeking to improve the effectiveness of their organizations. Peters and Waterman claim to provide 'lessons from America's best-run companies', while Pascale and Athos aim to 'strengthen our areas of weakness'.[1] In fact, these writers are primarily concerned with the factors that control and condition organizational culture at a strategic level. *In search of excellence*, for example, provides a detailed analysis of the strategic values that underpin the activities of a number of successful US companies. It does not, however, provide much

1

detailed information on how these values are disseminated, reinforced and managed on a day-to-day basis, nor does it provide much practical advice for managers wishing to introduce such values to their own organizations.[2]

In carrying out our case studies, one of our primary aims was to begin to rectify this omission. We wished to identify the practical techniques and processes used to manage culture. In particular, we wanted to identify the methods used to *change* organizational culture. The organizations we studied all claimed to have changed their culture significantly to meet changing business or operational needs. These claims were supported by measurable – and in some cases spectacular – improvements in the organizations' profitability or effectiveness. We hoped that, by studying the change processes involved, we would be able to identify practical approaches and techniques which could be used by managers faced with the need for such change in their own organization.

At the same time, our perspective was unusual. Very few commentators have approached the subject of organizational culture from a specifically human resources standpoint. The reader will search the index of *In search of excellence* in vain for any mention of personnel or human resources. Most of the other influential books on the subject talk at length about business strategy, about management structures and systems, about superordinate values or goals. They do not, however, say very much at all about the practical issues involved in managing the employees who actually constitute the organization and its culture.

In fact, with few exceptions, the techniques and approaches used to change the culture of the organization in our case studies have fallen squarely within the remit of the personnel function. Some of the organizations did cite non-personnel techniques used as part of the change process, including, for example, improvements in the planning or control of finances or material resources. However, these techniques were not generally seen as having a key impact on culture. Indeed, some managers found that, having initially set out to make such technical changes, their efforts were impeded by the existing culture. They were unable to change management systems without first changing the behaviour, attitudes and beliefs underpinning them. Hampshire County Council, for instance, found that they could not significantly impose their system of financial accountability until they had used personnel-based techniques to introduce a *culture* of accountability.

This is not to say that the personnel function should, or indeed could, be the primary initiator of culture change. In this respect the strategic focus of Peters and Waterman and other commentators is entirely appropriate. Culture must ultimately be a strategic issue and any culture change must be dictated by the strategic needs of the organization. Furthermore, most commentators agree – and this is borne out by our case studies – that significant culture change requires leadership and commitment at the most senior levels. Stanley M Davis, for example, comments that 'changing or purposefully managing a company's culture, directly or indirectly, has to be done in concert with the CEO'.[3] This view was echoed repeatedly by the managers we interviewed and in virtually all our studies change was initiated by the Chief Executive or equivalent. Major change is always traumatic and vision, determination and inspiration are required at senior levels to overcome the potentially debilitating effects of such trauma.[4]

At the same time, senior managers cannot assume that their vision of change will be communicated easily to the workforce. Even if employees acknowledge a theoretical need for change – because, say, the organization is no longer profitable or effective – this will not necessarily lead to changes in their everyday activities. It is always easier to stick with a familiar routine than to try a new approach. Without immediate and pressing motivation many employees will merely pay lip service to new strategic values while continuing to behave in exactly the same way as before.[5] In other words, the process of culture change needs to be managed, continuously and actively, at every level in the organization. This, in many of the organizations we looked at, was the task undertaken by personnel. We will examine the process in detail in chapter 5.

The research

The IPM's Working Party on Organizational Culture Change had two broad objectives. First, to identify the role of the personnel function in making organizations more effective in changing their dynamics and culture. And, secondly, to show personnel practitioners how to be more effective facilitators in the organizational and culture change process. The working party commissioned the Centre for Personnel Research and Enterprise Development at City University Business School to review the available literature and to undertake appropriate research.

In the autumn of 1987 a short questionnaire was mailed to the Chief Executive of one thousand of the largest UK public- and private-sector organizations. This questionnaire defined organizational culture change as 'any direct and systematic attempt to change the values, attitudes, perceptions or beliefs of a significant number of members of an organization or one of its constituent parts' and simply asked the respondents whether or not the organization had been involved in an attempt to change its culture during the last five years. If so, the organization was asked for a brief description of the change and methods employed and asked whether or not they would be prepared to talk to us further about their culture change. Approximately five hundred replies were received, nearly two hundred and fifty of which indicated that they had been involved in a culture change attempt. One hundred and eighty of these welcomed further discussions. This response rate is quite staggering, being four to five times the response rate expected from an unsolicited survey of this kind. It is clearly a reflection of the considerable interest in the subject in company boardrooms around the country. This high response rate left us with a problem: which organizations to include as case studies.

A short list of thirty organizations was drawn up, including organizations from both the public and private sectors, from different industrial classifications, sizes and geographical locations. These thirty organizations were telephoned in order to find out more about what they had actually done to change their culture and to explain what we required from them. Fifteen organizations were finally selected to be case studies. Throughout this sampling procedure the guiding principle was to select case studies from different sectors which differed in their methods and approach to culture change. This, it was felt, would maximize the learning to be gained from the research. We have given nine of the fifteen case studies in full in the text, but we have drawn on (and occasionally referred to) the others in our analysis.

A semi-structured questionnaire was used to guide the face-to-face interviews, which on average lasted about one and a half hours. Typically two such interviews would be undertaken for each organization as well as a number of conversations by telephone. The interviews covered the history of the organization, the reasons for change, the methods of change and the agents of change, as well as the product of change. Usually the organization provided supporting documents and occasionally articles or papers on the change. Draft case studies were circulated to the organizations for their comments. The organizations were allowed to add, delete and edit the reports as they wished; however, the decision whether or not to publish remained with the authors. In fact, very few changes were made by the organizations to the original scripts. One organization requested that large sections of the study be removed because they considered the information it contained to be competitor-sensitive. And, because of imminent privatization, we are able to refer to but not include in full the case study of *an area electricity board*. Otherwise, those changes that were made were invariably useful clarifications. Doubtless, the case studies that are presented have benefited from hindsight and are in part rationalizations after the event.

Limitations of the research

The major limitation is the fact that we have not measured culture or change. We have no objective evidence that any of the organizations actually succeeded in changing their culture. Our own view is that in some of the cases culture change is highly likely, in others less so. Therefore, the reader will have to exercise his or her own judgement. For us, it is a matter of probability. The more the organization has employed methods likely to change the common beliefs and attitudes of members, has used these methods extensively and consistently, and has supported the change with a realignment of its structures and systems, the greater the probability of cultural change. The reason why we have found it necessary to include more theory than we had wished, is to help readers to interpret the case studies and to make such judgements for themselves.

It should be noted that this sample is biased. Only those prepared 'to go public' are likely to offer research assistance; nobody offered us a culture change failure to look at. Occasionally we did feel we were part of the public relations machine. This is not particularly surprising for the development of the corporate image was part of the cultural change for many of the organizations. It is not unreasonable to conclude that the change attempts we have studied are perceived by the respondents as examples of successful change.

Hopefully we have made the limitations of the case studies quite clear and readers will heed the warnings. Individual studies should be treated with caution. Despite the weaknesses, we believe that the case studies represent a significant body of knowledge. This is particularly so when they are read as a coherent set of cases. It is the learning to be gained from the comparison of similarities and differences that we consider to be of greatest value.

The organization of the text

The book is in four parts. Part I is largely theoretical. It discusses the nature and formation of organizational culture. It is included to provide a framework to help readers interpret the case studies. As such it is not essential; for, as was made abundantly clear to us during our research, people have their own theories on culture and culture change. Part II is concerned with culture change and attempts to integrate our theoretical approach with learnings drawn from the case studies. The methods of change, the roles of agents of change and the processes of change are discussed. Part III concentrates on the role of the personnel function in bringing about culture change and Part IV leaves theory and interpretation to the reader; the case studies are presented without comment. Finally, there is a brief Conclusion with a discussion of the issues which remain for the future.

References

1   PASCALE R T *and* ATHOS A G. *The art of Japanese management*. Simon and Schuster, 1981
2   See, for example, THOMAS Michael. 'In search of culture – holy grail or gravy train?' *Personnel Management*. September 1985
3   DAVIS Stanley M. *Managing corporate culture*. Ballinger, 1984
4   See, for example, DEAL Terrence E. 'Cultural change: opportunity, silent killer or metamorphosis?' in Ralph H Kilmann, Mary J Saxton, Roy Sepra *et al. Gaining control of the corporate culture*. Jossey-Bass, 1985
5   See, for example, description of 'lip service' in DAVIS Stanley M, *op cit*

Part I

Understanding Culture

1

The Nature of Organizational Culture

'*Experience is the child of Thought, and
Thought is the child of Action*' –

Benjamin Disraeli

To begin we must clarify the nature of the beast. What is
organizational culture? What is its role and function in an
organization? Why is it important?

The definition of culture and the clarification of its nature
is not an idle academic pursuit. It has practical relevance.
When we know what culture is, we know what needs to be
changed for culture to change. When we appreciate its nature,
we can understand how it may be changed. When we know
its role, we can comprehend its importance.

What is organizational culture?

Most people seem to agree that culture exists and that it is a
useful concept. Far fewer agree on exactly what it is.

Definitions of culture abound. One text cites 164 different
definitions of culture. It concludes:

> Culture consists of patterns, explicit and implicit, of
> and for behaviour acquired and transmitted by
> symbols, constituting the distinctive achievement of
> human groups, including their embodiments in
> artifacts; the essential core of culture consists of
> traditional (ie historically derived and selected)
> ideas and especially their attached values; culture
> systems may, on the one hand, be considered as

products of action, on the other as conditioning elements of future action.[1]

This definition includes elements from many different approaches. It is certainly comprehensive, but, at this stage, it is probably more likely to confuse than clarify our practical understanding of culture in organizations.

In search of a definition

In general, definitions of culture tend to deal primarily either with the way we act or the way we think. At one extreme, culture may be defined as 'the way we do things around here'.[2] At the other, it may be defined as 'the way we think about things around here' or 'the fabrics of meaning with which human beings interpret their experience and guide their actions'.[3] Between these extremes, some authors have defined culture in terms of both thought and behaviour. An example would be: 'the commonly shared beliefs, values and characteristic patterns of behaviour that exist within an organization'.[4]

Not surprisingly, practical managers – including most of those interviewed for the case studies in Part IV – tend to view culture primarily in terms of behaviour. After all, managers are primarily interested in making practical changes in people's work, goals, methods and behaviours. By contrast, academics – along with a few of the managers interviewed for our case studies – tend to view culture primarily in cognitive terms. Again, this is not surprising. Academics are generally more concerned with 'why culture changes' than with 'why change culture?'

Our search for a definition of organizational culture and our understanding of it is not helped by some previous writers on the subject. Some consultancy based authors have drawn conclusions far beyond the available evidence. It is really quite extraordinary that, for example, Deal and Kennedy[5] and Peters and Waterman[6] have made statements about the nature of organizational culture mainly based on the statements of CEOs and senior executives of large multi-nationals; these interesting, but largely secondhand, executive stories are probably truly the myths of culture. It seems to us that many of these cultural statements are more likely the products of the corporate PR machine. The popularity of the works of these authors is thus a double-edged sword. For, while they have raised the consciousness of many boardrooms, they have not advanced the understanding of culture or of its change a great deal.

Edgar Schein[7] has defined culture as an unconscious and largely invisible entity which by definition is almost impossible to measure, study or change. There is something strangely fascinating about unconscious and invisible forces – witness popular interest in supernatural power, Freudian instincts, etc. Certainly, aspects of culture are unconscious and in a sense invisible. However, we can find few reasons for defining organizational culture in this way and some good reasons why it should not be so defined. If it is defined as such, it is difficult to measure, change or subject it to empirical investigation. Further, the relationship between culture as so defined and organizational behaviour and performance is unclear. One is reminded of the fact that differing schools of psychoanalysis are invariably able to interpret their clients' malaise in terms of their own theoretical assumptions and, further, their clients come to accept this view. Approaches which define culture as an unconscious and invisible entity offer little opportunity for reality testing and organizations should beware of consultants who take such an approach. This conceptualization appears to us to be both premature and unhelpful.

We are going to adopt a working definition of culture that describes it as an entity that is largely measurable, that can be subjected to empirical investigation and, being a determinant of behaviour, is of practical relevance. If future research shows that one needs to define culture as unconscious and invisible, then so be it.

**Culture is the commonly held and relatively stable beliefs,
attitudes and values that exist within the organization.**

This is our working definition of organizational culture. We
consider culture to be 'the way people think about things
around here'.[8] The characteristic patterns of behaviour in the
organization, the rites, rituals and symbols, are consequently
seen as manifestations. A representation of the elements of
organizational culture is given in the lilypond diagram in
figure 1.1.

Figure 1.1
Culture and behaviour

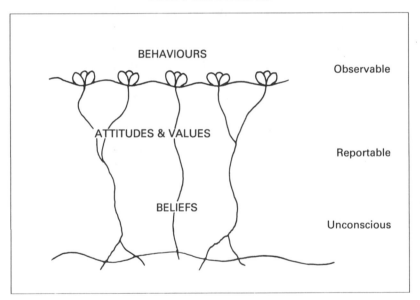

The elements of culture illustrated in figure 1.1 will be
considered in more detail in chapter 2. Briefly, though, the
diagram illustrates that the behaviour, attitudes and values of
members is dependent upon the sets of beliefs that individual
members possess, some of these beliefs being unconscious.
The beliefs of members are thus seen as the key element of

organizational culture. It is these that must be changed if culture is to change. Figure 1.2 gives the common behaviours, attitudes and beliefs, observed and inferred among managers at Cummins Engine Company.[9]

The elements of culture are the conscious and unconscious content and products of thought and reasoning. Culture pervades the decision-making and problem-solving processes of the organization. It influences the goals, means and manner of action. It is a source of motivation and demotivation, of satisfaction and dissatisfaction. In short, culture underlies much of the human activity in an organization.

Our working definition identifies an entity that clearly impacts upon organizational effectiveness. That is, defined in this way, culture is tied to behaviour and consequently is of practical relevance. As defined, culture is largely measurable, it is capable of change and it can be empirically studied. Further, our emphasis upon beliefs, attitudes and values as the major elements of culture enables us to draw upon previous empirical research on the nature of belief, attitude and value formation and change in developing our understanding of culture and the ways in which it can be changed.

Characteristics of organizational culture

Having settled on a potentially useful definition of culture, we will now explore its nature in more detail. Some of the key characteristics are:

- culture is learnt
- culture is both an input and an output
- culture is partly unconscious
- culture is historically based
- culture is commonly held rather than shared
- culture is heterogeneous

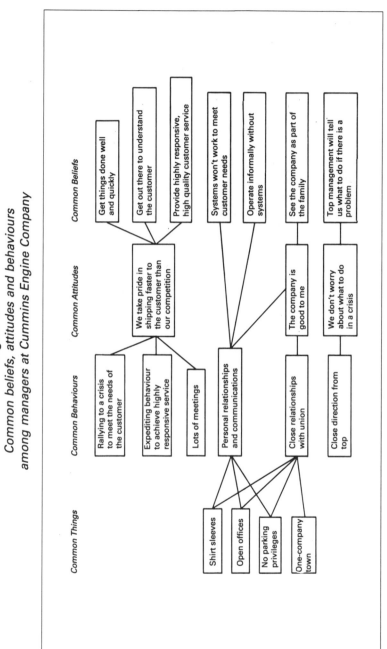

Figure 1.2
*Common beliefs, attitudes and behaviours
among managers at Cummins Engine Company*

Let us discuss these characteristics one by one.

Culture is learnt

Individual beliefs, attitudes and values are gained from the individual's environment. The culture of the organization is therefore gained from the environment common to its members. Both the internal and external environment of the organization influence culture.

The internal environment comprises the social and technical systems of the organization. Thus, in part, culture is the product of these socio–technical systems. They comprise the decision-making, planning and control procedures of the organization, its technology, the procedures for recruitment, selection and training, and the behaviour of other members – in particular, that of the manager and the work group. Culture has its roots as much in beliefs about the demands of the work environment as it does in the personal attitudes and values of individuals.

Externally, the organization is embedded in social, political, legislative, economic and technological systems. These represent the external environment of the organization. Those operating in different sectors have different markets, technologies and legal constraints. They have different skill and resource needs. These variations place different demands on organizations and create differing learning environments.

Culture is both an input and an output

Organizational culture is both the product of action and a conditioning element of future action (see figure 1.3). It is influenced by the socio–technical systems of the organization, but these systems are in turn influenced by the common beliefs, attitudes and values of the members. The strategies, structures, procedures and behaviour adopted by the management create the work environment for other members.

Figure 1.3
Culture as an input and output

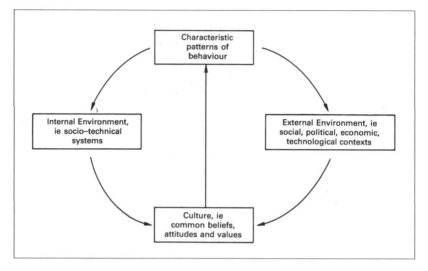

However, the managers, if they have been members of the organization for some time, are themselves a product of the culture. The strategies, structures, procedures and behaviour they adopt have been conditioned by the culture in which they have been immersed.

As culture is both an input and an output, it is likely to be self-perpetuating and highly resistant to change. This is particularly likely to be the case in career-based organizations and those with low labour turnover, standardized procedures for selection, induction and training, and those which operate in a relatively stable and predictable market.

Culture is partly unconscious

There are two ways in which the commonly held beliefs that exist in an organization are unconscious. First, members may unconsciously process information that influences the way they think. And secondly, the conscious beliefs, attitudes and values that underlie behaviour may repeatedly lead to success to the extent that they become taken for granted.

People process information at various levels of consciousness, and information processed below the threshold of awareness can influence behaviour – witness the impact of subliminal advertising on consumer behaviour. Similarly, our reasoning and problem-solving processes are occasionally unconscious. Everyone can recall instances where solutions to problems suddenly appear in an 'ah, ah' fashion after a period on the back burner, or during dreams or semi-conscious sleep states.[10] Thought can be unconscious and consequently so too can common patterns of thought or organizational culture. Consider the following story, which being secondhand may not be entirely accurate, but it is plausible and serves as an illustration:

> McKinsey's made a presentation to a management group of IBM that identified a problem that needed action. They gave a well-rehearsed presentation using slides and everything seemed to go very well. However, no action resulted. They consulted an internal IBM consultant for his opinion of what had gone wrong. At first sight he could see no reason. The points were well made and were pertinent to the problem. However, it did occur to him that IBM working meetings utilize flipcharts and not slides. At the next opportunity McKinsey used flipcharts at their presentation and action resulted.

This story illustrates a cultural phenomenon and yet one that was almost certainly unconscious. It is unlikely that the members of the group were aware of the factors influencing their behaviour or had ever discussed it. It would seem likely that when individuals repeatedly experience situations they are capable of unconscious learning which can influence their behaviour without awareness.

When solutions lead repeatedly to success they become

taken for granted and are likely to drop from awareness.
Edgar Schein has termed these unconscious beliefs, basic
assumptions. For example, one common assumption in
Western society is a value in personal property and privacy.
Children, of course, have to learn this and in early childhood
frequently transgress. However, by adulthood this assumption
is likely to be taken for granted. The meaning of gates and
fences around private dwellings and other signs and symbols
of private property have been learned, to the extent that
people transgressing them are frequently assumed to have
some ulterior motive. Through the processes of socialization
there develops a common and largely unconscious understanding of appropriate behaviour and the signs and symbols of
significance.

Assumptions also develop within organizations. The
decision of an organization to enter a new product market
will initially be hotly debated, but if it leads to success the
issues will drop from awareness and the new market will
become accepted as a natural part of the business. Social and
technical systems will develop to support this new initiative
and as a consequence the assumptions will become embedded
in the fabric of the organization. Over time the original
assumptions can be lost, while the systems and behaviours
continue. Parliamentary procedure in the UK abounds with
archaic rituals, the functions of which are no longer of any
relevance.

Culture is historically based

It has been suggested that the paternalistic culture of Japanese
companies has its roots in the historical relationship between
the Japanese rice farmers and the samurai. This was a
symbiotic relationship whereby the farmers provided food
and shelter for the samurai who in return protected the farms
from pillage.

Organizations are developed from the original assumptions,

strategies and structures made by their founders. Once the organization has made a strategic decision – reflecting its environment at that time – the degrees of freedom for succeeding generations are limited. The die has been cast and the original structures, procedures and assumptions may be present many generations after their foundation.[11] The original culture influences successive generations because decisions affecting the future of the organization are made within the context of the existing culture.

Culture as commonly held beliefs, attitudes and values

It should be noted that our definition refers to '*commonly held* . . . beliefs, attitudes and values' rather than the more usual '*shared* . . . beliefs, attitudes and values'. This is an important distinction.

A key feature of culture, in organizations and in society, is that, mostly, it is *not* shared. Generally, individuals within a given culture have not been able to discuss and reach a consensus on how to think and behave in a given situation. Nevertheless, they will still tend to think and behave similarly. They will tend to adopt similar interpersonal styles, rituals and modes of dress. They will tend to know immediately who has authority over whom and what. Similarly, within a given organization, individuals will often come to adopt similar ways of thinking or behaving, even though they may be widely separated geographically or functionally. It is this, perhaps, which seems to give culture its slightly mystical quality. In reality, of course, this common thought and behaviour results from common learning, common history and experience, and a common environment.

This is not of course to deny that the immediate work group may be an important cultural influence, which may result in shared beliefs, attitudes and values among those involved. However, group behaviour is only part of the cultural environment and it has perhaps been over-emphasized. Social psychologists, in particular, have tended to concentrate on small group behaviour and have emphasized the analogy between 'culture' and 'group norms' (ie the characteristic patterns of thought and behaviour shared by members of a given group).

The above analysis suggests that, in addition to the beliefs, attitudes and values unique to individual members, organizational culture comprises:

– the beliefs, values and attitudes uniquely common to the work group
– the beliefs, values and attitudes uniquely common to the department, function or unit
– the beliefs, values and attitudes uniquely common to the organization
– the beliefs, values and attitudes uniquely common to the society or parts of society from which members are drawn

The relative importance of these various cultural components will vary from one organization to another. If the organization operates through a series of highly autonomous divisions, for example, it is likely that the beliefs, values and attitudes of the division will be paramount. If it makes extensive use of team working, then the contribution of the work group is likely to be important. If it draws virtually all its employees from a narrow geographical catchment area, then it is possible that the culture of that particular society will play a significant role.

Culture is heterogeneous

Clearly, common beliefs form around objects of common concern. Issues of common concern at work relate to the purpose, tasks, methods, nature of authority and social relations of the organization. These issues will vary from one organization to another. Within a given organization, they may well also vary according to department or according to the level in the hierarchy. It is worth noting that, in this sense, our case studies' respondents represent a biased sample. The majority were senior managers in the organizations concerned and inevitably the case studies reflect the issues which concerned these individuals. There is therefore an emphasis on strategy, organization, the behaviour of others and the process of change.[12] If we had interviewed bank clerks or production workers, the issues of concern and associated beliefs would doubtless have been different. Concerns about unionization, demarcation, pay parity, the supervisor and promotion might well have been more apparent.

In practice, organizational culture is unlikely to be completely homogeneous. Most organizations are character-ized by sub-cultures which form around different roles, functions and levels. Probably very few beliefs, attitudes or values are common to all members. The typical medium to large organization is characterized by head office, branch, factory, production, sales, union, accounts sub-cultures. Most organizations probably comprise an executive culture with a common perspective and beliefs about strategic direction; a management culture focusing upon managing and resourcing; and a blue collar culture focusing on production or service.

Sub-cultures of greater or lesser significance exist in any organization. These sub-cultures can sometimes be beneficial if they increase a sense of common purpose and identity within a given department. Equally, though, they can be highly detrimental if they limit coordination or cause conflict across the organization. In an attempt to minimize these problems, a number of the case studies attempted, as part of their culture change process, to introduce an over-arching philosophy which defines a common purpose, common goals and common priorities. Such a universal philosophy may be beneficial, but to be effective it must be equally applicable to and similarly interpreted by all groups in the organization. This suggests that, to be effective, such a philosophy cannot simply be imposed from above, but must be developed with a clear understanding of the needs and characteristics of the various sub-cultures throughout the organization.

Types of organizational culture

Organizational cultures vary according to the nature of the beliefs, values and attitudes that are commonly held. These reflect differences in society, history and function. German, French, British, American and Japanese societies, for example, differ in their beliefs, attitudes and values. Organizations drawn from these societies are likely to vary accordingly. The cultures of organizations are also likely to reflect differences in their history. The culture may, for example, reflect the values and style of the founder, the history of industrial relations in the company, experience of economic recession and so on. Finally, organizational cultures are likely to reflect differences in function. The culture of, say, the Armed Forces – which have very specific functional needs – is likely to differ very significantly from the culture of an engineering or retail company. In practice, of course, the culture of a given organization is likely to reflect a combination of these various factors. The culture of the Civil Service, for instance, is a reflection of its relation to British society, of its historical development and of the nature of its operations.

Relatively few attempts have been made to analyse the different kinds of culture formed by the combination of these factors. However, two attempts to develop a cultural typology are worth considering. Geert Hofstede has undertaken a large study into the impact of *national* culture on a single multi-national organization.[13] On the basis of this study and a series of smaller projects, he has identified four dimensions on which national cultures appear to vary. These are given in figure 1.4. The research does not demonstrate, as has sometimes been suggested, that national culture transcends

Figure 1.4
Dimensions of national culture

Power distance: indicates the extent to which society accepts that power in organizations is distributed unequally. For example, a large power distance is indicated by a belief that 'supervisors consider subordinates to be a different kind of people'. The Philippines and Indonesia score highly on this dimension, with Austria and Israel scoring low.

Uncertainty avoidance: indicates the extent to which a society feels threatened by ambiguity and tries to avoid such situations by the use of formality and structure. For example, strong uncertainty avoidance is indicated by a belief that 'deviant persons and ideas are dangerous'. Greece and Portugal score highly, with Denmark and Sweden scoring low.

Individualism/Collectivism: indicates the extent to which society prefers a loosely knit social framework or a tight framework with absolute loyalty. For example, individualism is associated with a calculative involvement. Australia and the USA are individualistic societies, while Pakistan and Venezuela are collectivist.

Masculinity/Femininity: indicates the extent to which values in society are 'masculine' (eg assertive, domineering, uncaring) or 'feminine'. Japan, Venezuela and Mexico are 'masculine' societies; Sweden, Norway and Denmark are 'feminine'.

organizational factors. However, it does indicate that managers in different countries vary in the personal attitudes and values that they hold.

Hofstede's work is valuable in investigating the influence of national culture on organizations. Roger Harrison, on the other hand, has developed a typology more appropriate for analysing and comparing the cultures of individual organizations.[14] He has identified four theoretical cultural types and devised a questionnaire for their measurement. These are given in figure 1.5. This typology provides a

Figure 1.5
Power, role, task and people cultures

Power orientation: power-orientated organizations attempt to dominate their environment and those who are powerful within the organization strive to maintain absolute control over subordinates. They buy and sell organizations and people as commodities, in apparent disregard of human values and general welfare. They are competitive and have voracious appetites for growth. Within the organization the law of the jungle often seems to prevail among executives as they struggle for personal advantage.

Role orientation: such organizations would more typically be described as a bureaucracy. There is an emphasis upon legality, legitimacy and responsibility. Conflict is regulated by rules and procedures. Rights and privileges are defined and adhered to. There is a strong emphasis upon hierarchy and status. Predictability of behaviour is high and stability and respectability are often valued as much as competence.

Task orientation: in such organizations structures, functions and activities are all evaluated in terms of their contributions to organizational goals. Nothing is allowed to get in the way of task accomplishment. If individuals do not have the skills or technical knowledge to perform a task they are retrained or replaced. Authority is based upon appropriate knowledge and competence. Emphasis is placed on a rapid and flexible organization. Collaboration is sought if this promotes goal achievement. Task and project groups are common.

People orientation: this type of organization exists primarily to serve the needs of its members. Authority may be assigned on the basis of task competence, but this practice is kept to a minimum. Instead, individuals are expected to influence each other through example and helpfulness. Consensus methods of decision-making are preferred. And roles are assigned on the basis of personal preference and the need for learning and growth.

useful basis for discussing and investigating variations in organizational culture. However, there are grounds for believing that it fails to take into account certain significant aspects. Furthermore, as far as we are aware, no attempt has been made to validate the approach, ie to show empirically that the culture types actually do exist and to demonstrate that the questionnaire items do measure what they are supposed to measure.

To supplement these two theoretical approaches, figure 1.6 shows the range of beliefs actually observed or inferred from our case studies. We have not been systematic in their identification, but they provide a useful contrast with the cultural dimensions and types of Hofstede and Harrison. The list illustrates the wide range of different factors that can, in practice, influence the development of organizational culture.

An organization may have significant and idiosyncratic beliefs about any or all of the factors listed in figure 1.6. The combination of these various beliefs will contribute towards the development of the unique culture of the organization. When this range of possible influences is considered alongside the approaches of Hofstede and Harrison, the potential variety and complexity of organizational culture becomes apparent.

In practice, common beliefs, attitudes, values and assumptions may arise about the *ends*, *means* and *manner* of organizations. For example, some of our case study organizations were concerned with changing culture in respect of ends, such as quality or sales. Some were concerned with changing culture in respect of means, such as work methods or the extent of formalization. Some were concerned with changing culture in respect of manner, such as increased flexibility, cooperation and proaction.

Figure 1.6
Examples of beliefs identifiable in the case studies

Beliefs about the nature of the organization's environment:

– about the impact of legislation
– about supplier capability
– about customer expectations
– about competitor activity
– about stakeholder expectations

Beliefs about acceptable levels of organization performance in terms of:

– asset growth
– return on investment
– productivity
– wastage and product quality
– market share
– profitability

Beliefs about the organization appropriate for success:

– organizational structure
– reward and appraisal systems
– communications systems
– control systems
– decentralization of decision-making

Beliefs about the organization itself:

– its philosophy
– its identity
– its importance
– its role
– its history
– its market leadership

Beliefs about work behaviour (both one's own and that of others):

– work methods and roles
– management style
– formality
– dress
– cooperation
– interpersonal relationships
– productivity and quality
– absenteeism, time-keeping

Strength of organizational culture

A number of authors have referred to 'strong' and 'weak' cultures. These terms need to be used with care. Is a strong culture one where the central beliefs and attitudes are strongly held? Or is a strong culture one which is homogeneous – that is, the beliefs and attitudes are common to all the groups in the organization? Or is a strong culture one that is readily recognizable? Or alternatively one which promotes organizational effectiveness? These are not mutually exclusive definitions. A homogeneous culture can constrain the effectiveness of an organization as easily as it can promote it. Similarly, the strongly held attitudes may be in direct conflict with the objectives of the organization, or held by only a few members.

Internalization

We are going to define the strength of the culture of an organization as the extent to which the members have 'internalized' the beliefs, attitudes and values that exist within the organization. Members infer these beliefs, attitudes and values from the behaviour of other members, from written communications and from the systems, rules and procedures that are applied. Internalization is the reasoning process whereby individuals come to accept and agree with the beliefs, attitudes and values of other members. Over time, individuals come to accept as correct particular goals, methods and ways of doing things. These beliefs, attitudes and values become owned and valued. Behaviour becomes self-reinforcing; things 'should' or 'ought' to be done this way. Strong cultures are characterized by dedication, spontaneity and cooperation in the service of common values. However, these may not necessarily be the same as the organization's 'official' values. It is not uncommon to find an organization's publicity espousing one set of values – say 'quality' or 'customer service' – while the workforce is actually following some quite different set of values. Thus a strong culture can operate in direct conflict with the goals of senior management. Amongst our case studies, Jaguar, during the late 1970s and early 1980s, probably provides the best example of a strong employee- and union-based culture operating in conflict with the goals of senior management.

Identification

To identify with an organization means to have a positive attitude towards it. If the organization is seen as fair, loyal to its employees, positively valued by the public, etc, employees are likely to have a positive attitude towards it. Because employees desire to continue their membership, they are likely to behave compliantly.

Internalization of the organization's values results in increased identification. On the other hand, identification with the organization increases the likelihood that the individual will internalize its values, but does not guarantee it. A number of our case-study organizations had developed shiny new corporate images and had taken steps – particularly through various forms of corporate communication – to make the organization more attractive to its employees. This may well reduce turnover, but it does not necessarily result in a strong internalized culture.

Figure 1.7 shows a typology of employee involvement which relates to our present discussion. It is developed from the ideas of Etzioni.[15]

Our discussion leads us to an important conclusion about the development of a strong culture: namely, that it cannot be imposed. At best, it is possible only to create conditions likely to foster a change in beliefs and the internalization of new organizational values. These conditions may include the availability of valid information, openness and trust, and free choice. The same point was made by Chris Argyris some years ago:

Figure 1.7
Types of employee involvement

Moral involvement: represents a positive and intense orientation that results from the internalization of organizational goals and values and an identification with the organization. Spontaneous, cooperative and dedicated behaviour in the service of organizational goals can be expected.

Calculative involvement: represents a less intense orientation based upon exchange. The individual will work spontaneously and cooperatively if this is seen as profitable. There is, however, little identification or attachment to the organization itself which is perceived as a means to an end. The individual will leave if more lucrative opportunities arise.

Compliant involvement: results from an identification with the organization. Membership is valued and organizational values are espoused but not 'owned'. Within limits effort is above minimum and behaviour compliant.

Alienative involvement: the individual rejects organizational values and possesses a negative attitude towards the organization. Membership is not valued but continues because of lack of alternatives. Effort is minimal and may be subversive.

'Internal commitment' means that the individual has reached the point where he is acting on the choice because it fulfils his own needs and sense of responsibility, as well as those of the system. The individual who is internally committed is acting primarily under the influence of his own forces and not induced forces. The individual (or any unity) feels a minimal degree of dependence upon others for the action. It implies that he has obtained and processed *valid information* and that he has made an informed and *free choice*. Under these conditions there is a high probability that the individual's commitment will remain strong over time

(even with the reduction of external rewards) or
under stress, or when the course of action is
challenged by others [emphases ours].[16]

In an organization with a fairly 'weak' culture, changes in
policies, rewards, tasks and structures are likely to modify
organizational behaviour and cause a cultural shift. In stronger
cultures, changes in the infrastructure are less likely to change
the internalized beliefs, attitudes and values of individuals.
Individual behaviour may be modified, but there is unlikely
to be any significant shift in the way people think and behave.
Relatively strong cultures, as our case studies show, will
require more direct action. This might include training aimed
at influencing or developing specific beliefs and attitudes.

What is the function of organizational culture?

If a particular culture arises in an organization and is actively
maintained, it clearly serves some purpose for members of
the organization. What part does culture play? Edgar Schein
has identified some of the functions performed by culture;
these are given in figures 1.8 and 1.9.[17]

Culture identifies what is important in the external
environment, what the group attends to and monitors. For
senior executives this may be corporate performance,
competitor activity, market share, etc. Clerical staff, on the
other hand, may be primarily concerned with other groups
in the organization, with comparable groups in other
organizations, or with customers, suppliers or supervisors.
Common beliefs not only determine which of these factors
are considered important. They are a guide to the various
responses to the issues that arise from them. Such beliefs
may, for example, determine how the relevant parts of the
organization respond to issues such as declining market share,
changes in supervisory style or complaints from customers.

Figure 1.8

Functions of culture in resolving problems of external adaptation and survival

1 *Mission and Strategy:* obtaining common understanding of core mission, primary task, manifest and latent functions.

2 *Goals:* developing common understanding on goals as derived from the core mission.

3 *Means:* developing common understanding on the means to be used to attain the goals, such as the organizational structure, division of labour, reward system and authority system.

4 *Measurement:* developing common understanding on the criteria to be used in measuring how well the group is doing in fulfilling its goals, such as the information and control system.

5 *Correction:* developing common understanding on the appropriate remedial or repair strategies to be used if goals are not being met.

Figure 1.9

Function of culture in resolving problems of internal integration

1 *Common Language and Conceptual Categories:* if members cannot communicate with and understand each other, a group is impossible by definition.

2 *Group Boundaries and Criteria for Inclusion and Exclusion:* developing a common understanding on who is in and who is out and by what criteria one determines membership.

3 *Power and Status:* every organization must work out its pecking order, its criteria and rules for how one gets, maintains and loses power; consensus in this area is crucial to help members manage feelings of aggression.

4 *Intimacy, Friendship and Love:* every organization must work out its rules of the game for peer relationships, for relationships between the sexes and for the manner in which openness and intimacy are to be handled in the context of managing the organization's tasks.

Culture also determines the important issues within the organization. It identifies the principal goals, work methods and behaviour, how individuals interact, address each other, how friendship and personal relationships are conducted. Culture guides organizational membership, how the boundaries are maintained, who is an insider and who is an outsider. For the groups within the organization, culture may provide a common purpose and a coordination of activities. For members, common beliefs are important because they provide predictability in the social world and a common frame of reference.

Culture also performs a social function. It provides a medium in which friendships can develop. It provides an opportunity for the development of identity and a sense of belonging. The predictability of the social environment provides for security. It is interesting to note that two of our case studies have mentioned the potential trauma of cultural change and the need to provide emotional support during the change process.

The importance of culture to the organization

The research of Miles and Snow[18] found that the strategy of an organization, the type of people in power and its structure and systems reflect the dominant managerial ideology or culture. Furthermore, they found that these managerial ideologies tend to be more important than environmental factors in guiding organizational response.

Miles and Snow categorize organizations into three types according to the dominant ideology or management culture (see figure 1.10). They consider that managerial culture influences the organization's objectives, strategies and systems.

As we have seen, culture is both an input and an output. The managerial culture of an organization is therefore likely to be the product of past strategy, a moderator of current

Figure 1.10
Organizational culture and strategy

Cultural Type	Dominant Objectives	Strategies	Systems
Defenders	Desire for a secure and stable niche in market	Specialization; cost-efficient production, marketing emphasizes price and service; tendency to vertical integration	Centralized; detailed control; emphasis on cost efficiency; formal planning
Prospectors	Location and exploitation of new product and market opportunities	Growth through product and market development; monitors environmental change; multiple technologies	Emphasis on flexibility; decentralized control; use of ad hoc measures
Analysers	Desire to match new ventures to present shape of business	Steady growth through penetration; exploitation of applied research; followers in the market	Very complicated; coordinating roles between functions; intensive planning

strategy and a determinant of future strategy. Furthermore, while policy makers may attempt consciously to influence the culture of an organization, they too are often a cultural product. Policy makers who have spent their career in, say, a role-orientated culture are likely to develop future policy accordingly.

Culture influences what the executive group attends to, how it interprets the information and the responses it makes to changes in the external environment. Culture is a significant contributor to strategic analysis and the development of strategy. Since culture influences what other members of the organization attend to, how they interpret this information and react, it is a significant determinant of the success of strategic implementation. Culture influences the ability of the organization both to conceive and to implement a new strategy. The case studies suggested that some organizations are incapable of significant change until some form of crisis

Figure 1.11
The influence of organizational culture

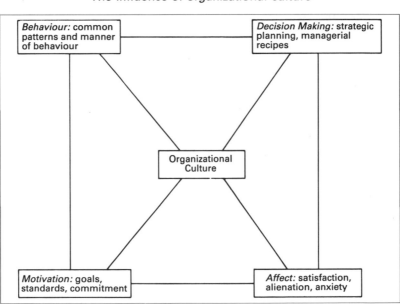

forces a stakeholder intervention and a shake-out at the top of the organization.

Figure 1.11 shows, in general terms, the influence of culture in the organization. It affects the decisions that are made, the goals and standards that are sought and the pattern and manner of behaviour. Further, dependent upon the degree of fit between organizational demands and personal beliefs, attitudes and values, it results in commitment and feelings of satisfaction, or antagonism, dissatisfaction, anxiety and stress.

An entity that represents the collective conscious and unconscious of the organization and that forms the basis for the interpretation of meaning, is a pervasive influence on organizational behaviour and as such a significant determinant of organizational performance.

Notes and References

1 KROEBER A L and KLUCKHOHN C. *Culture: a critical review of concepts and definitions*. Vintage Books, 1952
2 BOWER M, cited in DEAL T E and KENNEDY A A. *Corporate cultures: the rites and rituals of corporate life*. Addison-Wesley, 1982
3 GEERTZ C. *The interpretation of cultures*. Basic Books, 1973
4 MARGULIES N and RAIA A P. *Conceptual foundations of organizational development*. McGraw-Hill, 1978
5 DEAL T E and KENNEDY A A *op cit*
6 PETERS T J and WATERMAN R H. *In search of excellence: lessons from America's best-run companies*. Harper & Row, 1982
7 SCHEIN E H. *Organizational culture and leadership*. Jossey-Bass, 1985
8 To be more precise, this should read 'what people think about things around here'. There is little evidence that cultural differences affect the processes of thought, as opposed to the content of thought.
9 Adapted from SATHE V, *Culture and related corporate realities*. Irwin, 1985
10 For those who are interested in further reading on the subject of unconscious thought, we recommend DIXON N F, *Preconscious processing*. Wiley, 1987
11 See STINCHCOMBE A L. 'Social structure and organization' in MARCH J G *Handbook of organization*. Rand McNally, 1965

12   It should be noted that all our case study respondents were
      from personnel or a related function. There is therefore the
      possibility of bias when considering the evidence for the role of
      personnel in culture change. However, it should also be noted
      that the original contact was with the CEO of the organization
      and that we were passed on to personnel because of its central
      role in the management of change.
13   A brief synopsis of Hofstede's work is given in HOFSTEDE G,
      'Motivation, leadership, and organization: do American theories
      apply abroad?' *Organizational Dynamics*. Summer 1980. pp 42–
      63
14   HARRISON R. 'Understanding your organization's character'.
      Harvard Business Review. May–June 1972. pp 119–28
15   ETZIONI A. *A comparative analysis of complex organizations*.
      The Free Press, 1961
16   ARGYRIS C. *Intervention theory and method*. Addison-
      Wesley, 1970
17   Adapted from SCHEIN E H *op cit*
18   MILES R E *and* SNOW C C. *Organizational strategy, structure
      and process*. McGraw-Hill, 1978

2

■ The Formation of Organizational Culture

In this chapter we are going to discuss how organizational culture arises. As we have seen, beliefs, attitudes and values are the essential core of culture. We will therefore begin by looking briefly at the nature of individual beliefs, attitudes and values and at how these are formed. We will then investigate how individual beliefs, attitudes and values become commonly held by other members of the group or organization. Finally, we will consider the factors which influence the rate of change of organizational culture. Much of our discussion is well illustrated by the Toshiba case study in Part IV.

The nature and formation of individual beliefs, attitudes and values

As we have seen in chapter 1, the beliefs, attitudes and values of individual members of the organization form the building blocks from which culture develops. So – what is a belief, attitude or value? The answer to this question will help us to understand how the culture of an organization can be changed by changing the attitudes and beliefs of its individual members.[1]

What is a belief?

In simple terms, a *belief* refers to the information that an individual has about an object. Specifically, a belief links an object to some attribute. The object of a belief may be a person, a group of people, an institution, a behaviour, a policy, an event, etc. The associated attribute may be any object, trait, property, quality, characteristic, outcome or event. For example, the belief 'XYZ is a quality company' links the object 'XYZ' to the attribute 'quality'.

The reader should note that in common usage the term 'belief' is used in a number of different ways. First – as we are using it here – it may refer to the information or knowledge an individual possesses, for example 'I believe that Paris is the capital of France'. Secondly, it may signify faith or trust, for example 'I believe in God'. Or lastly, it may signify agreement, for example 'I believe in democracy'. In this last case, a belief is being used synonymously with 'value'. Many authors when referring to people's 'beliefs', by our definition, are referring to their values.

Beliefs are learnt. They may be gained directly from observation or experience. They may be inferred from existing beliefs. They may possibly be gained from some external source, such as written or oral communication. However, such information, unsupported by direct experience, is unlikely to be accepted as a belief unless the source is seen as highly credible or there is significant corroborating evidence.

Both beliefs and attitudes are formed – and changed – by the information to which we are exposed. If we receive additional information – supportive or contradictory – we will tend to adapt our beliefs accordingly. If employees learn that their organization has treated an individual badly, they may amend their beliefs about the organization's attitude to employee welfare. The process of belief formation is given in figure 2.1.

Our existing beliefs influence, directly and indirectly, the development of future beliefs, influencing the information that we attend to and the kinds of inferences that we draw. Over time, this results in the formation of a logically consistent network of beliefs – the *belief system*. The belief system has its roots in the past. Much of it is formed in childhood, from parents, teachers and friends. Our views on managerial style and the exercise of authority are likely to be based upon past relationships with parents, teachers and

Figure 2.1
Belief formation

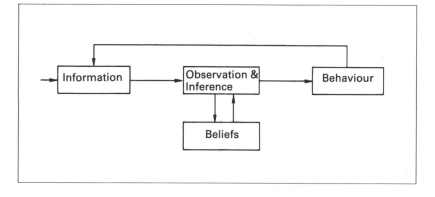

other authority figures. We may now be unaware of our original beliefs, but they have influenced – and indeed continue to influence – the development of our beliefs. A network of logically consistent, mutually reinforcing beliefs, partly rooted in our early life experiences, is likely to be both stable and resistant to change. (Also crucial is the impact of *language* – see figure 2.2.) In terms of the lilypond diagram in figure 1.1, the belief system can be seen as providing the 'pond bed', from which our attitudes and values – and our actions – grow.

Figure 2.2
Beliefs and language

Language provides a means for communicating meaning. However, it is not only a means of communication but also *an agency for the creation of meaning*. The language that we use influences the development of our belief system. In the same way that the Eskimos have different words for different shades of snow, the Hanunoo of the Philippine islands have names for 92 varieties of rice. This enables better discrimination and facilitates development of beliefs relating to different types of rice. Similarly, the Slave Indians, who live amongst the frozen lakes and rivers of Northern Canada have different terms for different forms of ice which relate not only to the nature of the ice, for example thin, brittle, hollow and so on; but also to its suitability to the mode of travel, by foot, by dogsled, by snowshoe.[2]

The functional demands of our environment give rise to different discriminations and terminologies and influence our belief system and interpretation of meaning. While carrying out the case studies, visiting the organizations and reading their literature, major differences were apparent in the language and terms used by the organizations to describe and conceptualize culture and its change. For example, in Mid-Essex Health Authority concepts such as 'the learning organization', 'theories-in-use', 'organizational development' and 'action learning' were to be found, but such terms were markedly absent in Jaguar and the electricity board, where the language was noticeably more 'ends-orientated' – 'product quality', 'absenteeism', 'productivity', 'budgets and targets' being the key terms. These differences in language and terminology reflect differences in the ways of thinking about the organization and have consequently influenced decisions that have been made regarding the goals and methods of change.

It is interesting to note therefore the use of new language and new concepts as part of many culture change programmes. The provision of a new language enables and encourages members of the organization to develop new beliefs. Examples include 'Just in Time', 'Right First Time', 'The Team you can Trust'. Similarly, Philip Crosby terms the organizational educators in his culture change programme 'The Thought Leaders' and much of Crosby's work is concerned with providing an appropriate language for the discussion and understanding of quality concepts:

> The quality education system (QES) ensures that all employees of the company have a common language of quality and understand their personal roles in causing quality to be routine (p. 8)
>
> The Absolutes of Quality Management must be understood by every single individual. These are the common language of quality (p. 88)
>
> The First Absolute: The Definition of Quality is Conformance to Requirements (p. 59)
>
> The Second Absolute: The System of Quality is Prevention (p. 66)
>
> The Third Absolute: Performance Standard is Zero Defects (ZD) (p. 74)

The Fourth Absolute: The Measurement of Quality is the Price of Non-Conformance (p. 85)

The culture of the company is going to change only when all employees absorb the common *language* of quality and begin to *understand* their individual role in making quality happen (p. 100) [emphases ours]

(Quotations from: CROSBY P B. *Quality without tears: the art of hassle-free management.* McGraw-Hill, 1986)

What is an attitude?

An *attitude* can be described as a learned predisposition to respond in a consistently favourable or unfavourable manner to a given object or idea. Like beliefs, attitudes are learned and are dependent upon past experience. However, attitudes also involve an affective evaluation in terms of, for example, like or dislike which predisposes the individual to respond in a particular way.

A person may believe that XYZ company pays a high salary, and demands a very high level of performance and personal commitment. If the individual positively evaluates these qualities, he or she will possess a favourable attitude towards company XYZ. On the other hand, a supervisor may believe that asking operators for their opinion of working practices will be time-consuming, will raise unresolvable issues and will undermine his or her authority. If so, the supervisor is likely to have a negative attitude towards work involvement and participative management. At any given time, therefore, a person holds a number of salient beliefs about a given object, action or event. These beliefs serve as primary determinants of the person's attitudes towards that object, action or event. The relationship between beliefs and attitudes is given in figure 2.3.

Most attitudes are developed over time. In practice, when we are asked for our attitude about something, we do not work through all our salient beliefs and evaluate them. We

Figure 2.3
Beliefs and attitudes

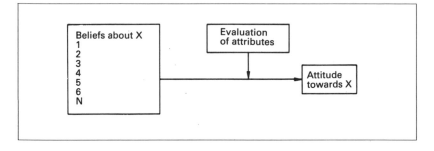

can give our attitude almost immediately. Equally, we do not necessarily need direct experience of an object to hold an attitude about it. Individuals frequently have attitudes, often stereotyped ones, towards concepts such as 'management', 'business' and 'trade unions' on the basis of very little direct information.

What is a value?

Conceptually, the distinction between attitudes and values is not clear-cut. However, in general terms, two types of value can be distinguished – instrumental and moral values. The former reflect a desire or preference and are virtually indistinguishable from attitudes. The latter carry a sense of obligation – of 'should' or 'ought' – and indicate what is correct or proper. Instrumental values result in feelings of satisfaction or dissatisfaction, moral values in feelings of pride or humiliation.

Values, like attitudes, are learnt and based upon the beliefs the individual possesses. However, unlike attitudes, they are cognitively evaluated in terms of their logical consistency with existing beliefs. To recap – in simple terms – beliefs refer to knowledge, attitudes to liking or disliking and values to agreement or disagreement.

In chapter 1, we defined the strength of a culture as the extent to which individuals have internalized the values of the group or organization. Individuals who have genuinely internalized the values of an organization are likely to engage in cooperative and spontaneous behaviour in their service. They have come to believe in (ie agree with) them. In these circumstances, behaviour is self-reinforced and traditional reward and supervisory controls will become much less necessary.

Beliefs, attitudes, values and behaviour

If we are to discuss an entity of practical significance, culture as defined needs to be related to behaviour and thus organizational performance. Figure 2.4 illustrates the relationship between beliefs, attitudes, values and behaviour.[3]

Figure 2.4
The relationship between beliefs, attitudes, values and behaviour

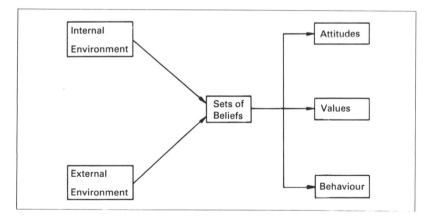

As the model shows, our attitudes, values and behaviour are dependent upon the *sets* of beliefs that we possess. However, different sets of beliefs may underlie our attitude, value and behaviour with respect to a specific person or object. Thus, our attitude towards customer service may differ from our value or from our behaviour. Typically there is considerable overlap in the beliefs underlying our attitudes, values and behaviour – hence the association between them. Yet this is not always the case. We find things attractive that we know to be morally unacceptable, incorrect or improper, and frequently there is little correspondence between what we say (ie our attitudes and values) and what we do (ie our behaviour), or between our espoused theories and our theories-in-use.[4] We know that people who value honesty will in some situations lie and cheat, though we also know that in some circumstances people will act in accordance with their values regardless of the consequences.

Research has repeatedly found only a weak relationship between people's attitudes towards an object and their behaviour towards that object. For example, despite extensive research, no clear link has been found between job satisfaction and job performance. The reason for this is that the way we behave is not influenced primarily by our attitudes towards objects, events, concepts or persons, but rather it is influenced by our beliefs about various situational contingencies: namely, our beliefs about the rewards and costs associated with the behaviour; our beliefs about the probability of success; our beliefs about our own capability; and our beliefs about the expectations of others. We may therefore have positive attitudes towards 'the job' or 'the organization' in abstract terms, but this may not have a significant effect on our behaviour. Similarly, a smoker may possess a negative attitude towards smoking cigarettes, but continue to do so because he or she also believes that there are negative consequences associated with giving up, or doubts his or her ability to stop smoking. To re-emphasize the point, our attitudes, values and behaviour are governed by the sets of beliefs we possess, but the set of beliefs underlying our attitude or value may differ from that which determines how we act.

For this reason, if we wish to improve customer service, rather than merely changing attitudes towards the concept of customer service, we must change beliefs about the rewards and costs associated with being helpful to customers, beliefs about the probability of being successful, employees' beliefs about their own abilities and beliefs about the social norms in the organization. Or, if we wish to encourage managers to behave more participatively, we need to change their beliefs about the practicalities of managing participatively.

It is clear that many of the beliefs that influence behaviour directly are gained from the work environment. Therefore, if we wish to link cultural change to a change in behaviour it is insufficient to change employee attitudes or values. One also needs to address aspects of the social and technical systems that impinge upon behaviour. For example, it may be necessary to change the work group norms, manager role behaviour, the reward system, the technology, the information and resources available, skill levels and so on.

Hopefully it is now quite clear that beliefs are the essential core of organizational culture and, if the culture of an organization is to be changed, it is the commonly held beliefs that exist within the organization that have to be changed. Further, if culture change is to be linked to behavioural and organizational performance, then beliefs about the various contingencies which impinge upon behaviour in the work environment must also be addressed. This is a key statement. It provides the rationale underlying methods of culture change and provides a criterion against which the likely effectiveness of change methods and actions (and the case studies in Part IV) can be assessed. That is, have they or are they likely to change the commonly held beliefs in the organization and have the social and technical systems been realigned to support the desired attitudes, values and behaviour?

Our analysis leads us to conclude that a major change in the technical systems of the organization, for example in the reward systems, organizational structure, technology, etc, may alone result in behavioural and cultural change. That is, behavioural and cultural change can be imposed. This, in part, was the approach taken in the Rank Xerox UK case study where the emphasis was to teach employees new techniques and behaviours, rather than to change beliefs, attitudes and values more directly. However, failure to consider existing attitudes and values may well result in dissatisfaction, minimal involvement and antagonism, and have a negative impact upon organizational climate. As figure 2.5 illustrates, organizational climate is seen as the consequence of the disparity, or otherwise, between the attitudes and values of members and their behaviour. Organizational climate is, in part, influenced by the relationship between how members would like or feel they ought to behave and what the work environment dictates that they do. If employees are required to act in a fashion contrary to their attitudes and values, then the climate within the organization is likely to suffer. Employee relations in the UK have not been helped by the frequent neglect of employee needs, attitudes and values, and an emphasis on the use of systems to control behaviour and a 'Now I've Got You' mentality. Certainly, people can be forced to comply – but there is a price.

On the other hand, if attitudes, values and behaviour are in harmony, a strong and effective culture is likely to result where employees are committed to the goals and methods of the organization. Consequently, the dissemination of information, consultation and participation are – as our case studies indicate – key components of the culture change process.

Processes underlying the formation of culture: observation, interaction and communication

As we have seen, beliefs are learnt. They are formed from the information we attend to and the inferences we draw. We gain information from our environment either directly from our own experience or indirectly from what we read or are

Figure 2.5
Organizaticnal culture and climate

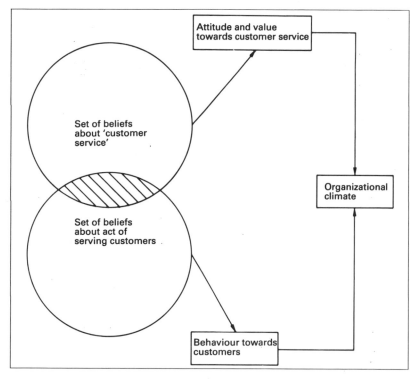

told. Because of this, the processes of observation, interaction and communication are central to the formation of beliefs. Equally, common and shared experiences and persuasive communications are fundamental to the formation – and the changing – of culture.

Observation and interaction

We naturally assume that our own experiences are valid. Our beliefs, attitudes and values are likely to be strongly influenced by directly observing the actions of others or participating ourselves in group tasks and discussions.

We frequently imitate the behaviour of others if we have seen that behaviour lead to desirable results. People act as role models for each other. Successful individuals – for example the chief executive or senior managers – often act as influential role models for more junior staff. Aspiring young managers may adopt modes of dress, conduct, management style and stated or implied philosophies.

Contact and interaction with other people, group discussion, role playing, skills learning and task performance all provide an opportunity to acquire and validate new information. They provide us with an opportunity to learn and to experiment with new forms of behaviour. In Hampshire County Council's Direct Labour Organization, for example, group exercises were used to experiment with unprecedented 'commercial' forms of behaviour.

Because it provides the opportunity for validation, participation is more likely to change beliefs than passive communication. A group discussion is more likely to form attitudes than listening to a lecture. Experiential learning techniques are more effective than traditional methods. However, while participation is more likely to result in the formation of new beliefs and attitudes, there is relatively little control over what beliefs and attitudes are formed. It is not possible, for example, to impose rigorous control on the scope or direction of a group discussion without severely undermining it as a 'participative' exercise.

Communication

Every day of their lives employees are exposed to passive communications intended to influence their beliefs, attitudes and behaviour. These include oral instructions from a manager, written memos, in-house journals, letters from the chairman, videos or conferences on company plans. By contrast with participative exercises, the information the individual receives through these media can be closely controlled. However, for the reasons explained above, passive communication is typically less persuasive than participation. There is no opportunity for the individual to validate the information through personal experience or interaction with others. Consequently, there is no sense of personal 'ownership' of the information.

The individual's acceptance of the information will depend on its credibility. As a general rule, therefore, face-to-face communication is more persuasive than anonymous contact. Video presentations are more effective than written forms of communication. On the other hand, written communications, which can be studied at length, will be more effective when the subject matter is complex.

In general terms, communications may be described in terms of a *source*, a *message* and a *receiver*. The characteristics of these elements will influence the persuasiveness of the communication (see figure 2.6).

Major determinants of organizational culture

As we have seen, common beliefs and attitudes result from a common environment and history. They are the result of common learning. Observation, interaction and communication are the processes by which common beliefs and values are formed. However, they do not in themselves explain why the culture of one organization differs from that of another. What factors determine which beliefs, attitudes and values are common to members of an organization?

As we indicated in chapter 1, culture results most immediately from the external environment, the structures, systems and technology of the organization and from the founder, manager and work group. Common beliefs, attitudes and values have their origins in all these sources. Figure 2.7,

Figure 2.6
Factors influencing the persuasiveness of communication

Source
The nature of the source will be a significant influence on the persuasiveness of communication. Relevant factors may include:

– credibility
– expertise
– status
– trust
– attractiveness

Message
The nature of the message itself will also influence the persuasiveness of the communication. Relevant factors may include:

– the perceived utility of the message (participants are more likely to be influenced by a message which is seen as personally useful or beneficial)
– the consonance of the message with the recipient's existing beliefs (recipients are more likely to be influenced by messages which conform with their current beliefs)
– novelty (recipients are more likely to be influenced by novel or unusual messages)
– repetition (recipients are more likely to be influenced by repeated messages)

Receiver
Finally, the nature of the receiver will also be a significant influence on the persuasiveness of communication. Relevant factors may include:

– the recipient's existing beliefs (recipients are more likely to be influenced by messages which conform with current beliefs)
– choice (recipients are more likely to be influenced if they can choose whether or not to accept the message)
– commitment (recipients are more likely to be influenced if they are able to feel a sense of personal commitment and 'ownership' of the message)

Figure 2.7
Culture in context

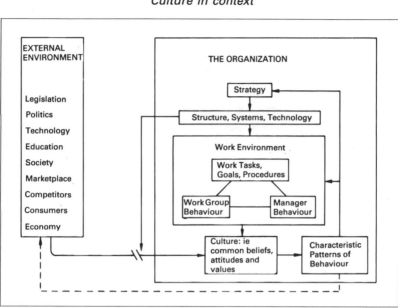

which augments figure 1.3, illustrates the major determinants of culture.

Impact of the external environment

An organization is embedded in social, political, legislative, economic and technological systems. Organizations operating in different sectors have different markets, technologies and legal constraints. They have different skill and resource needs. These variations place different demands and constraints on organizations and create differing learning environments. They influence the strategy of the organization and the structures, systems and technology that are adopted.

For example, the deregulation of the City created new demands and experiences for financial institutions not shared by other sectors. The differences in skill requirements between a manufacturing organization and a Civil Service department result in the recruitment of individuals from differing social and educational backgrounds. These variations are likely to be reflected in differences in manager behaviour, in work methods, in reward and training procedures, etc. Variations in external environment result in different experiences and demands which are reflected in differences in the socio–technical systems of the organization. These variations result in differing organizational learnings and hence differences in culture.

These broad contextual factors are likely to fix certain cultural parameters. For example, a company in the UK cannot easily adopt the culture of a Japanese company. For one thing, the social values in the respective societies are radically different. Similarly, organizational culture is likely to vary from sector to sector. A clearing bank would probably encounter significant problems if it tried to develop the same culture as, say, a computer company.

Impact of organizational structures, systems and technology

We shall discuss the impact on culture of the structures, systems and technology of the organization in terms of those used to maintain the boundaries of the organization, those resulting in its differentiation and those designed to integrate its activities.

Boundary maintenance An organization can influence the formation of its culture through the planned maintenance of its boundaries with the outside world. As we will see in chapter 5, recruitment and selection can be major cultural change mechanisms, especially when applied to key positions in the organization. One of the major functions of the traditional selection interview is often to select someone 'who will fit in'. Equally, though, more objective selection mechanisms can also operate conservatively, particularly when they are not validated or they are validated against internal criteria such as career progression. The sophisticated selection mechanisms developed by the Armed Forces and the Civil Service in the UK have been influential in the maintenance of their culture. By the same token, of course, selection methods can be used to make radical changes to the culture of an organization. Among our case studies, the switch from the recruitment and selection of engineers to sales professionals by the electricity board, or the use of a Realistic Job Preview at Toshiba both appear to have had significant cultural effects.

Beliefs, past experiences and values are incorporated directly into the organization with the recruitment of employees. The work of Geert Hofstede (see chapter 1) suggests that the culture of an organization is influenced by the values in the society from which its members are drawn. Common language, education, media, religion, political system, history, etc, result in common beliefs and values.

In extreme cases, culture may have its origins in the common learning and common experiences of a single local community, profession or trade. The Birds Eye Walls' chicken stripping plant at Kirkby on the outskirts of Liverpool is a classic example of an organization culture dominated by the local community from which its workforce is drawn. The culture of the National Health Service is heavily influenced by professionally trained medical groups with significant allegiance to their professional bodies. British Coal and British Telecom possess cultures influenced by the histories of their respective trade unions. In some cases, external factors can produce powerful cultural forces over which the organization has very little control.

The culture of an organization is influenced by its awareness of developments in its external environment. New ideas, beliefs, and philosophies are gained from external consultants, management education, developments in research, etc and strategies are influenced by, for example, knowledge of

competitor activity and customer requirements. Organizations
vary in the extent to which they monitor their performance,
the behaviour of competitors or the reactions of their
customers. They vary in the extent to which they utilize
external consultants or their managers attend external training
courses or conferences. In short, they vary in their openness
to new ideas and initiatives in their environment. We shall
expand on this idea a little later when we discuss the factors
affecting the rate of change of culture.

Differentiation Organizations tend to be characterized by
specialization. They are differentiated, vertically and horizontally, into groups with differing purposes, functions and tasks.
Skill and training needs vary from group to group, as do the
systems that are appropriate. Because of this, organizational
culture tends to be heterogeneous, reflecting the differentiation of the organization. In some organizations, such as
banks, retail chains, building society offices and police
stations, the sub-groups will be essentially clones, with the
same group replicated again and again throughout the
organization. In such cases the culture is also likely to be
replicated. In other organizations, the sub-groups will form
around widely differing functions. Most large manufacturing
organizations, for example, possess numerous distinctive
group cultures – research and development, manufacturing,
marketing and so on.

Integration Various formal systems of reward, coordination
and control may be used to provide integration across the
organization, although of course organizations differ in the
extent to which they are formalized. Implicit in these formal
systems are the organization's preferred goals and ways of
behaving: the organization's values. These, as we have seen
in the work of Miles and Snow (see chapter 1), reflect
management values and philosophy. Of course, these values
may in some cases be merely espoused by employees and not
reflected in actual behaviour. In general, such systems are

more likely to influence behaviour if they are related to desirable rewards and successes. Furthermore, as indicated earlier, such values and behaviours are more likely to be internalized if they are consistent with the individual's existing beliefs and values.

French, Kast and Rosenzweig[5] describe communication as 'the glue that holds organizations together', a description frequently given to culture. People exposed to the same information will tend to develop similar beliefs and attitudes and a common understanding. If used with care, communication systems can play an important role in forming common beliefs and attitudes. Videos, in-house magazines and conferences can all be important in forming culture. However, it should always be remembered that individuals are privy to several sources of information, both implicit and explicit. In-house magazines extolling the importance of a new management style are unlikely to be persuasive if other sources of information reinforce traditional beliefs and attitudes. There is little point in promoting, say, 'quality' as a paramount value, if incentive schemes continue to encourage high productivity at the expense of quality standards.

Among our case studies, Toshiba and Jaguar have made available to the workforce information previously confined to the Board Room. Many of the organizations we looked at formally cascaded information down the organization. At the same time, they encouraged employee 'ownership' of this information through discussion, involvement and participative meetings.

Similarly, a number of our case study organizations have introduced an over-arching ideology as a means of promoting an integrated culture. These organizations have attempted to develop common beliefs and attitudes about their overall purpose and principal mission, focused on concisely expressed concepts such as 'customer service' or 'quality'.

Corporate identity can also influence the culture of the organization. A positive attitude towards the organization increases the likelihood that individuals will conform to and

Figure 2.8
Recipes for success[6]

The recipe for success in an industry takes the form of managers' views of 'how to succeed' in their business environment.

A fashion retailer
To run a successful fashion retailing operation, management believe that they must:

– look for growth

– continually experiment with new products or ventures

– provide a constant stream of promotion opportunities

– attract new retailing talent

– continually adapt to changes in customer shopping habits

– closely monitor variable costs and centralize control of merchandise distribution

A milk processor and distributor
To operate a successful milk-processing and distribution business, managers believe they must:

– pursue greater volume of sales

– expand territory serviced

– monitor other distribution operations with a view to takeover

– optimize length and sales volumes of rounds

– increase sales per customer

– concentrate throughput into ever larger processing plants

The basic tenets of management recipes are that:

* faced with uncertainty or new situations, managers seek to relate such situations to their past experience

* an individual tends to adopt the recipe common within an industry. The commonality between recipes within an industry is greater than between industries

* the component parts of a recipe are likely to include views about how to cope with the particular business environment

internalize organizational values. Some of our case study organizations, such as Unisys and Marley, used corporate advertising to promote new and positive attitudes, not only among their customers, but also among their employees.

Impact of the founder

In many cases, culture formation is a process whereby the beliefs, attitudes and values of an individual or a small group of individuals become commonly held by other members of the organization. In this context, the creation of culture seems to require two essential ingredients: a vision of the future and power.

Vision of the future History suggests that leaders who are likely to influence the beliefs of others have clear beliefs of their own. In an organizational context these visions of the future have been termed management philosophies, ideologies or recipes for success (see figure 2.8).

Managerial recipes are drawn from the individual manager's experience. They are based upon his or her beliefs and assumptions, some of which may be unconscious.

It was frequently apparent in our case studies that managers' ideas and philosophies had been influenced by critical events or incidents in their past. Several mentioned the Peters and Waterman video *In search of excellence*. Others referred to their experiences in previous companies or during management education. Some of the influences on David Johnson's thinking as District General Manager of Mid-Essex Health Authority are given in his own words in figure 2.9.

Figure 2.9
Development of managerial recipes in Mid-Essex Health Authority[7]

Until recently, the concept of organizational development was unknown to me. My background has been in management science, working as a computer programmer for British Petroleum for a year before taking an MSc in Operational Research followed by five years as an operational research scientist in the Health Service. It was in 1974 that I decided to embark on a career as a health service administrator holding posts at the London Hospital, Middlesex Hospital and Royal National Orthopaedic Hospital. I took up my post as District

Administrator in Mid-Essex Health Authority in 1982 and, following the Griffiths Report in the Autumn of 1984, I was appointed as General Manager.

I was anxious at the time of my appointment to undertake some personal development for this new role and the National Health Service Training Authority offered a number of general manager programmes. One at Templeton College, Oxford, was attractive because it promised 'the programme will enable General Managers in the NHS to mix with senior managers from industry and commerce'. My assumptions that the NHS had something to learn from management in other organizations proved correct and, over a period of twelve to eighteen months in a series of 'retreats' to Templeton, a number of new concepts and perspectives were exposed.

The programme was led by Professor Rosemary Stewart. I was familiar with her work on the choices faced by individual managers, but it became rapidly apparent that there were also choices about how the organization functioned – the way it does things. It was also clear that, while we in the NHS felt that we were continually being reorganized, other sectors were also undergoing changes, in many instances on a more frequent basis. Some of the examples of change we explored also demonstrated that change could occur against a clear statement of the values of the organization (either existing or aspired) and that in these instances the upheaval seemed to be less traumatic. The introduction of general management into the National Health Service offered a culture shift or at least a change in the way we do things and placed less emphasis on prescriptive structural change – maybe the omens were good.

Also at Templeton, John Purcell introduced the concept of 'sophisticated human relations'. By this he means those companies who view their employees as their most valuable resource. Characteristics of such companies are often those who deliberately have above-average pay, flexible reward structures, employee appraisal systems linked to merit awards, extensive networks of communications, policies which aim to inculcate employee loyalty, commitment and dependency.

Purcell (1983) gives Marks and Spencer as an example of a 'sophisticated human relations' organization and quotes Lord Sieff (1981), Chairman and Chief Executive of Marks and Spencer as saying

Human relations in industry should cover the problems of the individual at work, his or her health, well-being and progress, the working environment and profit sharing. Full and frank two-way communication and respect for the contribution people can make, given encouragement – these are the foundations of an effective policy and a major contribution to a successful operation.

The conceptual framework that Purcell introduced was echoed by other Templeton speakers such as Stuart McAllister, one-time Personnel Director at Volvo. In the late 1970s, the company had embarked on a change in the way the organization functioned to a sophisticated human resource approach. There was a planned attempt to relate directly with employees – thus reinforcing the management line – and a flexible reward system was established.

During this period I also became familiar with the work of Peters and Waterman, *In search of excellence*. Concepts which Peters and Waterman use to characterize 'excellence', such as 'productivity through people', 'close to the customer', 'autonomy and entrepreneurship' and 'simultaneous loose–tight properties', and the evangelistic way they presented their thesis were compelling. Their clear rejection of the rational model of management should have been outrageous to a lapsed management scientist. And yet I felt comfortable with their propositions. My Operational Research course had a generous portion of behavioural science and, although my work with BP had been on linear programs, it has become clear to me that the success of the large oil companies is not solely about the optimization of the use of crude oil for its many purposes but also, and perhaps more importantly, the paternalism of the oil companies to the majority of their employees. My experience in the Health Service has also demonstrated that the pure management science approach to a people-dominated service has its difficulties. Issues such as quality of service and quality of life are not easily subject to objective measurement and analysis.

Links between Peters and Waterman and the Griffiths Report were evident. Griffiths criticized the NHS:

> Businessmen have a keen sense of how well they are looking after their customers. Whether the NHS is meeting the needs of the patient and the community is open to question . . . the process of devolution of responsibility is too slow. . . . Authorities are being swamped with directives without being given direction.

> Talking of the value of introducing general management
> (securing proper motivation of staff), he said
>
> > those charged with the general management responsibility
> > would regard it as vital to review incentives, rewards and
> > sanctions.
>
> During 1985 and the early part of 1986, therefore, I had various
> stimuli. Stewart, Purcell, Peters and Waterman, and Griffiths,
> had a degree of congruity. For me, Stewart offered the concept
> of choice about the way the organization functions, Purcell a
> particular way of working – sophisticated human relations which
> had a great many attractions – Peters and Waterman the value
> of people and Griffiths elements from all three.

Power   Power is the other essential ingredient of leadership. Power may be *personally* based in the form of charisma, expertise, attractiveness, likeability or trustworthiness. Alternatively, it may be formally based in the form of legitimate power. Our case studies suggest that both forms of power are required to influence culture. Leaders need to be able to persuade both their immediate colleagues and the workforce as a whole. They must also be able to drive change through the systems and structures via the strategy of the organization.

Individuals who possess both a vision of the future and personal and formal power are likely to have a significant impact on the culture of the organization. Founders of successful organizations are likely to possess both of these ingredients in abundance. It is not surprising that the culture of many successful organizations continues to be heavily influenced by their founders, even many years after their departure.

The role of the founder in creating organizational culture is relatively straightforward. The founder possesses both power and vision. He or she gathers like-minded individuals and they jointly experience the birth of the organization. The challenges, successes and failures of this period are likely to result in a highly committed group. Because of its attachment to the organization, the group becomes its core for some considerable time. The beliefs and values that founding members share (as Miles and Snow suggest) are reflected in the structures and systems of the organization. The small size of the young organization enables interaction and involvement in decision-making and ensures that managers are visible role models. If the fledgling organization is to survive, it must be successful. This success reinforces the original values and philosophies. The work of Stinchcombe is of interest here. He found that the structure and management of organizations reflects the values and ideologies prevalent at the time of their foundation.[8] As Edgar Schein states:

> Although the final form of an organization's culture reflects the complex interaction between the thrust provided by the founder, the reactions of the group members and their shared historical experiences, there is little doubt that the initial shaping force is the personality and belief system of the founder.[9]

Impact of the manager

Bosses tend to act as role models. Their behaviour represents the approved way of behaving. Individuals conforming to their behaviour are likely to be rewarded. Most of the organizations we studied considered management style to be an important cultural issue. The style adopted by managers reflects a combination of their personal values and their beliefs about the organization and the environment. For example, most autocratic managers probably do not believe, in general terms, that 'man is lazy'. Rather they believe that autocratic behaviour is most likely to be effective, given the needs of the job, especially if the manager is working under severe time pressures and has subordinates who are under-trained or themselves overworked. Similarly, there may be little value in a participative style if the organization is highly formalized, with rules and procedures for most things. Officers in the British Army are trained not to become too friendly with those under their command. This does not reflect social or personal values but simply acknowledges the potential difficulties of command in battle if this were not the case. In other words, the culture of an organization has its roots as much in beliefs about the demands of the work environment as it does in the personal values of individuals.

Edgar Schein considers that the major mechanisms of culture formation and reinforcement are: what leaders pay attention to, measure and control; their reactions to critical incidents and organizational crises; their deliberate role modelling, teaching and coaching; their criteria for allocation of rewards and status; and their criteria for recruitment, selection, promotion, retirement and excommunication.[10] Clearly, these are major cultural agents, but it should be remembered that these behaviours and the beliefs that underlie them are themselves, in part, a product of the culture within the organization.

Impact of the work group

A work group develops shared beliefs and values around its need to adapt to its external environment and integrate its internal environment. In these respects the group mirrors the overall organization. However, it is quite possible for the group's approach to conflict with the organization's philosophy and values.

Within the work group, interaction is likely to result in shared understandings. The exchange of information in discussion is likely to lead to consensus on the group's goals and ways of doing things. Once formed, this will be maintained by the pressure on individuals to conform.

Common and interdependent goals, tasks and functions provide the reason for interaction. Proximity provides the opportunities for interaction. The physical layout of an office or factory, as well as the nature of work routines, may influence patterns of interaction and the development of informal groupings.

When groups first form, a leader tends to emerge who influences the solutions to task issues. If these solutions are successful, they are likely to be adopted by the group. If they are repeatedly successful, the solutions will become taken for granted and will drop from awareness. This predictability of response reduces anxiety and provides security. At the same time, interaction and similarity of view promote the development of friendships. The group serves both a task and a social or emotional role and its culture forms around both. If members see the group as successfully providing for both task and social needs, it is likely that strongly shared beliefs and attitudes will develop. 'Successful' groups become very cohesive. They are resistant to change and react in concert to external threat. New members learn and are taught the characteristic behaviours and beliefs. Pressure is placed upon deviants to conform. If newcomers do not conform, they will tend to be ostracized and excluded from the group.

Shared experience of any kind will inevitably be a powerful social and cultural influence. For example, the founding group of an organization will share a common experience and history – sometimes quite traumatic – which are likely to lead to mutual understanding and empathy. This cannot be taught to or learnt by new members. Sometimes, when an organization grows beyond its original nucleus of members, it is difficult to overcome the feelings of alienation felt by newcomers who have not shared the founding experience. Equally, the founders may feel resentful that the organization is being taken over by 'outsiders'. For example, after Toshiba's original staff of 300 in 1981 had been increased to 1100 in 1986, an attitude survey found some dissatisfaction amongst the original employees: 'the image was of a team, linked by the common experience of crisis and revival, dispersed among a lonely crowd of strangers'. At any given time, in any organization, there will tend to be generations

representing the 'Old Village' and the 'Newcomers' each with
its own appreciation of what the organization is 'really' about.

Factors influencing the stability and change of organizational culture

The stability or rate of change in an organization's culture is
likely to be influenced by individual, group, organizational
and environmental factors. Figure 2.10 lists some of these
influences on the rate of cultural change. It should be noted
that some of these factors can operate to promote either
change or stability. Thus, for example, a crisis may promote
change and/or may result in feelings of insecurity which cause
rigidity and resist change.

Individual factors

An individual's beliefs and values generally tend to be stable.
They exist in a network of beliefs and attitudes which are
usually logically consistent, mutually reinforcing and resistant
to change. Our interpretations of the world need to make
sense to us and we do not change our habitual ways of
thinking lightly.

Because of this, we do not simply 'gulp down' organization
or group values. Rather, we interpret them from our own
point of view. In some cases, because of the pressure to
conform, we may decide simply to 'go along with' group
practices, even though we disapprove of them. In other cases,
we may come fully to adopt the group's values. In general
terms, as figure 2.6 indicates, we are more likely to internalize
beliefs, attitudes and values which are seen to be useful, to
be from a credible source and to be in agreement with our
existing beliefs and values.

Figure 2.10

Factors influencing the rate of change of organizational culture

Stability	Change
Openness to new ideas	Internally focused on rules and procedures
Customer surveys	
Monitors competitor activity and performance →	
	Criteria of success unclear
Monitors own performance	
Uses external consultants	← Internal training, internally validated
External training and management education	
	Predictable and stable market
Uncertain and volatile market	Dominant in market
Competitive market →	Powerful political lobby
	Success
Crisis	← Feelings of insecurity and threat
Crisis seen as a challenge	
Authority can be challenged	Strict regard for authority and status
New ideas, innovation and risk-taking valued →	
Senior management bought in when required	'Home-grown' management
	Career-based, 'jobs for life'
Multiple-level entry into organization	Single-level entry into ← organization
Powerful external stakeholders	'Ultimate' authority unclear
	Board all from within company or industry
Non-executive directors from outside industry	
	Low labour turnover, → cohesive work groups and strong conformity pressures
Selection procedures objectively validated on regular basis	← Selection based on ad hoc interviews, or traditional selection and recruitment → procedures which are not validated, or validated against subjective, internal criteria

Group factors

As we have seen, group solutions to the need for external
adaptation and internal integration are shared. Shared beliefs
and values are likely to be stable. The group imposes
pressures on those with alternative or deviant views to
conform. As an illustration, the work of Irving Janis on
Groupthink given in figure 2.11 illustrates the persuasive
force of a group.[11]

Figure 2.11
Groupthink

Irving Janis has analysed the decision-making process of a
number of American presidential administrations. He has
identified what he terms as Groupthink. Groupthink is defined
as the deterioration of mental efficiency, reality testing and
moral judgement in the interests of group solidarity.

Illusion of invulnerability
Members of one group believed that they were invincible. For
example, on the eve of the disastrous attempt to invade Cuba in
1961 (the Bay of Pigs invasion), Robert Kennedy stated that with
the talent in the group they could overcome whatever challenged
them with common sense and hard work and bold new ideas.

Tendency to moralize
The group studied had a general tendency to view the United
States as the leader of the free world. Any opposition to this
view was characterized by the group members as weak, evil or
unintelligent.

Feeling of unanimity
The group reported that each member of the executive
committee supported the President's decision. Later on,
however, members indicated that they had had serious doubts
at the time the decisions were being made. For example, Arthur
Schlesinger and Theodore Sorensen both reported that they had
had reservations about the decisions being made with respect
to South East Asia during the Kennedy years. Both men admitted
regretting their hesitancy to let their views be known at the

time. However, at the time they believed that everyone else was in total agreement and that they had the only differing view.

Pressure to conform

Occasionally, President Kennedy would bring in an expert to respond to questions that members of the group might have. The purpose was to have the expert in effect silence the critics instead of actively encouraging discussion of diverging views. Other forms of informal pressure to conform are used on Cabinet and staff members. In one instance, Arthur Schlesinger reported that Robert Kennedy had mentioned informally to him that, while he could see some problems associated with the particular decision, the President needed unanimous support on the issue.

Opposing ideas dismissed

Any individual or outside group that criticized or opposed a decision on policy received little or no attention from the group. Even valid ideas or relevant arguments were often dismissed prematurely. Much evidence indicated strongly that the invasion of Cuba would fail, but it was given little consideration. Thus, conflicting information with group goals can be distorted or ignored as individual members strive for agreement and solidarity.

Members who identify with a group – that is, who have positive attitudes towards the group and wish to remain members – are more likely to conform to group opinion. Identification reduces turnover. Groups with stable membership are likely to develop strong cultures. Long tenure increases the likelihood of individuals sharing experience and identifying with and internalizing the values of the group or organization.

Beliefs and attitudes which result in failure will be modified; failure is 'stamped out'. Those which result in success will be 'stamped in'. Those that lead repeatedly to success will be taken for granted and may drop from awareness. Group members become unaware of the assumptions they are making. Patterns of behaviour and thought become habitual and unconscious and consequently more resistant to change.

Organizational factors

The culture of an organization has a tendency to become stable because it, being both an input and an output, tends to be self-perpetuating.

The beliefs and attitudes within the organization are drawn initially from its external environment. The beliefs of individuals within the organization determine their behaviour, which acts as a role model for others. When coupled with power, as in the case of senior executives, beliefs influence the internal environment of the organization in a more formal way. This may be through the development of strategy, or through the design and implementation of the structures and systems of the organization. If effective, these reinforce existing beliefs and influence the beliefs of new members joining the organization. In other words, beliefs influence the internal environment which in turn influences beliefs. If there is no new input from the external environment, this will result over time in stability.

The systems and structures also influence the boundaries of the organization. We have already discussed one of these boundary filters: namely, the recruitment and selection procedures erected to select 'appropriate people'. Others exist, most notably those that monitor factors such as the external performance of the company, competitor activity, customer requirements, developments in R & D or in management practice, legislation, new technology and the economy. Organizations may tend to be externally focused (that is, aware of ideas and developments in their environment), or internally focused (that is, concerned with internal procedures, rules or power struggles). Clearly this difference in focus reflects a difference in the openness of the organization to new ideas, new beliefs and attitudes. Open, externally focused systems are more likely to change while closed, internally focused systems are more likely to stabilize.

We are not suggesting that culture changes automatically as a result of organizations monitoring their performance, the reactions of their consumers, clients, competitors or whatever. The interpretation of and reaction to such information will be influenced by the prevailing culture that already exists within the organization. Thus, the openness or closedness of the organization is as much a product of culture as it is a determinant of it.

Environmental factors

Changes in an organization's environment will probably influence its culture, though stabilizing factors within the organization will often moderate or slow down any environmental change.

However, if an organization fails to respond to environmental change, it may well go out of business. There are numerous examples of companies hitting hard times precisely because of their failure to respond to changes in the marketplace, customer need, etc. The term 'cultural drag' would seem appropriate here. Clearly, organizations operating in different business sectors are also likely to operate in different environments varying in volatility and unpredictability. As a result, the culture of organizations from different sectors is likely to differ not only in type but also in stability.

Change in Western society over the last three or four decades has resulted in changes in expectations and values among employees. Common values in society place constraints upon the kinds of organizational culture acceptable to members. For example, since the Industrial Revolution there have been substantial changes in social values regarding the work ethic, working conditions, leisure, equal opportunities, employee rights and the quality of working life. All these changes affect the kinds of values and practices that will be satisfying to people at work. They affect the type of organizational culture that will be acceptable.

Large, dominant multinationals can to some extent influence aspects of their external environments. This is perhaps more obvious in the USA where more visible attempts are made to influence governmental, legislative and economic decision-making. Among our case studies one or two organizations had attempted to influence their external environment. Jaguar and Toshiba had imposed 'quality' requirements upon their suppliers or distributors which had had a knock-on effect on other organizations, including Johnson Matthey, who had been on the receiving end. However, for the most part, organizations are subordinate to environmental demands. At best they adopt a responsive posture and develop a dynamic equilibrium with their environment so that external changes result in internal adaptation. They monitor these changes and are responsive to them. Other organizations, as we have already discussed, are more internally focused. They operate as a closed system. They are more concerned with internal rules and procedures. Consequently, the culture of the organization is likely to stabilize and significant changes in the environment are likely to threaten the organization's survival.

In virtually all our case studies some form of crisis was the instigator of cultural change. It would seem likely that crisis and intervention by external stakeholders are the only means whereby some organizations can break out of the circularity that is created by operating as a closed system.

Notes and References

1 Much of our discussion on the nature of individual beliefs, attitudes and behaviours is drawn from the work of Isaac Ajzen and Martin Fishbein. See, for example, FISHBEIN M *and* AJZEN I. *Belief, attitude, intention and behaviour: an introduction to theory and research.* Addison-Wesley, 1975

2 Those who are interested in cross-cultural studies of cognition will find an essential source book to be: TRIANDIS H C. *Handbook of cross-cultural psychology.* Allyn and Bacon, 1980

3 For ease of understanding we have simplified Ajzen and Fishbein's 'Theory of Reasoned Action'. They suggest that our behaviour is in fact determined by our attitudes towards behaviour, our beliefs about the social norms and our motivation to comply. See FISHBEIN M *and* AJZEN I. *op cit*, or AJZEN I *and* FISHBEIN M. *Understanding attitudes and predicting social behaviour*. Prentice-Hall, 1980. Criticism of their approach is given in EISER J R *and* VON DER PLIGT J. *Attitudes and decisions*. Routledge, 1988

4 The distinction between espoused theories and theories-in-use was made by Chris Argyris and Donald Schon (see ARGYRIS C *and* SCHON D. *Theory in practice*. Jossey-Bass, 1974). Interestingly, their assumption appears to be that theories-in-use are in some way more fundamental than those espoused. However, our analysis suggests that rather than one being more fundamental than the other, the differences between them is simply due to a difference in the set of beliefs underlying what we say and what we do: a difference between what we would like or think we ought to do and what the work environment dictates that we do

5 FRENCH W L, KAST F E *and* ROSENZWEIG J E *Understanding human behaviour in organizations*. Harper & Row, 1985

6 From JOHNSON G *and* SCHOLES K. *Exploring corporate strategy*. Prentice-Hall, 1984

7 From ATTWOOD M *and* JOHNSON D. *Making general management work – a case study on organizational change and development in a District Health Authority*. Paper presented to Centre for Management Learning, Lancaster University. September 1987

8 STINCHCOMBE A L. 'Social structure and organization' in MARCH J G. *Handbook of organization*. Rand McNally, 1965

9 SCHEIN E H *Organizational culture and leadership*. Jossey-Bass, 1985

10 SCHEIN E H (1985). *op cit*

11 JANIS I. *Victims of groupthink: a psychological study of foreign policy decisions and fiascos*. Houghton Mifflin, 1973

Part II
Changing Culture

3

♟ Methods of Culture Change

In this chapter we are going to concentrate on the lessons gained from the case studies. Those intending to apply the lessons need to take account of the process issues discussed in chapter 4. For the present, let us consider why organizations attempted to change their culture, how they attempted to change it and the factors that appeared to facilitate change.

Why did the organizations attempt to change their culture?

The answer is quite simple. The organizations attempted to change their culture in order to implement a strategic change. Most of the case studies began with a strategic review in response to some crisis or opportunity. The strategic review required a change in organizational objectives, work methods and behaviour. As we know, culture can act either to promote or constrain business strategy. It is likely to be the self-sealing, embedded product of past strategy and, unless carefully managed, will act to negate any future strategy which requires a major change in the way people think or 'do things around here'.

In all the case studies culture change was strategy driven. None of the organizations set out to change their culture for the sake of it. In fact, one suspects that some of the organizations did not attempt to change their culture at all but, rather, they set out to implement a new strategic direction by introducing new work objectives, methods, systems, structures, training and people – and changed the culture quite fortuitously. However, most were aware that in order to change behaviour they needed to change people's beliefs and attitudes. They realized that to change the strategic direction they needed to change the culture of the organization and took planned steps to do so.

Important among our findings was the observation that culture change did not occur in a vacuum, but was linked to organizational effectiveness via strategic planning. One of the best examples of this would appear to be given by Rank Xerox UK who have formally integrated their Leadership Through Quality programme into the business planning process (see figure 3.1). In planning cultural change organizations need to consider not only how to change the culture of the organization, but also how to link the change with organizational goals and effectiveness. The changes which occurred in the case study organizations were ultimately driven by business demands, not by the need to change culture.

How did the organizations change their culture?

In order to change the culture of an organization you need to change the common beliefs, attitudes and values that exist within the organization. Our case study organizations attempted to do this in six main ways, namely: by changing the people in the organization; by changing people's positions in the organization; by changing beliefs, attitudes and values directly; by changing behaviour; by changing the systems and structures; and by changing the corporate image.

Figure 3.1

Linking cultural change and organizational strategy

During his time at Burroughs David O'Brien had introduced a process called 'Business Development Planning' that had been used successfully by his account teams – sometimes with customers – to determine key strategies and objectives. He introduced a similar process at Rank Xerox UK, but tailored to the distinct requirements of the new situation in Rank Xerox and developed as a comprehensive approach to implementing an integrated management process. A similar process of Business Systems Requirements Review was used at the functional level to identify rules, system requirements, management processes and resources required to deliver the objectives defined by the BDP output. The vehicle used to implement the strategic requirements was a renovated Leadership Through Quality programme and the use of consensus management and cross-functional teams.

The integrated planning process is given below:

Integration of Leadership Through Quality and Business Planning at Rank Xerox UK

Level of Responsibility within the Organization	Definition of Role	Planning Process	Methodology	Outputs
Direction	What are we going to do?	Responsibilities	Business Development Planning	Mission Strategy Responsibilities
		Corporate Mission Critique		
		Environment Appraisal		
Function Management	What do we need to do it?	Objectives	Business Systems Requirements	Management Process Systems and Rules Resources
		Objective Setting		
		Organization Delegation Resourcing		
Operational Management	How are we going to do it?	Activities	Leadership Through Quality	Quality Improvement Projects Operational Improvements Team Commitment
		Planning Approval		
		Execution Monitoring Control		
Operations	Doing it		Teamwork	

By changing people

If you change the people you may change the pattern of
beliefs and attitudes in the organization, particularly if you
change people in key positions. Consequently, recruitment,
selection and redundancy were frequently part of the change
process.

Toshiba, in order to promote cooperation on the shop
floor, took considerable care in wording their recruitment
literature which referred to assembly operators rather than
specific jobs or trades. They also used a video as a Realistic
Job Preview to aid the self-selection of those with the
attitudes appropriate to a clockwork organization (see figure
3.2). The area electricity board as part of its change from a
technical to a sales culture, recruited sales professionals and
subsequently increased its sales staff by sixty-three per cent
over five years. It is not unreasonable to assume that the
sales professionals brought into the organization had different
experiences, knowledge and attitudes to the engineers who
had been recruited in the past.

Figure 3.2
Self-selection at Toshiba

The following is a transcript of the video presented by Geoffrey
Deith, then the Managing Director of Toshiba Consumer
Products, to job applicants.

Toshiba the Commitment

Toshiba is one of the oldest and largest electrical engineering
companies in Japan, covering all fields from heavy engineering
to microchips. It has 98,000 employees, but I want to talk about
one job, the one you are applying for and to give you the flavour
of the company and what working for the new company in
Plymouth will be like. That's exactly what it's going to be: a new
company, with brand new ideas and new ways of doing things.

We'll be taking on some three hundred people at the
beginning. We want to find some of the best people we can get.

We're looking for *expertise*, whether as a truck driver, an engineer or a computer analyst. We're looking for expertise in the people that we employ.

The next quality we're looking for is not often talked about in British companies. It's *enthusiasm*. Does it frighten you, the idea of enthusiasm? We almost have a tradition, don't we, of not being seen to be too enthusiastic about what we do. But in the new Toshiba company we'll be looking for people with enthusiasm, because we're going to need that in the years to come.

The next quality, *idealism*, is even stranger. Let me tell you a story of when I was in America. I visited this office equipment manufacturer, where all the work benches were covered with billiard cloths made of the usual green baize. So I said to the man taking me round, 'This looks very splendid but isn't it expensive?' 'Well, you see,' he replied, 'we turn the desks upside down on the benches and slide them along, and we don't want to scratch the furniture.' Then I asked him, 'Supposing there was a screw on the bench, or someone dropped one by accident, wouldn't that scratch the desks?' 'A screw?' he said, 'Is someone wasting a screw? Do we have accidents? Where is the accident? I don't want to waste a screw for five cents and scratch a five-dollar desk!' There was a manufacturer who was idealistic. He had a very efficient manufacturing operation, with nothing out of place.

In the new Toshiba company we are looking for that sort of idealism, and that comes from *commitment*. We are putting together a team of three hundred people absolutely and utterly committed to an efficient manufacturing operation: not half-hearted, not doing our best, but doing it right.

These are the four qualities we are looking for and there's a fifth quality, *attention to detail*, absolute detail. Many of you have already worked with our colleagues from Toshiba and we have often admired the detailed way they investigate things, the way they leave no stone unturned in their planning and the way they make sure the right things happen by doing it in detail.

What have we done to ensure that we get the right operation here in Plymouth? Well, in forming Toshiba Consumer Products, TCP – what a title, TCP! We're going to have to live with the jokes over the years – we have taken some fairly basic decisions. Everyone will be on monthly staff. Shall I say that again? Everyone will be on monthly staff. The term 'hourly paid' will mean nothing in the future. There will be one dining room and the same type of coat for everyone. Why? To ensure that everyone in the company feels an important part of the team. We are convinced that, if people have the right organization and the right enthusiasm, we don't need many of the old-fashioned ways of motivating people. We'll have the same holidays, the same sick pay entitlements. This has been done so that everyone who works at TCP feels an important part of the team.

What else have we done? Toshiba has put down a lot of money: the capital for the factory, to set it up and to run it efficiently in the future. We've set up a new way of communicating with each other. It's called an advisory board. It's elected from all parts of the company. The whole company is represented round the table. It will advise the company on conditions, on future prospects and on anything the members feel they have advice to offer about. There will be a separate presentation to show you how it will work. You may be surprised that it has the unqualified backing of the trade union. But you shouldn't be surprised, because if industry, especially manufacturing industry, is to survive then we must find new ways of doing things – and ways how a new, lean and hungry company can be competitive.

These are things we have done. What are we asking you to do? If it doesn't sound too simple, we are asking that people come to work. There is a word – 'absenteeism'. I don't ever want to use it again. We are paying people on monthly staff to be here on all working days. So the first thing we are asking is for you to come here for 230 days a year or whatever it is.

It is important that people do come. If you have a bad accident or are in hospital, then we understand but there are very few other reasons why people can't come. I've no doubt in my mind that a lot of absenteeism is due to one of two reasons. First, people know that there isn't really a job for them to do. Secondly, it comes from people having other responsibilities and looking after people when there is no one else to look after them. But we're trying to say right from the word go to anyone who may have a problem looking after a child with a cough or cold at home, because there are no other parents in the area, that perhaps you should think again about coming to Toshiba Consumer Products. Because we won't have any spare people. It will be a lean and hungry company. We need everyone here all the time. I hope you'll appreciate that we want to say everything important first before the start so that we can get the right team of the right people that can work together.

We're expecting high standards of workmanship. Many people

think of workmanship as a high standard filing at a bench but it's also high standards of planning, buying and accounting. We're looking for, striving for, very high standards in whatever we do. So we're asking people if they want to move into a company which is aiming at such high standards.

If we can put together the qualities and attributes of the people and if we can mould them into a system which uses the team to good advantage, then we can have a really good factory, a manufacturing unit that works like clockwork. We don't want surprises. We want a clockwork factory. We don't want to get into a situation where we have to use our juggling expertise to get out of trouble. We've got a very good start, with only about ten models. We've got an excellent production line laid out. There's a lot to be said for a clockwork organization. Some of the happiest operations are the very efficient ones, where people can do what they came for in the first place. For people who want to be part of a clockwork organization that is therefore competitive, that can make television sets as good as any in the market place, that are reliable and good value for money, for those people who want to join that sort of company, then TCP is for them. Others might want to think twice. Some might not like the idea of a clockwork-like factory.

I hope I've given you some idea of the flavour of the company. It's a tremendous step forward in organization and a tremendous step forward in conditions; but with it is the responsibility of living up to high standards. Thank you.

Jaguar increased the recruitment of engineers and technical specialists in its attempt to rebuild the technical expertise lost during the BL days. Abbey National Building Society has steadily increased the number of graduate trainees as part of the process of becoming a more commercial organization. And Hampshire County Council recruited new managers in its Direct Labour Organization to replace the District Surveyors.

While people have not been made redundant in order to change the culture of the organization, the redundancy of key individuals and those with more intransigent attitudes has been mentioned as promoting cultural change by a number of organizations. Unisys considered that the early retirement of traditional Sperry and Burroughs employees facilitated the creation of the new company (see figure 3.3). Abbey National found that there were pockets of managers who were uncomfortable with the new ways of running the business and

Figure 3.3
Changing people at Unisys

Not all the changes were positive. The company had to shed some four hundred staff in the merger process. Unisys endeavoured to treat staff as well as possible and, wherever possible, job losses were achieved through early retirement. In addition, outplacement consultancy and counselling was made available to the staff to ease their transition period. Interestingly, this process may itself have contributed to the speed with which the change was achieved. Many of the longer serving staff found it hard to come to terms with the new organization and chose to leave. At retirement dinners, for example, it was not uncommon to hear retiring staff say 'it will always be Burroughs [or Sperry] to me. . . . I will never use the name Unisys'.

these were approached with generous early retirement packages. In all 150 – approximately twenty-five per cent of management – left under such arrangements. Jaguar also reduced its workforce coincidentally with the initial stages of change. As it was recognized that employee commitment was essential to the long-term survival of the company it was decided to make one large cut rather than a series of small ones; the workforce was reduced by over thirty per cent during 1981. Xerox in discussing its Quality programme states the case more openly:

> We clearly identify which executives are with us and which are not with us. We are patient with those that have to make the change but, in the end, if they do not adapt, they have to leave. Quite simply if you do not want to be a quality performer, you do not work here.

All the companies have recognized that the way labour reductions are handled is an important issue for the future of the company. Feelings of insecurity and anxiety among those who remain have to be handled sensitively if commitment and loyalty to the organization are to result. Both Abbey National and Unisys used individual counselling and outplacement to help people make the transition.

People have changed at the top of the organization. A change in the leadership of an organization can bring with it new ideas and visions of the future which, when coupled with power, can act as a major stimulus to cultural change. A surprisingly large number of our case studies have had changes in their chief executives. Witness the arrival of Sir John Egan at Jaguar, David O'Brien at Rank Xerox UK, Geoffrey Deith at Toshiba, George Russell at Marley, David Johnson at Mid-Essex Health Authority, Eugene Anderson at Johnson Matthey and Peter Birch at Abbey National Building Society. Of course, change at the top is in itself unlikely to change the culture of an organization, particularly if the new executive is drawn from the same industry – a point well made by George Orwell in *Animal farm*.

By changing places

Sub-cultures develop in the organization around differences in function, role and level. Culture can, therefore, be promoted by reshuffling the pack and moving different people with different experiences and learning into key positions. The electricity board moved sales staff into management positions which previously had always been occupied by engineers; while in Abbey National the early retirement of older and more traditional managers enabled high flyers to be moved into key positions. Also at Abbey National, the decision was made to move managers around more frequently. Those who had been in their posts for more than seven years were, with their agreement, moved to fresh pastures.

Normally this involved moving a branch manager to an adjacent branch. Interestingly, in practically all cases, there were 'reportedly marked improvements in performance, both in the branch left behind and in the one to which they moved.

By changing people's beliefs and attitudes

In chapter 2 we identified direct experience, in the guise of observation, interaction and participation, and persuasive communication, as the processes underlying belief formation and change. The corresponding practical methods used by our case study organizations have been: role modelling, participative group methods such as circles and briefing groups, role playing, counselling, management education and formal communication.

While these are practical methods for changing the beliefs, attitudes and values of employees, it should be noted that relatively few of our case study organizations had culture change as their explicit objective. Thus, for example, quality circles were used to identify and resolve quality problems and – as an aside – to increase employee involvement or participation; the workshops at Mid-Essex Health Authority were used to draw out the implications for the District and individuals of the general management role; and the 'kick-off' meetings at Unisys were used to introduce the new company's policies and objectives – what these methods were also probably doing was changing people's beliefs and attitudes and thus the culture of the organization. Typically, the purpose of the method of change was to implement a new strategy, not to change culture.

Through the use of role models Most of the organizations in our sample have recognized the importance of individuals, particularly senior managers, acting as role models for the desired attitudes and behaviours. People learn by observation and are likely to emulate those behaviours that they believe are likely to lead to success.

The Royal Bank of Scotland, in developing a more participative style of management, have used senior managers as role models on training courses. Thus, selected senior managers take question and answer sessions because they have a personal style that is open and participative. Training centres are important in presenting the approved form of behaviour and a number of our case study organizations have circulated videos throughout the company in order to present senior managers as the appropriate model.

The development of a participative style among managers and the training in participative techniques may therefore be a central culture change strategy. It changes what managers pay attention to, monitor and control, their criteria of reward, promotion, selection and retirement, and their deliberate teaching and coaching. It changes the nature of the role models in the organization and provides managers with the skills to manage participatively. However, these changes need to be supported by an integration of style and system.

Through participation   Most of the organizations have used formalized group discussions in the guise of, for example, morning meetings, team briefings or quality circles as part of the cultural change process. The purpose of these formalized and usually cascaded discussions is manifold: to increase the involvement of employees as a means of encouraging identification and commitment to the group task, the group or organization; to improve organizational communication and control; to solicit group experience in problem solving; to promote participative management practice.

The Royal Bank of Scotland used circle activities in its branches to identify ways of improving customer service. Small groups of branch employees meet to discuss customer service issues and related topics. Toshiba uses participative employee circles with the emphasis upon product quality. It is similarly the case at Jaguar, but here good quality and productivity schemes originating from the circles can earn cash awards. Managers at Toshiba hold five-minute morning meetings to discuss the day's issues and deal with any outstanding problems. Both the electricity board and Jaguar use team briefing but primarily as a means of one-way communication. Jaguar's emphasis is upon management control through the feedback of productivity and quality achievements and targets.

Mid-Essex Health Authority has used a series of management workshops to promote 'a learning organization'. The workshops began at the top with Authority members, consultants and senior managers who clarified the Authority's mission, debated the implications of the general management role and identified the key tasks facing the Authority. The outputs from these initial workshops resulted in the setting up of other task groups, team building workshops, and personal and organizational development workshops which linked personal and organizational development needs. In turn these groups have spawned other workshops on, for example, financial management, inter-personal skills, stress and time management, and resulted in individual managers originating development groups in their own units to work through the local implications of the change.

Both the Royal Bank of Scotland and the National Freight Consortium have attempted to introduce a more participative management style. The experience of NFC is summarized in figure 3.4.

Group discussion is potentially an excellent mechanism for the development of shared beliefs and attitudes, but whether or not attitudes are likely to change and what attitudes are likely to do so is dependent upon the specific nature and content of the discussion. If an open discussion is held in an appropriate climate it is likely that group beliefs and attitudes will be discussed and perhaps that some of the group's assumptions will surface and be tested against reality. Assumptions underlying behaviour are more likely to surface when talking through an intended behaviour change. That is

Figure 3.4
Participative management at NFC

In the early 1980s the Government made the decision to sell off the National Freight Corporation. The management could not afford to buy the company on its own, so the support of all employees was sought. This involved a major exercise in communication, which improved senior management's ability to communicate and promoted the participative style.

The fact that the vast majority of employees are share holders also has a big impact on the need for management to communicate. There are regular newssheets and discussions with directors about financial results, and the Board publish a quarterly 'Best View' of the financial out-turn for display in all branches to enable the employees to decide whether to increase their capital stake. In support, line and supervisory personnel have been trained in presentation skills.

When one of the senior managers was booked on a training course run by Management Centre Europe and had to back out due to pressure of work, the Chairman, Sir Peter Thompson, attended instead. He was so enthusiastic about the course that all senior managers were later sent for similar training and over a quarter of a million pounds was spent. The aim was to develop a more participative management style. Personnel had introduced appraisal, goal-setting systems etc. before, but only lip service was paid to them. Suddenly senior managers saw the relevance of integrated systems and management style.

'In every part of our business there is an individual who is accountable for its profit and its development. He is the person who takes the decision, but in doing so we expect and require him to listen to and take account of the views of those he manages. The success of the business and the harmonious industrial relations they have enjoyed for the last six years, is testimony to the importance of our participative management style' (Quote from Chairman's report, NFC Annual Report, 1987).

when the group is focused on task issues. Whether group discussion results in feelings of 'groupness', commitment and a sharing of beliefs and attitudes, as opposed to having a boomerang effect and increasing the intransigence of traditional beliefs and attitudes, is dependent upon the nature and content of the discussion, group composition and climate, and leader's skill.

There is likely to be more control over the content and structure of group discussion run as part of a training course. Hampshire County Council and Sainsbury's have developed group role-play exercises, targeted at specific beliefs, attitudes and behaviours. Sainsbury's introduced region by region a training package combining videos, role-playing exercises, discussion and skills training in its attempt to develop positive attitudes towards customer service.

Through the use of formal communication   Communication has been widely used by the organizations. Most organizations have 'communicated like mad'. Jaguar Cars used conferences, videos, posters and in-house magazines as part of its attempt to change employee attitudes to productivity and quality, and a Speak-Up scheme to increase employee involvement. Unisys used information bulletins, audio tapes and magazines as well as internal computer communications systems. Customer orientation was reiterated again and again in the Unisys published documents and briefings. A typical edition of the Unisys quarterly news briefing, for example, contained articles entitled 'Protecting Customer Investment', 'Putting the Customer First', and 'Responding to Changing Demands'. At the same time Unisys also made major use of its external corporate advertising on television and in the media to promote the values of the new company among staff as well as customers. The corporate affairs department has also been heavily involved in change at the area electricity board where there was a similar recognition of the potential value of external advertising – in this case among the local community – in promoting internal change. Similarly, Jaguar through its 'Hearts and Minds Programme' for employees and their families has attempted to extend its quality image into the local community, from where it recruits the majority of its employees.

Through counselling A leading paper manufacturer needed
to make significant reductions in staff in order to cut its costs
and improve its profitability. The company's primary difficulty
therefore was to maintain staff commitment and promote a
new proactive and positive culture, while at the same time
achieving the kinds of staff reductions that were required.

It was decided that these objectives could only be achieved
through a process of extensive and highly personalized
communication. The proposed changes would ultimately
affect all employees in the company, and it was felt essential
that there should be complete commitment to the proposals
from the most senior levels downwards. Once the plans had
been drawn up by the project team, but before any changes
had been announced, the senior management of the company,
led by the Chief Executive, began a gradual cascade process
which they called 'bringing on board'. At each level
of management, they carried out one-to-one interviews,
explaining in detail the intended changes, outlining the
implications for the individual concerned and defining what
would be expected of those working in the 'new' organization.
The individual was then asked whether he or she could be
fully committed to working in the organization on the terms
that had been laid out.

This process of individual counselling was carried out, as
quickly as possible, throughout the management of the
organization, down to the level of sales manager. In total,
some 300 individuals were interviewed, and at least half of
those in very extensive and detailed sessions. The interviews
were for the most part carried out by the Chief Executive or
other senior managers. The personnel function was involved
both in the original project team which determined the
method of operation and in the preparation of detailed
'counselling packs' which were provided to the manager
conducting the interview. The whole process was carried out
over a period of two weeks.

Because of the need to reduce staff, the 'bringing on board'
interviews were also accompanied by counselling interviews

for those individuals who were not seen as having a role in the new structure. Although it was possible to lose some staff through voluntary redundancies and early retirement, there were inevitably a number of compulsory redundancies. Every effort was made, not only to provide a redundancy counselling and support service as appropriate, but also to ensure that the reasons for the changes were explained as fully and clearly as possible.

Once the process of informing management was complete, the process was extended to all field sales staff, this time through a series of group presentations. Once again, redundancy counselling and support was provided for those who did not have a place in the new organization.

Similar problems of maintaining staff commitment at the same time as making significant reductions in staff numbers have been faced by Abbey National and Unisys, who both also employed redundancy counselling and outplacement support.

Through management education   Management education has been a strategy central to culture change at Abbey National, which has cascaded management education down the organization. The top two layers of management were sent on externally run courses and then the external consultants were contracted to devise and run the customized internal programme for the rest of the staff.

Management education is the central component of the Crosby Quality approach devised by Philip Crosby and used by BP Chemicals and Johnson Matthey in our case studies. As Crosby states:

> The individual's role in causing quality must be understood by each and every person in the company. . . . The overall educational aspect requires executive education, wherein senior management can learn its role; management education, wherein those who must implement the process learn how

to do it; an employee education system, wherein all the employees of the company learn to comprehend their roles; and workshops, wherein special functions such as purchasing, accounting, quality, marketing and so forth can learn how to do the individual and special things that are important to their world.
(P B Crosby. *Quality without tears, the art of hassle-free management*. 1987. p. 88)

Both BP Chemicals and Johnson Matthey used the standard Crosby package. Company executives and senior management attend the Quality College for a couple of days to learn the Absolutes of Quality Management and then company trainers attend the two-week course. The latter then educate the rest of the organization using fifteen two-hour modules which are pre-packaged with supporting videos, posters etc. A quality improvement team is then used to manage the development of quality throughout the organization.

By changing behaviour

We agree with Philip Crosby that culture change is a matter of changing values and attitudes rather than teaching people a bunch of new techniques or replacing their old behaviour patterns with new ones. However, training in new skills is likely to change people's beliefs about their capabilities. People are unlikely to change their beliefs and attitudes about, for example, producing a quality product, if they believe they are unable to perform the necessary tasks. Rank Xerox UK has attempted to change employee attitudes towards quality by training in the calculation of non-conformance costs, bench marking, etc. Similarly the Crosby approach, used by BP Chemicals and Johnson Matthey among our case studies, places emphasis upon quality skills training. By training in new skills, people's beliefs about their capabilities are changed.

Sainsbury's has included 'check-out' skills training as part of their customer-service package and has found it necessary to provide briefing and presentation skills training for the managers charged with managing the change. The electricity board, with the support of the Industrial Society, has provided training in how to run briefing groups for its staff. And Abbey National has trained its managers in presentation skills to support the development of a participative style.

By changing the structures, systems and technology

Many of the organizations have engaged in some form of restructuring. It is likely that major structural change will make some impact upon the culture of the organization. It influences the work and functional groupings within the organization, as well as impacting upon the communication networks. However, the effect on culture of such change is rather unpredictable. It would appear that structural change is not particularly useful as a means of changing the culture of an organization in any specific way.

Reward, appraisal, monitoring, budgeting and control systems, on the other hand, can be linked to specific behaviour and are, as a consequence, capable of changing people's beliefs and attitudes towards performing in particular ways. As we discussed in chapter 2, such systems alter the situational contingencies in the work environment.

Jaguar has introduced new quality control systems, as well as customer tracking surveys. The area electricity board introduced a scheme where non-sales staff receive cash bonuses for providing sales leads. Unisys, Abbey National and Rank Xerox UK, among many others, have introduced pay systems linked to desired performance. Abbey National Building Society has introduced new appraisal systems, and both it and the electricity board have used assessment centres to identify management potential appropriate to the new culture. Abbey National also found that its planning and budgeting systems had to be aligned to support the change to a more commercial organization, and Johnson Matthey changed its planning and decision-making procedures as part of its cultural change.

A number of the organizations have introduced employee share ownership schemes. This has been done at the Royal Bank and Jaguar but, more significantly, at National Freight Consortium, which was an employee buy-out. A MORI poll at NFC found that sixty-six per cent of the shareholders believed that share ownership had resulted in people working more effectively.

By the corporate image

A number of our case study organizations have attempted to develop their corporate image. Typically, the main purpose is to develop positive attitudes among both customers and staff towards the organization, the intention being that employees will identify with the organization and will become committed to it. As we have already discussed in chapter 1, identification results in members wishing to remain with the organization; it only promotes, rather than guarantees, that they will internalize the organization's values. In this regard, we believe, some of our case studies have had rather optimistic expectations of the implications for organizational commitment. A positive attitude towards the organization is not the same as a positive attitude towards one's job, product quality, absenteeism or any specific behaviour.

Our case study organizations have attempted to develop their corporate image through formal communications – both internal and external advertising – the development of a corporate name and logo, employee involvement, social events for employees and their families, and the publication of success.

The area electricity board and Unisys have used corporate affairs and advertising professionals to promote the corporate

image both internally through, for example, videos and
externally through TV advertising – the employees and their
friends watch the adverts as well as potential customers.
Unisys ran a company-wide competition among employees in
order to identify the name of the new company. The
electricity board and Hampshire County Council both chose
their logos with care, 'The Team You Can Trust' and
'Hampshire Works'. Both the board and Toshiba have
introduced new workwear, the latter with the deliberate
intention of promoting a single-status organization. Jaguar
has been the most active in promoting social events for
employees and their families through its 'Hearts and Minds'
programme. And Jaguar and Unisys have taken careful steps
to publish the successes of the company. Unisys deliberately
publishes sales successes in the in-house journal, and Jaguar
has showrooms on-site of their vintage cars and provides a
book of the history of the company for employees in order to
reinforce its earlier image of 'grace, pace and space'.

   In summary, organizations have attempted to change their
culture by changing people, changing places, changing beliefs,
changing behaviour, changing the structure, systems and
technology, and changing the corporate image. The case
studies revealed that an organization will use a wide variety
of these methods in an attempt to change its culture. Thus
new people are recruited, others are lost, people are moved
around, training is cascaded, briefing groups are introduced,
new skills are learnt, the rewards systems are realigned and a
new shiny image is created, all these changes being led by
organizational strategy.

What factors facilitate culture change?

Most of the case studies began with some form of precipitating
event: financial crisis, a declining market share, a change
in customer expectations, intervention by stakeholders,

competitor initiatives, change in legislation or impending privatization.

These precipitating events are not trivial. They provide the justification for the upheaval that is to follow. They justify the expenditure on training, on new systems and structures and on redundancies. They lend credibility to the changes, to new visions, ideas, beliefs and to new ways of doing things.

The visibility of the criteria of success can be reasoned to be influential in promoting change. Organizations with clear and agreed criteria and methods of measuring acceptable performance are more likely to be aware of and respond to changes in their fortunes. In general, there would appear significant differences between public- and private-sector organizations in this regard and in the extent to which the criteria are related to performance in the internal or external environment.

It appears that the political structure or constitution of an organization is a significant factor in influencing its capacity to change. The nature of the stakeholders differs in publicly quoted, privately owned, partnership and public-sector organizations. In some public-sector organizations it's unclear where the power base lies. As the Griffiths report on the NHS stated '. . . if Florence Nightingale were carrying her lamp through the corridors of power at the NHS today she would almost certainly be searching for the people in charge'. Relatedly, organizations appear to differ in the extent to which they utilize their governing body as a stimulus for change. Some are graven in the image of the organization. Sir John Egan is both Chairman and Chief Executive of Jaguar and all the Board are executive directors, while companies such as ICI or, in our case studies, the electricity board make a greater use of non-executive directors drawn from outside the industry.

An organization that is externally focused is likely to be more able to change its culture than one that is internally focused. By externally focused we mean that the organization is aware of its external environment as opposed to being focused on internal procedures, rules, systems and power structures. For example, an externally focused organization monitors its own performance and the behaviour of its customers and competitors, sends top management on education and training courses and to conferences on new development, and utilizes external consultants. In short it is open to new ideas and developments in its environment.

In many of the case studies there was a change in the leadership at the top of the organization. Perhaps the most traumatic example was at Johnson Matthey where Charter Consolidated intervened and replaced the Chief Executive and some of the directors. A less public revolution has occurred at Abbey National Building Society. Since Peter Birch joined as Chief Executive in 1984 the majority of the top management level has changed. New leadership brings with it new ideas, recipes for success, visions for the future and experience. On a number of occasions it was noticeable that the Chief Executive's learning experience in one organization was transferred to the new organization. David O'Brien brought the business planning process to Rank Xerox from Burroughs. Geoffrey Deith had previous experience of a company advisory board similar to that introduced at Toshiba and Eugene Anderson had introduced the Crosby Quality approach at Celanese prior to joining Johnson Matthey.

Culture change is likely to be promoted by change in the strategy of the organization. Most of the case studies begin with a strategic review and a clarification of the organization's objectives, values and behaviours. Such a review identifies the changes in behaviours, beliefs and attitudes that are required and promotes the relevance of the cultural change to organizational effectiveness. It also promotes the acceptance of the need for change among the staff.

Power and commitment are necessary to drive change. The fact that power is concentrated in a few hands or that there is a clear authority structure would appear to be conducive to change – though obviously also a potential obstacle to change.

Both Marley and Johnson Matthey found it necessary to 'tighten the reins' in a decentralized organization. In at least five of the companies we studied the Chief Executive or Chairman was described as being a very impressive, authoritative or charismatic figure – each possessed both a legitimate and personal basis for influence.

The use of a cultural change strategy that uses role models and methods of participation and persuasive communication, targeted at specific beliefs, attitudes and behaviours, is likely to promote cultural change. This is particularly the case when methods are cascaded down the organization and there is top commitment. Change is also likely to be promoted when a philosophy of simple central concepts such as 'Just in Time', 'Hampshire Works' or 'The Customer is King' is used and the message is visible, given high profile and repeated. The use of signals, for example logos or workwear, to signify that something new is happening will also appear to have a role to play.

Finally, these changes need to be reinforced by a realignment of the structures, systems and policies of the organization so that changes in culture become embedded in the systems and structures. One needs to change people's beliefs about what is rewarding, what is feasible, etc and these beliefs are gained in part from the social and technical systems of the organization. To attempt to change people's attitudes towards product quality but leave in place incentive schemes which reward productivity, or to fail to change the expectations and behaviour of supervisors or work colleagues, or to provide poor quality materials or outdated machinery, or to fail to provide knowledge of quality performance and reward it, will not result in the desired behavioural change but will instead raise doubts about the commitment of management to product quality, result in dissatisfaction and anxiety, and have a negative impact upon the climate within the organization.

4

Process, People and Power in Culture Change

It takes time for people in a newly established social system to develop commonly held beliefs, attitudes and values or a culture. As culture matures we expect to find visible signs of a coherence and continuity. Changing a culture also takes time, a long time. Most commentators agree that we need to think in terms of years rather than months. Mature cultures are inherently stable and self-reinforcing systems. Any attempt to introduce change is likely to arouse resistance in the same way that a foreign body activates the defence immune system in an individual. In this chapter we want to explore some conceptual ideas which can be applied to our case studies and may prove useful in helping us to gain more insight into the conditions and processes accompanying successful cultural change.

First, we shall look at two established models which are applicable to the process of change. Their potential value lies in enabling us to anticipate and prevent unnecessary problems arising. Secondly, we shall present a framework of three interrelated roles which should prove helpful in clarifying the behaviours which are instrumental in bringing about organizational culture change. Finally, we shall relate these three roles to the concept of power. This variable will enable us to understand why each of these roles is most effectively played by different people inside or outside the organization.

Process in culture change

There are two analytical frameworks which are often used to describe the process of change, ie a series of interrelated actions directed at achieving the change goals. There is the organizational decision-making model (see figure 4.1 overleaf) and the force field model shown in figures 4.2 and 4.3 (pages 106–7). The very simplicity of these models makes them applicable to a wide variety of situations. Their value is in highlighting the importance of a number of considerations in managing change, rather than in portraying the true flavour of events accompanying change. To convey the latter we would need a very complex, 'messy' and impractical diagram.

Organizational decision-making model

This model is a familiar tool encapsulating the ideal stages which management teams go through in solving organizational problems or in developing new opportunities. It is a rational model which identifies key stages and emphasizes their interdependence in the change process. If diagnosis at the problem stage is inadequate, the chances of arriving at an effective solution at the choice stage is decreased. Or an excessively authoritarian approach at the problem and choice stages may lead to lack of commitment and indifferent performance from those who have to make the solution work during the implementation stage.

Some further comments on figure 4.1 are needed. As we have already seen from the earlier chapters, planned culture change has to be part of the corporate strategy of an organization if it is going to have any chance of succeeding. As a rule a review of strategy is triggered by poor performance or some crisis, rather than a feeling that 'we should be doing even better than we are at the moment'. Sometimes it is triggered by the anticipation of future problems arising in the absence of 'preventive' action. In our case studies Abbey National falls within this preventive category, but the others belong more to the poor performance or crisis category. Locating mission and strategy in the centre of the model is therefore appropriate.

By mission we refer to the agreed statement of the

Figure 4.1
Organizational decision-making model

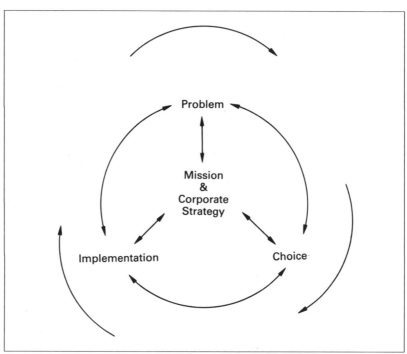

organization's overall purpose which senior management arrive at in the process of developing the organization's strategy. It is a statement which tries to highlight the type of organization it is and the nature of its business. The mission statement which was agreed by senior managers on workshops in the Mid-Essex Health Authority may be summarized as: 'In Mid-Essex our task is to provide and promote a high standard of health care in order to improve the quality of life, within the resources available, and which are accepted by society'.[1]

The three other elements in the model – problem, choice and implementation – represent stages which we associate with the problem-solving paradigm. In the problem stage we include such activities as clarifying the nature of the problem, seeking further diagnostic information and so on. The choice stage includes formulating possible courses of action or solutions, evaluating alternatives and choosing between them. The implementation stage covers planning how to put the chosen solution(s) into effect, implementing the plans and adjusting the plans in the light of feedback information or evaluation.

A criticism levelled at similar problem-solving models is that organizational change does not occur in quite such a neat and rational way. The broad pattern is recognizable, but there is an awful lot of patchwork and repairs involved! This is one reason why it is nearer reality to show these elements in an interactive rather than in a unidirectional relationship. Certainly the strategic rationale for bringing about cultural change needs to be a constant influence throughout the process of change.[2] The notion of development and progress in the model is expressed through the outer ring of arrows. Readers may find it instructive to analyse the case studies in terms of the model. It is a way of structuring the sequence of events in culture change, in comparing and contrasting different approaches and in assessing the extent to which organizations followed 'good practice' or the application of available knowledge.

For example, take the Abbey National case study. About ten years ago the marketplace in which it operated showed significant change. Building societies were more consciously vying with each other in an effort to improve their league table position. The cartel, which had been operating to fix rates of interest to be paid on investments or charged on mortgage loans, began to weaken. The high interest rates led the clearing banks to become more interested in the mortgage business. General deregulation encouraged new entrants into the market. All these changes have brought about increased competition for individual building societies.

It was against this background in 1984 that Abbey National took a serious look at its future strategy. Some changes in its human resource management systems had already been taking place (eg the patronage-based system of promotion had been removed), but the need was recognized for a more profound change in the culture of the organization. Staff generally needed to become more commercially oriented.

Thus we see that the Abbey's concern with its existing organizational beliefs and assumptions arose as a result of formulating its future strategy. It in effect identified mismatches between the strategy it was developing and the existing culture. Once the 'problem' had been sufficiently understood, the question was what to do about it and how to bring about the sort of changes that appeared to be needed. The choices made led to a specific training programme being selected as the main vehicle for culture change. It was also recognized that various human resource systems had to be modified to match the culture that would support the agreed strategy.

The activities involved in the implementation stage included the careful planning and execution of the training programme and changing other human resource systems (eg performance-related pay replacing across the board increases). These activities were carefully thought through in content and approach so as to apply current knowledge regarding the conditions necessary for effecting the desired changes (eg sending top managers first on the course, replacing key personnel who were unsympathetic toward the changes). While there has been no evaluation in the scientific sense, the normal feedback information available has enabled management to conclude that the results they are aiming for are being achieved with respect to culture and performance.

The organizational decision-making model is therefore a possible way in which we can represent the process involved in culture change. Its main value is in reminding us of three important but simple guidelines:

- planned culture change must be grounded in corporate strategy

- sufficient attention must be devoted to each of the equally important sets of activities
- implementation is most effective when those involved can experience ownership of the problem and solution (normally achieved by involvement in the early stages of decision-making).

Force field model

This model has its origin in the work of Kurt Lewin[3] who pioneered research into changing behaviour of individuals and social systems. The model can be used to portray a target of change or goal, such as a measure of change or of quality of customer service, as the function of two sets of forces: the driving forces and the restraining forces. If we want to bring about change, then we must disturb the equilibrium by strengthening the driving forces, weakening the restraining forces, or both. The model therefore encourages us to identify the various forces impinging on the target of change, to consider the relative strengths of these forces and to explore alternative strategies for modifying the force field. One useful generalization from the model is that attention should be given to both the driving and restraining forces when trying to bring about change. Concentrating on the driving and neglecting the restraining forces will create undue stress in the system and result in undesirable consequences such as resistance to change, employee resignations and absenteeism, industrial disputes and so on.

Figure 4.2 illustrates the use of the force field model. On the basis of some of the findings from our case studies (discussed in chapter 3), we would hypothesize that these two sets of forces will have an important influence on an organization's propensity to change. Thus, if driving forces for change are strong (eg there has been change of leadership at the top, powerful influences from shareholders or competitors are being activated), restraining forces against change are weak (eg the organization is not successful, the environment is unstable), then the probability of change taking place will be high. In figure 2.10 we made similar use of the force field model in helping us understand the factors influencing the rate of change of organizational culture.

Figure 4.2
Force field model relating to an organization's propensity to change

Forces Driving Culture Change	Forces Restraining Culture Change
Change at the top →	← Career-based organization
Powerful external influences →	← Low turnover
Vision of the future →	← Success
Powerful leader →	← Stable environment
Acceptance of need to change →	← Criteria of success not visible
Externally focused →	← Lack of clear authority
Crisis or opportunity →	

A second useful characteristic of Lewin's model is its three-stage process of change which is shown in figure 4.3. We have already pointed out on several occasions that organizational culture change is very difficult to achieve. Two difficulties will almost certainly be encountered: coping with resistance to change and ensuring that changes achieved persist after the sponsors and supporters of the change have gone. What conceptual guidelines can Lewin's model provide us with in dealing with these difficulties?

Three stages of change

In several of our case studies the culture change effort focused on the beliefs, attitudes and values relating to quality of products or customer service. This was particularly true with respect to Toshiba, Jaguar, Johnson Matthey, BP Chemicals and Rank Xerox. According to Lewin, if we want to change the level of quality of customer service, the first stage is to unfreeze existing forces, possibly by showing the inadequacies of current beliefs and policies for the tasks that have to be done to regain competitive advantage. The second stage is to introduce change aimed at re-establishing the equilibrium of forces at a new level, by strengthening/weakening existing forces or introducing new forces. If effective, these two stages will result in an increase in the quality of customer service.

Figure 4.3
The three-stage model of change

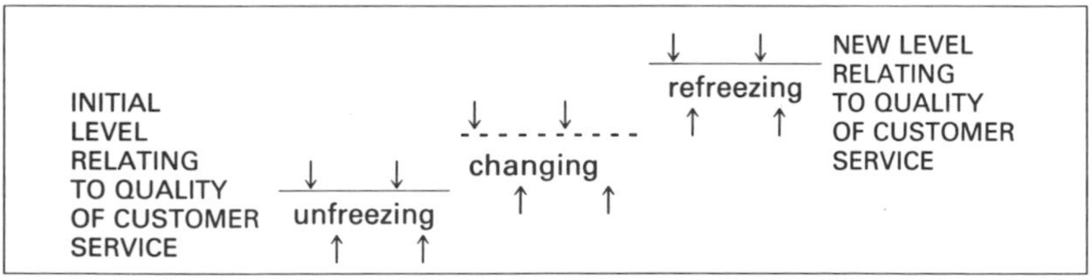

The final stage of refreezing recognizes that changes in quality may have been brought about by the one-off investment of resources (eg a training programme) being devoted to achieve this outcome and by the extra but temporary attention being paid to achieving it by top management. The only way to ensure that the new level of customer service is a stable and inherent feature of the organization is to ensure that the forces changed are those which will continue to operate in normal circumstances (eg methods of rewarding performance, structural characteristics). If these conditions are met and the effects of the planned cultural change are successful in terms of performance criteria, then the belief system underlying the new quality-oriented behaviour patterns will become frozen or embedded in the organization.

Resistance to change

Much has been written about the topic of resistance to change. The conditions which are most likely to bring this type of behaviour about include:

- the need for change is not recognized by those affected by it
- there is an increase in the level of uncertainty relating to one's future job, its rewards, power and status (matters which are important to the needs of individuals and groups)
- the change strategy adopted fails to take sufficiently into account the conditions under which people learn and display new behaviours in the organizational setting

Let us briefly look at each of these within the context of the force field model and identify some of the effective guidelines being applied by those organizations which were trying to improve the quality of their customer service.

Developing the need for change   The need for change will be self-evident to those involved in formulating an organization's strategy, but it also has to be developed in others. In many of the case studies the training or educational approach dominated the unfreezing stage. Thus we see that at Johnson Matthey 150 senior managers and key middle managers were sent on a one-week Crosby quality education course and this was followed up by 55 individuals attending a two-week course to prepare them to run quality courses for the rest of the workforce. The educational process continued on the job with the formation of quality improvement teams to develop a change strategy for improvement with the help of a Crosby consultant.

A variety of techniques may be used to unfreeze existing beliefs and to implant new ones. They include the use of group learning methods and of learning experiences which make people aware of contradictions between their beliefs and behaviour (cognitive dissonance technique). These disconfirming experiences lead to dissatisfaction with things as they are and a readiness to explore the benefits of new beliefs and behaviours. But the rejection of old beliefs and behaviours will not occur until there is something more attractive to replace them.

Reducing uncertainty   Again training plays an important role here, because it is one of the main vehicles through which people learn about the why, what and how of any planned change programme. It is also through training (including opportunities for practice in a supportive environment) that individuals acquire the new skills, knowledge and attitudes which will enable them to maintain the level of competence which they had been experiencing to date. It is therefore not surprising to find that training played a prominent role in the case studies.

A second factor which helps to reduce uncertainty is the credibility of those involved in driving through the changes. This is where a relatively standardized quality improvement programme such as Crosby scores. The fact that many organizations have used it, and found it of value, means that it has predictable outcomes and it is something which top management will find easier to sell to their organization. Its clear goals and rational process also ensure that people will have a good idea of what it is all about.

A participative management approach to change is a third method of reducing uncertainty. If people feel involved in the planning of change and have some influence at the implementation stage, they are more likely to experience ownership of the changes and to have an opportunity to protect their interests. They will also be better informed as to developments taking place. There are of course situations where the benefits of participation may not be readily achieved. These are where some individuals have more to lose than gain from implementing planned changes. Anticipated losses may be in terms of various rewards such as promotion, power and status, or even in terms of a growing gap between their values and those of their changing organization. Within the context of cultural change, where it is difficult for such individuals to adapt it is often in their interest, and that of their employer, to part company on a mutually satisfactory basis. Abbey National went about this in one way, Toshiba in another. Different approaches used will reflect different situational factors – including different cultures!

It is during the change stage of Lewin's model that resistance may become acute and it is at this stage that the reassurance of external consultants is often needed if the change programme is to remain in being.[4] We had no case study where resistance to change led to premature termination – although for obvious reasons only those who perceive themselves as success stories are likely to welcome scrutiny and publicity! For every success story there are no doubt many unsuccessful ones. In one of the more convincing studies comparing seventeen successful and unsuccessful organization development case studies, Greiner[5] was able to identify two distinguishing features. First, those falling in the successful change category followed a similar and consistent route in the stages of the change process; these were very similar to the Lewin three-stage model of change. Secondly, the change approach in the success stories involved the sharing of power: that is, the power which normally resided in the formal authority and influence of management was redistributed so that significant alteration occurred in the traditional practices used by the organization in making decisions. This second feature is consistent with the participative approach advocated above and with the comments made earlier in relation to the organizational decision-making model – the desirability of involving the implementers of change in the early decision-making stages.

One interesting way of testing out the validity of the guidelines to emerge from the present 15 case studies would be to approach the 250 organizations in our sample who claimed to have attempted culture change and to study a further group of less successful cases.

Reinforcing behaviour changes on the job   Formal training is a temporary tool more appropriate to the unfreezing and changing stages of the force field model. If the newly achieved level of quality of customer service is to be maintained across time (ie if the refreezing process is to take effect), then other more stable forces have to be brought into play. In other words the more visible signs of culture which encourage or discourage particular beliefs and behaviours need to be compatible with the changes which have been introduced.

A change strategy which seems to have been common across the case studies was to change beliefs and behaviours at the top of the organization and then to work down the hierarchy. This is an effective approach, as people tend to emulate the behaviour of those they look up to.

A systems orientation also appears to have been present in the 15 organizations. This is implicit in the force field model, where effort is made at an early stage to identify those system characteristics which have a bearing on the variable one is trying to change. Thus, if a customer-oriented culture is the change goal then the organization's human resource policies and procedures (eg appraisal system) must recognize and reinforce appropriate behaviour and performance. It is not just human resource systems which are relevant; changes in the structure of the organization can provide powerful reinforcements. An example is the establishment of a quality

office at Rank Xerox, with the manager reporting to the
director of strategic development.

The most effective reinforcement of culture change is
success. If feedback information routinely available within an
organization indicates that success is being achieved and
maintained, then the newly introduced beliefs, behaviours
and organizational characteristics will become a stable feature
of its culture. The key role which communication plays in this
context is obvious and is discussed elsewhere.

People in culture change

The term 'change agents' is commonly used to refer to those
people who play a significant part in bringing about change
within an organization. Our case studies suggest that there
are three key roles which change agents play and that the
incumbents of these roles can come from within or outside
the organization. The roles have been labelled initiator,
coordinator and facilitator.

Initiators

As Schein[6] points out, the founder is the person who has
most influence on culture during the early years of a company.
We had no actual example of this from our cases since we
were concerned with culture change rather than culture
creation, but Toshiba came close to it. Legally Toshiba was a
newly established company in 1981; in reality it shared much
the same staff, technology and factory as Rank Toshiba which
it replaced. The reason why we may treat this example as
analogous to a new organization is that it provided the newly
appointed chief executive officer (CEO) with an opportunity
to establish the culture of the factory in much the same way
as a founding member would have done. A possible difference

between the founder of a company and the newly appointed CEO of a pseudo-greenfield factory such as the present one is that the CEO was probably appointed to his post because of the managerial beliefs he held, whereas a founder is normally self-appointed. We are told that he was charismatic and visionary, and as a result of his educational and work experiences he had firmly held beliefs relating to the importance of employee involvement, a flexible workforce and an integrated management team. These beliefs were reflected in the policies, practices and management systems which were eventually implemented in the new organization. Within the context of our model of organizational culture we would expect these beliefs to become part of the commonly held guiding beliefs of this company. An interesting method of concertinaing the time required to bring this about was the self-selection procedure adopted by Toshiba (see chapter 3).

It was not only at Toshiba that the CEO played a key role in initiating culture formation and change. The part played by Sir John Egan at Jaguar is now well known. Sir Peter Thompson at the National Freight Consortium was equally instrumental in effecting cultural change. As a result of a chance attendance on a management training course, he was convinced of the need to develop a more participative management style in the organization. All his senior managers were subsequently sent on a similar course.

The initiator role does not necessarily rest with the CEO/Chairman. In the case studies there are examples where individuals in the personnel function played, or at least shared, this role. In each case where this was most apparent, the individual imported the new cultural elements from their last employer.

The initiators of change are often individuals who have recently entered the organization at a senior management level. Apart from the power they wield, there are three good reasons for this. First, they are sufficiently free of the organization's cultural influences to be able to look at it in a novel way. Secondly, their learning experiences in another organizational culture provide them with a familiar and workable model to follow. Thirdly, because of the circumstances of their appointment they are often expected by others in the organization to change things in order to improve performance and therefore they are oriented toward change.

There are instances where the initiator role is played by outside agents. Thus we find that in the Mid-Essex Health Authority case study it was government-sponsored initiatives which instigated change. The change from consensus management to general management was recommended in the Griffith Report.[7] However, the strategies for putting Griffith into operation, and the precise shape of the culture which developed, depended a great deal upon the district general manager (ie the CEO).

Similarly in the Johnson Matthey case study, the largest single shareholder (Charter Consolidated) was instrumental in bringing about change, including the appointment of a new CEO. This individual had worked previously in a company which had applied the Crosby total quality improvement programme. It was therefore not surprising to find that this programme was used as a central part of the effort to change the culture of the organization.

So we find that at an early stage of the change process outside agents or stakeholders may take on the initiator role by forcing certain financial, structural and personnel changes on the organization. However, planned organizational culture change, as opposed to other types of change, is normally initiated by the CEO.

In a more covert way there are other outside change agents influencing the thinking of CEOs. Academics, researchers and consultants may stimulate CEOs to take on the initiator role in cultural change by presenting attractive alternative theories and methods in managing organizations. This may be done through their publications or in face-to-face situations on courses. Examples include: Philip Crosby (see Rank Xerox, Johnson Matthey, BP Chemicals); Peters and

Waterman, and Rosemary Stewart (Mid-Essex Health Authority).

Coordinators

The initiator role is primarily one of giving direction, inspiration and support. Whether something is going to be successfully implemented is going to depend on a coordinating structure, either in the form of an individual coordinator or a coordinating team, or both. Mid-Essex Health Authority was the only case study where an individual was specifically recruited to the coordinator role and she was subsequently made head of the personnel function. Within the context of culture change it is the human resource systems which are most likely to be used as the levers of change and therefore it makes sense for the coordinator role to be located in that function. While the early educational element of the Crosby[8] total quality improvement programme is usually made the responsibility of personnel (see, for instance, the Johnson Matthey case study), it is worth noting that at a later stage a coordinating quality improvement team is established to manage the development of quality throughout the organization and line managers are involved in this.

On the basis of our case studies it seems that coordinators are appointed to a specific aspect of the change effort, such as when a training programme is used as an instrument of change. Presumably where other coordinating functions are needed it is the most appropriately placed line manager, or the CEO, or the management board, who will fulfil the coordinating role as part of their normal responsibilities. This finding (ie absence of an omnipotent change agent cum coordinator) is not surprising when we consider the complexities of organizational politics.

Facilitators

Whereas initiators make their main input at the start of a change effort (problem and choice stages) and coordinators toward the end of the decision-making cycle (ie implementation stage), the facilitators may be involved throughout the cycle. Within the context of the organization development literature, the term change agent and facilitator are almost synonymous. When in a facilitator role an individual will be helping others (either as individuals or as teams) to learn and change by the use of appropriate techniques and with available resources. All those involved in the change process are potential incumbents of the facilitator role, but we are here using the label to refer to those individuals who directly interact with others (either as individuals or groups) in order to help them achieve specific learning or change goals. Normally those taking on this task will have had some training in the role. Terms used in our case studies in referring to those playing this role, include: trainer/instructor, organization development manager and consultant.

It is worth differentiating between two groups of facilitators: the internal or external consultants and the line managers or supervisors. We usually think of the former category when discussing the facilitator role, but the latter is an important development which is becoming more common. One of the best ways of getting people to change their beliefs and behaviour is to train their line managers and supervisors to act as trainers, and as leaders of participative group meetings such as quality circles. There are two good reasons why this approach is often successful. First, subordinates are likely to model their behaviour on their manager when they find the rewards attached to his or her position attractive; if they find that certain behaviours and beliefs are actively supported by their trainer managers, this can create a more powerful force for change than a consultant trainer or a professional trainer from the personnel function. Secondly, by involving managers in the role of trainer, they will not only gain more insight into the new behaviours and beliefs which are being promoted, but will become more committed to the cultural change goals. The more academically minded reader will recognize that the first point has its theoretical justification in the social learning theory of Bandura,[9] and the second point in the cognitive dissonance theory of Festinger.[10]

The strategy of utilizing the role model potential of managers was first widely used in Blake and Mouton's Managerial Grid[11] organization development programmes in the 1960s. It was used in several of our case studies, most notably by those following the Crosby programme (ie Johnson Matthey, BP Chemicals, Rank Xerox).

The use of consultants in the case studies was mainly confined to a training input. This can be deceptive when trying to identify the nature of their role as facilitators of culture change. Their training input not only involved content but also process. It is this latter aspect which will determine the probability of successful change, and consultants experienced in helping organizations bringing about the culture change will put this expertise at the disposal of the client. Using their knowledge they will, for instance, be able to advise on the process models likely to lead to successful outcomes (eg the value of the two models described earlier as a means of ensuring that enough drive is generated to maintain the change effort and reduce resistance to change to manageable proportions), on the benefits of initiating change at the top and cascading the programme down the organizations and so on.

There are at least three important contributions which consultants make: the obvious one of applying their process skills to aid effective decision-making on the part of individuals (eg the CEO) or groups (eg the management board); the less obvious one of strengthening the credibility of a culture change programme, or of the initiator of the programme, through their personal prestige (this is the political dimension); and the ability to make relatively independent and objective observations regarding existing and espoused culture (this ability stems from appropriate training, familiarity with available diagnostic tools and, if one is an·outside consultant, minimal exposure to the organization's culture).

If our case studies had been in more depth, it is probable that the facilitator role of the management consultant would have been more clearly revealed. The literature suggests that there is a tendency for respondents to play down the role of consultants, unless this area is explicitly explored by the researcher. Thus we find that in a survey of the use of consultants, Mackay[12] talks about their 'invisibility'.

Power

In the change literature there is one variable which is of overriding importance. This is power. The concept of power refers to the ability to cause others to perform actions that they might not otherwise perform and therefore to change the behaviour of others. In managing change it is important to understand not only who are the people who influence change but what are their sources of power. By understanding the sources of power which different individuals had in our case studies, we shall be in a better position to understand the roles which they played in cultural change. This limited objective will prevent us from entering into an unnecessarily lengthy discussion of the concept.

A framework which will be found useful in understanding the sources of power is that of French and Raven.[13] They put forward a five-category typology as shown in figure 4.4.

Earlier on we saw how external stakeholders played a role in initiating change in two of the case studies. They were able to do this on the basis of the legitimate, reward and coercive powers they possessed as ultimate owners (in the case of the National Health Service) or shareholders (in the case of Johnson Matthey). The framework also makes it more

Figure 4.4
Sources of power[13]

LEGITIMATE: power is derived from the position which the individual holds

REWARD: power is derived from the ability to give or withhold the rewards which others seek

COERCIVE: power is derived from the ability to administer the punishments which others try and avoid

EXPERT: power is derived from the belief in others that one possesses the knowledge and skills needed to succeed in an area of interest or of concern

REFERENT: power is derived from the belief in others that one's knowledge, skills and behaviour are attractive and worth identifying with or imitating

obvious why CEOs play such a key role in bringing about culture change. They obviously have legitimate power. They also have strong reward and coercive powers available. Some, such as the Chairmen/CEOs of Jaguar and Toshiba were often described as charismatic leaders and therefore can also be said to have strong referent powers. The combination of these is a powerful base from which to initiate culture change and to ensure that momentum for change is maintained.

Generally speaking those heading the human resource function are in a less favourable position to initiate change. If they have general manager status reporting directly to the CEO, they will enjoy legitimate power when changing the systems for which they are responsible. They should also enjoy expert power, but are less likely to have strong reward and coercive powers except toward those for whom they are directly responsible. Their opportunities for developing referent powers are also likely to be much less than CEOs'. For these reasons it is not surprising to find that those heading the personnel function are not often seen as initiating culture change.

However, the legitimate and expert power bases of the personnel function will enable it to have a significant influence on the human resource levers of cultural change, such as selection, placement, training, communications and reward systems (see chapter 5). Some will also have expertise in the special skills associated with professional facilitators or change agents, such as process consultation and survey feedback skills.

French and Bell[14] provide a good comprehensive discussion of these latter techniques in their textbook on organization development. Power may also be derived from their expertise in identifying and recruiting suitable management consultants to help in the process of cultural change or in negotiating the cooperation of unions in the planned changes. These last two examples are interesting illustrations where the power of a function stems from expertise in operating in the organization's external rather than internal environment.

When we try to account for the power base of a function or department, the most obvious factors which come to mind are the numbers of departmental staff and the assets controlled. The work of Hickson et al[15] is useful in drawing to our attention three less obvious factors which influence the department's contribution to the functioning of the total organization and therefore its perceived power. The first is the department's ability to minimize, reduce or absorb the uncertainty impinging on the organization. Thus the personnel function will enhance its power if its training programmes and its choice of outside consultants reduce the uncertainty accompanying cultural change. The second factor is the department's degree of substitutability. If the work of the personnel function cannot be readily performed by other departments, then the degree of substitutability is low and power that much greater. The third factor is the degree of centrality held by the department, ie the extent to which other departments are dependent upon it in the work flow. In a manufacturing organization maintenance will derive considerable power from this dimension, personnel less so. However, there are circumstances where personnel can demonstrate its ability to influence conditions affecting work flow. This is more likely to occur where they are part of a labour-intensive organization, where industrial relations are unpredictable and staff recruitment and retention are difficult. The reader may like to consider our cases in the light of these factors, when trying to account for the part played by the personnel function in organizational culture change.

The power base of consultants (internal and external) is almost always heavily dependent upon their expertise. That is why their role is largely limited to that of facilitator of culture change, although as we have pointed out the stimulus of charismatic consultants (referent power) can be considerable on CEOs initiating change within an organization. Peters and Waterman, and Philip Crosby are obvious examples in relation to culture change. But there are many others from the recent past, including: John Humble, Peter Drucker, Blake and Mouton, Fred Herzberg.

The relative absence of organization development (OD) consultants in our case studies was something of a surprise. Readers interested in this area will be well aware of the fact that the OD literature is very much concerned with planned cultural change and that the OD consultant is increasingly conscious of the power variable in bringing about organizational change.[16] In Mid-Essex the influence of OD technology and thinking was overtly visible; in the others it was present in a more disguised fashion. The covert influence is apparent in the heavy use of group learning and change techniques.

So it does seem that the influence of OD is there, but without the blatantly idealistic and humanistic value systems with which the movement became closely associated and without the high profile of an OD consultant. This is an observation worth making because it does highlight again the distinguishing feature of our cultural change case studies: the omnipresent influence of the CEO and corporate strategy in initiating and driving through culture change. This is in marked contrast to one of the best known OD programmes of the past – the Managerial Grid. The first three phases of the Grid are concerned with beliefs, attitudes, values and managerial style; only in the fourth phase is corporate strategy the centre of attention.

References

1 ATTWOOD M *and* BEER N. *Development of a learning organization – reflections on a personal and organizational workshop in a District Health Authority*. Paper given to an Association for Management Education and Development Conference. 1987

2 JOHNSON G *and* SCHOLES K. *Exploring corporate strategy*. London, Prentice-Hall, 1988

3 LEWIN K. *Field theory in social science*. New York, Harper and Row, 1951

4 LIPPITT R, WATSON J *and* WESTLEY B. *The dynamics of planned change*. New York, Harcourt, Brace & World, 1958

5 GREINER L. 'Patterns of organization change'. *Harvard Business Review* 45, 1967, pp 119–28

6 SCHEIN E H. *Organizational culture and leadership*. London, Jossey-Bass, 1985

7 *Griffith Report*. National Health Service Management Enquiry. London, DHSS, 1983

8 CROSBY P. *Quality is free*. New York, McGraw-Hill, 1979

9 BANDURA A. *Social learning theory*. Englewood Cliffs, NJ, Prentice-Hall, 1977

10 FESTINGER L. *A theory of cognitive dissonance*. Stanford, California, Stanford University Press, 1957

11 BLAKE R *and* MOUTON S. *The managerial grid*. Houston, Texas, Gulf, 1964

12 MACKAY L. 'The future – with consultants'. *Personnel Review*. 16(4), 1987. pp 3–9

13 FRENCH J R P *and* RAVEN B H. 'The bases of social power' in *Studies in social power* edited by D Cartwright. Ann Arbor, University of Michigan, Institute for Social Research, 1959

14 FRENCH W L *and* BELL C H. *Organization development: behavioral science interventions for organization improvement*. Engelwood Cliffs, NJ, Prentice-Hall, 1984

15 HICKSON D J, LEE C A, SCHNECK R E *and* PENNINGS J M. 'A strategic contingency theory of intraorganizational power'. *Administrative Science Quarterly* 16, 1971, 216–29

16 GREINER L E *and* SCHEIN V E. *Power and organization development: mobilizing power to implement change*. Reading, Massachusetts, Addison-Wesley, 1988

Part III

The Role of Personnel

5

The Role of Personnel

*'It is . . . a question of who the priests are: I suspect they are
the Personnel Officers, exercising their care of souls . . .
Compared to their counterparts in the Christian church the
Corporation priests still have a lot to learn.'*[1]

As we have seen in the preceding chapters, the culture of an
organization develops from the beliefs, attitudes and values of
its individual members. If we wish to change organizational
culture, we will need to influence the thoughts and behaviour
of individual employees. Not surprisingly, therefore, the skills
and techniques of personnel practitioners – who, after all,
should be the organization's experts in human resource issues –
are likely to play a crucial role in achieving culture change. In
this chapter we shall look at the practical role played by
personnel in implementing culture change and at the kinds of
skills and interventions needed to carry out this role effectively.

The personnel role

In most of our case studies, personnel – or some related
specialist function, such as organization development – acted
as a practical change agent. Once senior management had
determined its desired strategic goals and values, personnel
management techniques were used to influence and change
values and behaviour accordingly.

Many of the techniques used are not in themselves
particularly innovative. Most trainers could develop role-
playing exercises similar to those used by Hampshire County
Council or institute team-briefing processes like those used
by Jaguar. The importance of these techniques lies in their
strategic focus. They are being applied consciously to develop
or reinforce cultural values, which have been explicitly

determined and articulated by senior management. In
Hampshire, for example, these values might be expressed by
terms such as 'accountability' or 'entrepreneurship'. In Jaguar
or Rank Xerox they might be expressed in terms like
'customer service', 'reliability' or 'quality'. In effect, these
organizations have adopted familiar personnel management
techniques as the medium for, in the words of Peters and
Waterman, 'creating and instilling a value system'.[2]

To place these techniques in context, it is perhaps worth
reiterating some general points about the nature and
components of organizational culture. As we have seen,
culture can be thought of as the system of interlocking
values, attitudes and beliefs that underline individual and
organizational behaviour. This system is itself likely to be
influenced both by external factors – political, economic,
social and technical – and by the attitudes and behaviour of
its constituent individuals. In some cases, like Marley among
our case studies, the culture may be strongly influenced by
charismatic founders. In others, like some of the public-sector
organizations among our case studies, the culture may be
conditioned by the operating needs or environment. Over
time, the original beliefs and assumptions will tend to become
unconscious and the organization develops a stable culture
which seems to work for its particular circumstances.

This stable culture is likely to be a powerful influence on
employee behaviour. It is also likely to be highly self-
perpetuating. Traditional approaches are reinforced because
they conform to the accepted ethos. Innovations and external
interventions are resisted because they contradict cultural
norms. As Deal and Kennedy point out, 'the force of the
culture can neutralize and emasculate a proposed change'.[3]
Many of the managers we interviewed commented that
change had initially been resisted because employees had felt
that the traditional ways were still the best. One manager
spoke of an 'arrogant' assumption among middle managers
that they could cope with any developments without changing
their methods of operation.

Nevertheless, circumstances do change. A strong, internalized culture may easily lose touch with a changing external environment. Some of the 'excellent' companies cited by Peters and Waterman and others have run into difficulty precisely because their strong cultures have not been able to adapt easily to a rapidly changing market. Among our case studies, problems had arisen because of changes in profitability, market-share, legislation and countless other areas. It is at this point that the need for culture change arises. Managers need not only to define new strategic values, but also to find ways of communicating these to the workforce. More importantly, they need to find ways of breaking into the self-perpetuating cultural cycle. They need to re-establish contact between the external environment and the values and behaviour of their workforce. In short, they need to provide a practical impetus to change deeply rooted activities and values. In most of the organizations we studied the personnel function created this impetus. The personnel function was used to develop mechanisms to raise awareness of the organization's external and strategic needs and to influence values and behaviour accordingly.

As we indicated in chapter 1, culture can be thought of primarily in terms either of thought or behaviour. Not surprisingly, therefore, there has been something of a debate not only among cultural theorists but also among practising managers about whether culture change interventions should be directed at behaviour or at values. Most commentators agree, in line with Schein and others, that visible behaviour is only a manifestation of underlying values. Some have argued that these values, being intangible, can only be changed by changing behaviour. Others argue that behaviour cannot be truly changed unless underlying values are changed first.

In practice, as our case studies demonstrate, the distinction is likely to be academic. Although the focus varied, most of the case-study organizations attempted to change both values and behaviour simultaneously. In Rank Xerox, for example, where the focus was explicitly on changing behaviour, the notion of 'total quality' was used to provide a conceptual framework for change. Changes in behaviour were related to changes in attitudes. Equally, in Toshiba and Unisys, where much of the emphasis was on changing attitudes and values, there was constant reinforcement from changes in operational practices. In cases where behaviour was divorced from underlying values, change was not lasting or significant. A number of managers commented that initial attempts to implement new management systems foundered because they were introduced in isolation and not related coherently to changes in strategic values.

Culture is an interlocking system, which involves all aspects of the organization. In implementing culture change, personnel practitioners need to develop a comprehensive and integrated programme of human resources initiatives. It should not be assumed that culture can be changed simply by the introduction of, say, a new appraisal system, new reward practices or new methods of training. All of these are likely to have an effect on culture and each of them could be a crucial element in a culture change programme. In isolation, though, these personnel mechanisms are likely to be subordinated to the existing culture. At best, employees will pay lip service to them. At worst, they will be disregarded entirely. It is a standing joke in some organizations that the first task of a newly appointed manager is to throw away the pile of uncompleted appraisal forms left by his or her predecessor. Equally, some managers still perceive training as an unnecessary and irritating intrusion into their day-to-day activities.

In considering the personnel mechanisms detailed below, it is important to remember that, in each case, they were used as part of an integrated package of culture change initiatives. The practitioners involved, working in conjunction with senior and line management, analysed the strategic needs of the organization in relation to the current values and behaviour of the workforce. They then intervened, consciously and systematically, in the areas where change was needed. In most cases, these interventions were designed, not only to reinforce strategic values, but also to reinforce each other. Human resource activities, often trivial in themselves, were perceived as part of a unified strategy, directly coordinated with the overall goals of the organization.

The mechanisms of culture change

The techniques used to change culture in our case study organizations covered the whole range of personnel practice. They included, for example, initiatives in the following areas:

- recruitment and selection
- induction
- training and development
- communications
- payment and reward
- appraisal
- employee relations
- terms and conditions of employment
- organization structure
- counselling and redundancy
- social activities

Recruitment and selection

Recruitment is one of the most immediate points of contact between the internal culture of an organization and the outside world. As we have seen in chapter 3, it is often the most direct channel for introducing new ideas into an introspective and self-perpetuating culture. If the recruitment process is carried out thoughtfully and systematically, it is possible to exert a strong influence on the 'incoming' culture.

This in turn can be a powerful influence on those already working in the organization.

At its simplest and most common level, this might involve the appointment of a senior manager with an innovative or charismatic approach. In a number of our case-study organizations, the Chief Executive or other Directors had been appointed precisely because they had achieved significant and distinctive change in other organizations. In some cases, this was because the organization wished to emulate change processes carried out elsewhere. In others, it was simply felt that the individual had the necessary vision and force of personality to drive through whatever changes were needed.

This kind of strategic approach is often taken with the appointment of top-level staff. It is used much less commonly at lower levels in the organization. In fact, there is no reason why most managerial and even supervisory appointments should not be approached from a more strategic perspective. In drawing up person specifications, recruiters should be encouraged to give serious consideration to the overall strategic aims of the organization as well as to short-term operation demands. If, for example, there is an urgent need for change to be implemented at all levels in the organization, it may well be appropriate to give this a high priority in the person specifications of middle management posts.

There is no reason why strategic considerations should not play a significant part in selection for any post capable of having a strategic impact. Hampshire County Council, in appointing managers to the newly independent Direct Labour Organization, had to find individuals capable of achieving unprecedented commercial objectives. Similarly, Toshiba and Unisys had to appoint managers who would be able to lead the companies towards newly defined strategic objectives. Other organizations encouraged the appointment of marketing, rather than technical staff, at senior levels, with the aim of moving towards greater customer orientation.

Recruitment can have a significant cultural impact at all levels in the organization. If managers are trying to foster a

particular culture in the organization generally, it is clearly
sensible to ensure that this message is communicated to those
contemplating joining the company. Candidates looking to
work in a paternalistic environment, for example, are unlikely
to be comfortable or successful in a company which is moving
towards a culture of independence or entrepreneurship. In
appointing staff to their new organization, Toshiba used a
pre-recruitment video, in which the Chairman outlined the
company's expectations of its new staff. Those who felt
unable to live up to these were able to withdraw prior to the
selection process. In effect, the company had defined its new
strategic values to the workforce even before they took up
employment. This can be seen as an attempt to pre-empt and
control the normal process of cultural development.

Some organizations – though none included in our case
study sample – have taken this a stage further. They have
attempted to use psychological selection techniques, such as
personality questionnaires and interest inventories, to select
staff who will conform with their existing or desired culture.
They argue that to sustain a culture of, say, innovation, they
need consistently to recruit employees who are interested in
and capable of innovatory performance. This is clearly an
extreme example and some may find it unwelcome.
Nevertheless, it demonstrates that some employers recognize
the potential power of recruitment as a device for managing
culture. It is, after all, likely to be easier to recruit the right
people in the first place than to change their attitudes and
values later.

Induction

Induction, however it is carried out, is the first real contact
that employees have with the organization that is paying their
salaries. It is an opportunity to affirm corporate values and
objectives while employees are still likely to be comparatively
receptive and before they have been subjected to dissenting

views. It is also an opportunity to provide employees with an organizational context for their own duties and responsibilities. Many of the organizations we looked at saw induction as a crucial point for communicating a strategic perspective to employees before they became too blinkered by the pressures of day-to-day work.

Many organizations still seem to underestimate the value of induction. It is not uncommon for employees, even after quite lengthy service, to have no real idea of their organizations' products or activities, let alone their strategic values and goals. At one level, this is simply bad performance management. It is unreasonable to expect employees to be motivated towards good performance if their activities have no organizational context. Equally, though, such organizations are failing to manage their corporate culture. Employees are not told what values and behaviour are expected of them, nor how these are related to the organization's objectives. Employers cannot then be surprised if employees develop their own, *ad hoc* perceptions, which may be totally at odds with the organization's intended aims and values. In one company we heard of – not, fortunately, one of our case study examples – shopfloor quality control consisted of hiding faulty components among batches of good ones. The employees believed that their priority was high production rather than high quality. They would have been shocked – or at least, highly amused – to hear that their product was being marketed on the basis of quality.

In this case, the problem was no doubt compounded by other factors, such as an unhelpful incentive bonus scheme and generally poor communications. Nevertheless, one of the crucial factors was that the employees had never been told, clearly and explicitly, what priorities were expected.

Most of our case study organizations recognized the importance of defining, at the earliest opportunity, the kinds of values and behaviour expected under the changed culture. This underlies Unisys' concept of 'kick-off' meetings. Another organization we encountered used one-to-one counselling to bring staff 'on board' the new culture. If such a culture is to be successfully maintained, this process needs to be continuous. Any new employee entering the organization needs to be 'brought on board'.

This is not to say that the induction process needs necessarily to involve heavy propaganda. Some organizations have successfully adopted a proselytizing approach, but in many cases, this may simply lead to cynicism. Equally, induction cannot operate in isolation. There is no point in affirming particular corporate values during the induction process, if these are not evident elsewhere. If new employees who have been told that 'quality is all important' find that, in practice, production levels are given priority, the cultural message will soon be undermined. Induction, by itself, cannot change culture. Nevertheless, it is a powerful reinforcer of other cultural initiatives.

Training and development

Most of our case study organizations used training in various forms as a primary tool of culture change. This included developmental programmes, such as those arranged by the Abbey National and Hampshire County Council, as well as practical skills training, like that introduced by Marley and the Unisys. In virtually every case, the development of training programmes was explicitly linked to the strategic and cultural needs of the organization.

This strategic perspective is worth stressing. In the past, there has been a tendency to view training, with the exception of top management development, in the context of immediate operational needs rather than longer-term strategy. Even in those organizations where training is carried out on a more systematic basis, training needs are often assessed only by analysing the specific operational requirements of individuals in their immediate jobs. Little attention is paid to the strategy in which the job is carried out. As a result, resources are often wasted in providing training which is peripheral to the organization's strategic needs.

In recent years, this perspective has begun to change. It is now much more common for training, at all levels in the organization, to be perceived as a strategic and cultural mechanism. In a number of organizations we looked at, for example, 'customer orientation' was seen as a primary cultural value. As a result, practical training was provided in techniques such as telephone communication with customers. In Hampshire County Council, there was a need to develop a more commercial perspective on the Authority's operations. Consequently, business games and role-playing exercises were used to develop relevant new skills and values.

The training used by our case study organizations falls into three broad categories. First, and most straightforwardly, there was practical skills training. The value of this should not be underestimated. Many of the culture changes we examined could not have been achieved if employees had not felt capable of coping with the demands of the new culture. It is unreasonable to expect employees to adopt, say, a more entrepreneurial or innovative approach, if they lack basic operational skills. Similarly, employees cannot be expected to be 'customer-orientated' if they cannot communicate effectively with their customers. Many organizations, in setting up grand programmes of culture change, forget to provide these basic building blocks. In Unisys, by contrast, much initial effort was expended on providing practical training in the new company's products. It was recognized that employees could not be expected to provide a high level of performance if they lacked basic skills or knowledge. This may seem an obvious point, but it bears repeating. Too many organizations, in striving to achieve significant culture change, expect their employees to run before they have learned to walk.

The second form of training used by our case study organizations is concerned with the development of new attitudes or values, linked to changes in work performance and behaviour. Such developmental training can prove a key factor in achieving culture change, although its design may prove problematic. In most of the cases we looked at, developmental training was used to raise awareness of factors or approaches crucial to the desired culture. In Hampshire County Council, role-playing exercises and business games were used to heighten awareness of commercial issues. By simulating the constraints and pressures of a business environment, the training encouraged managers to confront commercial issues not previously part of their responsibilities. Managers were asked to consider how concepts such as 'profitability' and 'return on investment' might be applied to operations formerly carried out on a 'public service' basis. At the same time, role-playing exercises were used to foster awareness of different perspectives within the organization. Managers were, for example, encouraged to view their operations from the perspective of their customers. Above all, managers were urged to consider the issues from a strategic viewpoint, to develop personal views on organizational goals and values, to identify potential problems and to provide suggested solutions.

The value of this training was manifold. It gave managers a 'dry run' to practise and develop the skills needed to operate in the new environment. It raised an awareness of unfamiliar issues or approaches. It provided a greater understanding of the problems or pressures facing those attempting to manage the changes at a strategic level. By involving managers at an early stage in the development of systems and policies, it encouraged a sense of commitment. It allowed managers to gain a wider perception of how their roles fitted into the organization as a whole. It provided a mechanism by which individuals could share ideas, perceptions and problems, with the aim of improving communications and, if possible, arriving at a consensus view. All these factors combined to produce changes in attitude and approach which were central to the successful development of the new operation. Furthermore, the process of shared learning and experience itself fostered a sense of unity and common commitment to the new culture.

Abbey National also used training as a vehicle for developing and promoting changes in attitudes, values and approaches. In this case, the training aimed to provide a conceptual framework for management thinking, encouraging managers to approach their responsibilities in a more systematic and strategic manner. The objective, as in Hampshire County Council, was to raise awareness of the aspects of the management role most relevant to the new cultural needs of the organization. The training was presented with a high level of enthusiasm and energy, with the specific aim of fostering strong personal commitment among participants. In retrospect, Abbey National also acknowledged the value of 'cascading' the training process down the organizational structure. After each manager had undergone training, his or her subordinates would undergo the same or a similar process. The enthusiasm of the subordinates placed pressure on the managers to adapt their behaviour in accordance with the training. In cases where no management change had been evident, subordinates were encouraged to question the reasons. In this context, managers were unable merely to pay lip service to the principles involved, but had to change their behaviour in accordance with their colleagues' and subordinates' expectations.

There are numerous similar examples among our case studies of training being used to promote changes in attitude or behaviour. In most cases, as in Hampshire and the Abbey National, the aim has been to highlight particular issues or approaches and to provide a new or more coherent focus for the employee's activities. In Unisys, management training was used to develop the role of the manager as 'leader and coach', using a number of key themes as a framework. In this case, video techniques were used to facilitate speed of communication and consistency of approach. Similarly, the 'total quality' concept, adopted by Rank Xerox, Johnson Matthey and BP Chemicals International, provides a conceptual focus for employee performance. By encouraging awareness of 'total quality' or 'conformance to customer requirement', the training provides a yardstick by which employees can evaluate their performance and, if necessary, change their behaviour accordingly.

Finally, training can also influence attitudes and behaviour through a process of 'role modelling'. In other words, the style and content of the training itself displays and defines 'acceptable' or 'legitimate' behaviour for the trainees. Question and answer sessions can be conducted by senior managers in an 'open' manner, confirming that this is appropriate behaviour in the organization. This 'open' style can then be developed and reinforced in the formal training process, using group work and various forms of action learning. Once again, this approach can be cascaded down the organization, so that the behaviour of managers authorizes similar behaviour among their subordinates.

Communications

Communication was probably the single most important mechan- ism of culture change among the case study companies. One of the managers interviewed commented that, in attempting to change culture, his company 'communicated like mad'. On another occasion, when we tried to define the notion of organizational culture to a group of managers, one of them commented: 'But when you talk about culture, you really just mean communications, don't you?' Culture is more than just communications, but, in virtually every case we looked at, communication techniques played a critical role in changing culture.

In a sense, this is obvious. After all, employees cannot be expected to adopt new values or behaviour if they do not know what these are. Nevertheless, communications are often undervalued. Many organizations – some of them quite large – still lack effective mechanisms for communicating with their staff. These organizations encounter major problems even in disseminating practical information, let alone in communicating cultural values. Other organizations, which previously had comparatively sophisticated channels of communication – ranging from formalized briefing methods to company videos – lost these during the depths of the recession. When cost cutting became a priority, communications became dispensable.

Above all, there are many organizations which possess effective channels of communication, but which do not use them for strategic ends. In these organizations, there may well be media such as company publications, briefings, even videos, but little attempt is made to relate them to cultural needs. Characteristically, the communications media are edited by comparatively junior members of staff, not privy to strategic thinking. At best, they convey a vague sense of organizational 'well-being' – recent successes, new projects, the occasional exhortatory message from the Chairman. At worst, they are simply a waste of precious resources.

Ironically, some personnel managers have in the past tried to distance themselves from the communications role. In attempting to define a more 'commercial' role for themselves, they have rejected communications responsibilities as peripheral to the 'bottom line'. Editing a site newspaper or information sheet was seen as an onerous duty, which only served to confirm perceptions of personnel as a 'soft' function, irrelevant to real business needs. When the opportunity arose, many personnel practitioners were only too glad to ditch their responsibilities in this area.

In fact, as our case studies demonstrate, communications media are a vital element of culture management. Edgar Schein has suggested that, at the most visible level, culture is manifested in the organization's artifacts and creations. Communications media are usually among the most explicit and influential of these articles. Handled skilfully, therefore, they provide a powerful tool for directing culture change.

In Unisys, publications and even free audio cassette magazines were used to convey key cultural messages. The company needed to demonstrate its success, quickly and explicitly, to overcome the potential traumas of merger. Publications reported successful new projects, sales and marketing achievements, improvements in profitability. Staff were made aware of the company's achievements, reinforcing an ethos of success and high performance. These publications also stressed the company's stated values of customer orientation, teamwork, innovation, high ethical standards and quality, relating these to practical achievements by employees. By reporting success, the company was providing a real-life focus for abstract statements about values and culture. BP Chemicals International used a similar technique as part of their 'total quality' programme. The company's staff magazine included regular reports on the impact of 'total quality management' on particular departments or operations. The effect, again, was to bring culture down to earth, providing a practical focus to which employees could easily relate.

Communications techniques were also used to ensure that a consistent cultural message was being relayed to all staff. In large organizations, messages about values or culture commonly become distorted or lost as they are transmitted down the line. Senior managers – who are, for example, aware of low-price competition – may affirm loudly that 'quality' or 'customer service' are paramount. By the time this message reaches the shopfloor, it becomes adulterated, so that supervisors tell their staff that, yes, quality is important, but not if it gets in the way of productivity. Without good communications, employees are likely to develop their own sets of values and priorities, based on limited perceptions or short-term expediency, which may be totally at odds with the organization's real needs.

Modern information technology has made it easier to deal with this problem. A large number of the companies we looked at had used media such as video, audio and even computer networks to convey consistent messages swiftly throughout the organization. The Toshiba pre-selection video, for example, was intended to ensure that all received an identical account of the company's expectations and values.

Jaguar, Abbey National and others made extensive use of video as a means of communicating quickly and consistently with a large number of employees across a wide range of locations.

Jaguar also developed a formalized 'team briefing' system as a means of disseminating information and messages amongst its staff. Although perhaps less efficient than video, team briefing has the major advantages of being more personal and encouraging a 'two-way' response. It encourages involvement in the ideas and information being put across. To ensure consistency, the team briefers were provided with core material about the organization as a whole, which they could supplement with more localized material. This enabled employees to relate corporate aims and values to their own immediate activities. Toshiba also made use of five-minutes briefing sessions at the start of each day, with similar objectives.

Many of our case study organizations provided short, memorable and repeated reminders of cultural values. In Unisys' staff magazine, there are continual references to 'customer awareness' and 'customer orientation', stressing the primary focus of the company's activities. The company provides each manager with a 'management creed'. This is a short statement of management values, posted in the manager's office. In BP Chemicals International, staff who have undergone training in 'total quality' are asked to wear a 'quality badge', as a continuing reminder of the values and requirements involved.

These techniques may seem gimmicky, but they provide a powerful and immediate focus for cultural thinking. Generally these kinds of techniques need to be handled with a degree of light-heartedness to pre-empt charges of propagandizing or indoctrination. This was evident in the humorous injunction at Unisys training courses that the names of the former companies would not be mentioned on pain of forfeit. The instruction was followed in a semi-serious spirit, but the basic message – that the company was entering a new era – was powerfully conveyed.

In many cases, the communications techniques described above were administered primarily by the personnel function. The personnel function, for example, generally provided training in team briefing and other interactive skills. Similarly, the function was often responsible for devising memorable ways of communicating cultural values to employees on a day-to-day basis. Sophisticated media, such as videos and magazines, were of course generally produced by experts. Nevertheless, personnel still had a significant input to ensure that appropriate cultural messages were being relayed. Personnel effectively acted as the link between strategic thinking and the communications experts. This is an important and powerful role, which needs careful managing. If the link breaks down, the communications media can lose their credibility and become counter-productive. In one case we came across – not one of our final case-studies – the company newspaper continued to exude bland well-being long after senior management had been forced to adopt harsh measures to deal with a financial crisis. The result was a high level of cynicism and suspicion which did not assist the company's chance of profitability.

Payment and reward

There has long been a debate among personnel theorists about whether or not financial remuneration can positively influence work behaviour. Conventional personnel wisdom, drawing on Herzberg, suggests that pay is merely a 'hygiene factor', which demotivates if it is unsatisfactory but does not generally motivate. In recent years, an increasing number of organizations have rejected this view, arguing that, if used carefully, pay can be a very powerful motivator. For many practitioners, the effective management of remuneration has become a critical part of the personnel brief.

Whichever view one accepts, however, there is no doubt that an organization's approach to remuneration does convey

strong cultural messages. Remuneration is paid in return for
an employee's contribution to the operations of the
organization. The nature of the payment – the standards set
and conditions attached – therefore speaks eloquently of the
organization's expectations of its employees. To take a simple
example, if salary increases are given solely on the basis of
length of service, employees will tend to assume that the
organization does not give major priority to high performance.
Conversely, if salary increases are entirely performance-
related, employees may well assume that company loyalty is
a lower priority.

This is not to say that any single approach to remuneration
is necessarily 'right'. There has been a tendency in recent
years to assume that, for example, performance-related pay
is necessarily 'better' than service-related pay. In many
organizations, where the overwhelming need is to improve
performance, this may be true. However, it is possible to
conceive of situations where loyalty and long service may be
a higher priority than raising performance. Equally, some
organizations – such as cooperatives and some charities –
operate successfully with absolute pay parity. In these cases,
the major priority may be the creation of a sense of unity and
common purpose.

In other words, an organization's remuneration system
should be related to its cultural values and objectives. If it is
not, the organization may well be sending its employees
conflicting and confusing cultural messages. There is little
point in trying to foster a culture of initiative and
entrepreneurship, if employees are rewarded solely on the
basis of long service. It will be impossible to develop a sense
of company loyalty if employees only get salary increases by
threatening to leave. It will be difficult to promote a concern
for 'quality' if employees are rewarded solely on the basis of
high productivity.

By the same token, the reward system can be a powerful
reinforcer of the organization's stated values and objectives.
If employees perceive that certain kinds of behaviour will

lead to financial reward, they are more likely to respond accordingly. Many of our case study organizations recognized that attempts to change beliefs and behaviour would be more effective if they were supported by an appropriate payment system. Abbey National, for example, realized that, to promote a more commercial and performance-orientated culture, the payment system would need to be related much more closely to individual and organizational performance. The Society scrapped across-the-board pay rises and introduced individual performance-related pay. It also introduced a simple profit-share scheme, taking care to explain how individual performance at all levels could contribute to profitability.

Unisys, in promoting a culture of high achievement and innovation, developed a totally performance-based pay system under which individuals could receive increases ranging from 0 per cent to 20 per cent. In other organizations, even when there was no dramatic move towards performance or profit-related pay, efforts were made to link the payment system more closely to cultural and strategic ends. In Hampshire County Council's Direct Labour Organization, for example, the incentive bonus scheme was revised. This was, first, to ensure that it was more closely related to performance. Secondly, from a management perspective, the new system was 'pre-evaluated' to encourage a higher level of forward planning and to ensure that, as far as possible, the payment of bonuses was related to the fulfilment of customer requirements. In this case, the scheme was designed to influence the behaviour not only of those receiving the bonus, but also of those responsible for authorizing its payment.

Appraisal

A large number of our case study organizations mentioned the introduction or revision of appraisal schemes as an important element in their change programmes. Marley, for example, referred to the introduction of an improved appraisal system, based on a modified 'management by objectives' approach. Unisys also moved towards a 'management by objectives' system, and a number of other organizations mentioned similar developments in appraisal techniques.

Appraisal is always likely to be a key tool in effective performance management. It is not surprising, therefore, that it should also be a useful tool in influencing attitudes and behaviour. The appraisal system is another of the organization's cultural artifacts and, like the payment system, its form and contents send out clear cultural messages. The employee will not take very seriously attempts to foster a culture of, say, high performance, if there is no mechanism for evaluating performance. Equally, most employees will pay little attention to the organization's stated strategic objectives, if these contradict the personal objectives set out in the appraisal process.

There are still many organizations where, even if appraisal is taken seriously, it is not related explicitly to the strategic or cultural needs of the business. Often, appraisal is still based on assessing vague behavioural or character traits, rather than the achievement of clearly defined objectives. Even if it is related to objectives, these are frequently determined solely by the whim of the departmental manager, rather than originating from organizational needs or goals.

Effective appraisal – whether or not it is based on a formal 'management by objectives' approach – should create a strong link between corporate objectives and the objectives laid down for individual employees. Appraisal should become another element of cultural communication, translating strategic aims and values into personal objectives. Employees are much more likely to respond to clearly defined, mutually agreed individual objectives, than they are to grand statements about corporate values, however eloquently these are articulated. After all, as we saw in Part I, if we wish to change culture, it is much more important to change attitudes to *behaviour* than to change attitudes towards concepts or ideas.

The role of personnel is to ensure, first, that appraisal is taken seriously and, secondly, that it is related to strategic thinking. The system has to be coordinated centrally and has to be designed so that it concentrates on the areas of performance that are critical to achieving organizational goals. If, for example, the organization believes that greater customer orientation is crucial to its future success, appraisers should be encouraged to set objectives accordingly. In many organizations, appraisal systems remain unchanged for years. Ideally, though, it may well be appropriate periodically to revise appraisal forms – or at least any accompanying briefing material and appraisal training – to meet changing strategic and cultural needs.

An effective appraisal system is important also in relation to pay and to training and development. It is now widely accepted that the appraisal process should be separated from decisions on salary if it is to function effectively as a development tool. Nevertheless, any effective system of performance-related pay does need to be based on credible performance appraisal. Remuneration will not work as a tool of culture change if there is no clear link between behaviour and reward. Equally, appraisal must be used also to identify training and development needs. If employees are unable to achieve culturally determined objectives because of lack of skills or knowledge, attempts to change culture will soon founder.

Employee relations

Relationships between management and employees, however these are manifested, are likely to be a crucial element in determining organizational culture. If relationships tend to be confrontational, it is likely to be difficult to disseminate management-driven values or objectives among the workforce. Management's efforts to foster a particular culture will probably result in opposition, cynicism and the creation of unhelpful counter-cultures. If, on the other hand, relationships are more relaxed and there is a commonality of purpose, employees will be more receptive to management-driven culture change.

Many of our case study organizations prepared the ground for culture change by endeavouring to improve the general employee relations climate. Toshiba provides one of the clearest examples. Before setting up the new organization in 1981, the company reached a detailed agreement with the EETPU, designed to foster a climate of greater cooperation. The agreement gave the EETPU exclusive bargaining rights, ensured single status among the workforce and included provision for disputes to be settled, in the final instance, by 'pendulum' arbitration. Perhaps more importantly, the company agreed to provide extensive formal processes for consultation and communication.

Some of these provisions may, in industrial relations terms, be controversial. This is not the place to debate, for example, the general rights and wrongs of 'single union' agreements. Nevertheless, it is evident that Toshiba's employee relations agreement was a crucial element in fostering the culture needed for success. Management and the workforce moved away from adversarialism towards participation and coopera-tion. The 'company advisory board', in particular, provided an invaluable mechanism for involving employee representati-ves in the company's business. This in turn promoted a greater understanding and awareness of the company's strategies and values, and greater commitment to its objectives. In effect, the advisory board short-circuited the traditional division between strategic aims and values and the day-to-day activities of the workforce.[4]

Not all the case study organizations were able to redefine their employee relations activities from first principles, like Toshiba. Nevertheless, even organizations operating in more conventional industrial relations climates made strenuous efforts to improve relationships. These organizations saw good industrial relations as essential to the management of change and the effective promotion of new cultural values. In setting up the new Direct Labour Organization, Hampshire County Council made strenuous efforts to involve the relevant unions. The Authority encouraged a process of continuing informal discussion as well as formal negotiation, in an effort to increase understanding and involvement. In addition, this helped to highlight potential problems at the earliest possible stage, before management or workforce could become entrenched in confrontational positions.

Throughout our case studies, consultation, involvement and improved employee relations are a recurrent theme. The Royal Bank of Scotland developed a system of service circles – a variation on the more familiar quality circle – as a means of involving staff in the cultural development of the organization. These circles allowed staff to formulate their own attitudes to customer service issues and other work-related topics. Staff could identify for themselves the most effective means of fulfilling the bank's strategic needs at an operational level. This fostered a strong and practical commitment to the otherwise abstract concept of, say, 'customer service'. It also ensured that those with the most detailed and direct knowledge were involved in the design of new practices or policies. This increased the staff's sense of ownership and ensured that the new systems would be practicable. The service circles also provided an additional channel of communication between senior management and the workforce, bypassing the traditional management hierarchy. In this way, cultural messages could be reiterated and reinforced from several directions.

The companies which used a 'total quality' approach also made extensive use of quality circles and similar systems. Again, these encouraged the workforce to develop practical responses to strategic needs and objectives. Staff became directly involved in the implementation of new cultural values, identifying the implications of these values for their own operational context. Through this process of involvement, the new culture begins to take root.

Terms and conditions of employment

An organization's terms of employment, like its salary structure, speak volumes about its attitude to its workforce. Policies and practices in this area can therefore send out significant cultural messages, which may either reinforce or contradict more explicit efforts to manage culture. Attempts to promote a general culture of cooperation and common purpose, for example, may be severely undermined if there is a clear status division between managers and other staff.

Equally, there will be little point in trying to foster a customer-orientated culture, if staff dealing with customers find that their terms of employment are worse than, say, staff at Head Office.

Many organizations still spend small fortunes on disseminating grand statements about corporate culture which are promptly and continuously undermined by their employment practices. Employees are unlikely to be impressed by exhortations to 'pull together' or 'share in our common purpose', if their managers are clearly giving greater priority to personal status.

Many of our case study organizations recognized this and took care to ensure that the cultural messages sent out, whether explicit or implicit, were consistent. Toshiba, for example, as part of its initial agreement with the EETPU, introduced 'single status', on the Japanese model, for all its staff. This included common terms and conditions, a single canteen and even a universal mode of dress. The aim was to reinforce the sense of common purpose that underpinned all the activities of the new organization.

Organization structure

There is likely to be a close relationship between the structure of an organization and its prevailing culture. Charles Handy has commented that 'it will be argued that many of the ills of organizations stem from imposing an inappropriate structure on a particular culture'.[5] In practice, the organization will probably develop, whether consciously or not, a structure which reflects its original cultural and strategic needs. For example, if the organization's priority is to ensure reliability and the avoidance of error with comparatively little concern for innovation or individual enterprise, its developing structure is likely to resemble a conventional Weberian bureaucracy. There will be a clearly defined hierarchy, with very precise spans of responsibility and control. Individual freedom of action will be limited and there will be tight checks on all activity. This kind of structure has developed, for example, in many administrative areas of the public sector. By contrast, if the organization's priorities are for entrepreneurship and initiative, the developing structure will probably be much less formal. There will be much greater development of responsibility and much more individual freedom. This kind of structure is often found in small, research-based high technology companies.[6]

The strategic needs of most organizations are likely to be very varied and their structure may display a corresponding complexity. The organization may, for example, need to juxtapose a reliable manufacturing unit with an innovative research operation or an entrepreneurial sales function. Ideally, each of these functions would have developed a structure – and indeed a culture – best suited to its particular needs. If this has happened, the organization will then need to solve the difficult problem of integrating the various operations with the overall strategic needs of the organization.[7] It will also need to resolve the interfunctional frictions likely to arise from conflicting perceptions and values. If the organization can manage to sustain this delicate balance between 'differentiation' and 'integration', it will probably come close to achieving Peters and Waterman's ideal of 'simultaneous loose–tight properties'. Such organizations would be 'rigidly controlled, yet at the same time allow (indeed, insist on) autonomy, entrepreneurship and innovation from the rank and file'.[8]

In reality, few organizations – even among those cited by
Peters and Waterman – live up to this counsel of perfection.
Most· avoid the issue by developing a prevailing structure
appropriate to their priority needs, which conditions all their
operations. For example, a large multi-national company,
operating in a traditionally stable market, will probably
display a bureaucratic structure which promotes reliability
and discourages risk-taking. If it operates a research outfit or
a sales function, these will probably be subordinated to the
priorities of the company as a whole. They will be low-key
and lacking in influence, operating with an unsatisfactory
structure and in an unconducive culture.

This may be frustrating for staff working in the low-priority
functions. Nevertheless, this imperfect compromise works
well enough for most organizations, as long as the overall
structure and culture is appropriate to their priority needs.
Problems arise when the priorities of the organization change.
In the case of the multi-national cited above, the bureaucratic
structure would probably become inappropriate if the market
suddenly became unstable. In this context, the company
would probably be seeking a much higher level of innovation and personal initiative, while saddled with a
structure unconducive to such a culture. This problem faced
many of the oil majors after the oil price crashes of the
1970s.

Many of our case study organizations also recognized that
major structural change was likely to be a pre-condition of
fostering a new culture. Hampshire County Council realized
that it would not be possible to develop an entrepreneurial
culture in the direct labour force while this was part of the
essentially bureaucratic structure of the organization as a
whole. It was necessary to take the Direct Labour
Organization out of the traditional Authority structure and
set it up as an independent operation in its own right. It even
became necessary for the DLO to override some of the
formal control mechanisms operating elsewhere in the
Authority. The success of the DLO's restructuring and culture

change is undoubted. It has, however, led to problems of integration like those referred to above.

In Toshiba, the company's cultural messages reflected changes in production methods and organizational structure. The company moved towards a greater 'task orientation', with less demarcation and a high level of flexibility. At shopfloor level, this was achieved through a grading structure based on the range and flexibility of job skills. At more senior levels, it was achieved through a reduction in the number of management layers and the development of management teams not committed to specific functions. This 'loosening' of the traditional structure was accompanied by promotion and greater awareness of overall company values.

In Marley, the company underwent a process of decentralization, devolving management control from Head Office. Head Office became an enabling rather than a controlling function. These structural changes reflected the company's overall intention of moving from paternalism towards a culture of greater initiative and independence. In Unisys, on the other hand, the new organization was consciously designed as a very 'flat' hierarchy, with few management layers. The intention was that the customer should be as close as possible to senior management. This in turn reinforced the company's general culture of accountability and customer awareness.

Organizational structure can be a key element in the management of culture. It is unfortunate, therefore, that structural changes are still commonly carried out on a short-term technical basis and tend not to be related to strategic need. As John Child has commented, '. . . most of the literature on organizational design treats it as a purely technical matter, a question of adjusting structure to suit prevailing contingencies'.[9] It is also probably true that, except in some large companies with formal organization development functions, there tends to be a lack of knowledge about organizational issues. Line managers are unlikely to have the resources, inclination and overview needed to handle such issues, except on the basis of short-term technical expediency. On the other hand, the personnel function is not commonly perceived as a repository of organizational wisdom and many personnel practitioners would probably not be capable of taking on such a role.[10] Structural development can make a major contribution to the achievement of strategic and cultural objectives. If these are to be fully exploited, personnel practitioners will need to strengthen their skills and influence in this important area.

Counselling and redundancy

To change culture, it is necessary to change the behaviour, values, attitudes and beliefs of individuals. Most of the mechanisms outlined above attempt to influence the attitudes and behaviour of employees *en masse*. It is assumed that, if consistent messages are sent out to the workforce as a whole, the general pressure to conform will act as a powerful motivation for change.

There is, however, considerable value in communicating directly with employees as individuals. After all, if the intention is to change behaviour and attitudes, managers are likely to be more influential in direct face-to-face contact than through more formal mechanisms. Furthermore, individual employees are likely to have personal reservations about change which are not shared generally by their colleagues. If these individual reservations are not understood and overcome at an early stage, they may well become aggregated into general opposition. For example, employees may resist attempts to foster a new culture because of unnecessary doubts about their own abilities. If these can be resolved at an individual level, change may proceed much more smoothly.

One organization we came across used an extensive process of individual counselling – described as 'bringing on board' – as the first stage of their culture change programme. The personnel function acted as facilitators and, to ensure consistency, produced common briefing material for the line managers conducting the counselling. During this process, managers described the proposed changes, explained the implications for individuals and defined expectations of those working in the new organization. The individual was then asked whether he or she could be fully committed to working in the new organization on the terms described. Reservations or problems could be discussed and, if possible, resolved. If staff accepted the new terms, they were formally 'brought on board'. If not, they could be considered for redundancy treatment. In this way, while achieving necessary reductions in its workforce, the company ensured that the remaining employees were fully committed to the company's strategic aims and values.

Unisys, which needed to shed staff from the two former companies, identified through counselling those individuals who felt unable to accept the values and culture of the new company. In most cases, these were long-serving employees who were strongly committed to their old company. These generally left on premature retirement terms. It was not uncommon to hear such individuals declare, at retirement parties, that they refused to use the name 'Unisys'. The departure of these individuals not only removed potential opposition to change. It also acted as what Terrence Deal has described as a 'transition ritual',[11] signifying the end of the old order and the creation of the new.

Abbey National also discovered that some managers were unable to accept their new culture and the expectation of changed behaviour. These managers were given premature retirement. All of these organizations, incidentally, stressed that retirement or redundancy was always handled as generously and sympathetically as possible. In the words of one manager, 'there could be no question of leaving the feeling that those who, through no fault of their own, could not adapt would be abandoned on the junk heap'. Financial terms were generous and counselling and outplacement were generally provided where appropriate. This was partly for moral reasons, but it was recognized that the redundancy process could itself send powerful cultural messages to those remaining in the organization. If the organization was seen to be behaving ruthlessly or arbitrarily, this would lower morale and diminish commitment to the new culture.

Social activities

Many of the organizations we looked at used informal or social activities to foster and reinforce cultural development. In Toshiba, Geoffrey Deith consciously shifted resources away from the traditional social club, which received comparatively little support, to organized trips and events for all the workforce. The aim was to reinforce the sense of common purpose through 'out of work' activities involving all levels and functions. The informal environment of a social event helped to dissolve unnecessary or outdated formal distinctions. In Hampshire County Council, the newly independent Direct Labour Organization arranged a series of social activities aimed at building up informal relationships between staff. It was hoped that these informal relationships would encourage a sense of community in the work environment.

In Marley, the organization of inter-functional social activities helped to break down traditional barriers between functions. Such activities have encouraged staff from different departments and even different sites to talk to one another, often for the first time. These informal communications have then developed into more formal, work-related contacts. This has assisted the company's move away from paternalism towards a more developed culture which communicates horizontally as well as vertically.

The culture of an organization is determined as much by informal behaviour and attitudes as by formal structures and practices. 'Out of work' activities can therefore play an important role in influencing culture. Such activities need to be directed and coordinated in relation to the organization's cultural objectives. Otherwise, like Toshiba's former social club, they may prove a waste of resources or even be counter-productive. Events held solely on a departmental basis, for example, might simply reinforce unproductive formal divisions.

If social activities are to be useful, as well as fun, they need to be coordinated centrally. Again, forging the link between strategic thinking and informal activities would seem to be an appropriate role for the personnel function. In practice, many personnel managers have traditionally handled social activities by default, finding themselves unwillingly elected Chairman of the Sports and Social Club. Ironically, in recent years, some practitioners have tried to divest themselves of such responsibilities, seeing them as 'non-productive'. It may well be that, in attempting to manage culture, personnel professionals will need to re-evaluate such apparently 'soft' management tasks. Approached from a strategic perspective, they may be far from trivial and may contribute significantly to organizational effectiveness.

Some conclusions

Organizational culture is a complex matter. It is difficult to pin down and even more difficult to manage. This is because, in a very real sense, culture involves everything. It influences – and is influenced by – issues ranging from major strategic decisions down to the layout of the entrance hall or the way people address one another. In simple terms, culture is the all-embracing structure of values, attitudes and beliefs that underlies all the organization's activities. It is formed, usually over many years, through a combination of dominant personalities, trauma and positive re-inforcement. In most organizations, it is deeply rooted and very difficult to change.

Nevertheless, culture change may, on occasions, be crucial to an organization's success or even survival. Just as an appropriate culture can be a strong asset, so an inappropriate culture can be a strong liability. If circumstances change, the organization may need to change its prevailing culture very quickly, to respond effectively to new operational needs. In the cases we looked at, the reasons for change were numerous – new market demands, new production methods, new legislation – but in virtually every case significant and rapid change was needed for the organization to take effective advantage of its new situation.

The personnel function is not generally in a position to initiate or lead such changes. Change must be strategically driven and must be supported by the full commitment of the Chief Executive or equivalent. Nevertheless, even if such commitment is present, culture change will not happen simply by some process of osmosis. It needs to be managed, continuously and actively, throughout the organization. Furthermore, given that culture is likely to be all-persuasive, it cannot be assumed that any single change mechanism, such as a new reward system or a training programme – will be sufficient. Such mechanisms, if used in isolation, are likely merely to be subsumed under the prevailing culture.

In most of the organizations we looked at, the personnel function acted as change agent. It influenced culture through repeated and varied initiatives, using a wide range of personnel activities and techniques. Some of these were aimed at changing attitudes and values directly. Others were intended simply to affect behaviour, on the assumption that this would influence underlying values. Some were intended to facilitate management's role in influencing culture. Others were directed at the workforce as a whole. Some involved major formal exercises. Others made use of low-key, informal activities. Some were innovative. Others were very conventional.

In each case, however, these initiatives were linked to a clear strategic and cultural vision. The practitioners involved, supported by senior management, used personnel techniques to communicate strategic objectives and create the climate within which these could be achieved. The techniques were applied consistently and repeatedly, reinforcing one another, so that the workforce received a coherent series of cultural messages. By this slow but inexorable process, culture was changed.

Some sceptics, considering how personnel is perceived in their own organizations, might query whether the personnel function is really capable of playing a part in changing culture. After all, it is still not uncommon for personnel to be seen merely as an administrative or support function, peripheral to 'bottom line' activities. Furthermore, some personnel practitioners, striving to maintain a detachment from the organizational mainstream, have collaborated in this perception. From this perspective, it is certainly difficult to see how the function can have any significant impact at a strategic or cultural level.

By contrast, in most of our case study organizations, personnel occupied a unique and invaluable position, outside the hurly-burly of everyday operations but, at senior levels, close to strategic thinking. The function was held in high regard, and senior management in particular recognized its potential for improving individual and organizational effectiveness. In this context, with a high level of senior support and commitment, personnel practitioners could exert considerable influence as agents of culture change. The impact of such change on our case study organizations, in terms of profitability and effectiveness, speaks for itself.

Such influence never comes easy and will only be justified by practical, 'bottom line' results. It may well be difficult for some personnel practitioners, hindered by outmoded perceptions, to break out of this 'Catch 22' and prove they have a real contribution to make. Nevertheless, as this book demonstrates, culture *is* important and the personnel function has a potentially crucial role to play in its management. In their influential book, *Corporate cultures*, Terrence Deal and Allan Kennedy argue that the effective management of culture will become a critical component of organizational success.[12] If this is the case, the unique skills of the personnel profession should be able to play a major part. Some individual practitioners, however, will need to develop a much higher level of strategic knowledge, vision and commercial awareness if they are to prove themselves up to the task.

Notes and References

1   JAY Antony. *Management and Machiavelli*. Revised ed., Hutchinson, 1987

2   PETERS Thomas J *and* WATERMAN Robert H. *In search of excellence*. Harper and Row, 1982

3   DEAL T E *and* KENNEDY A A. *Corporate cultures: the rites and rituals of corporate life*. Addison-Wesley, 1982

4   For a detailed account of this process see TREVOR Malcolm. *Toshiba's new British company*. Policy Studies Institute, 1988

5   HANDY Charles. *Understanding organizations*. 3rd ed., Penguin, 1985

6   See, for example, descriptions of small, high technology companies in LLOYD Tom. *Dinosaur & Co*. Routledge, 1984

7   For a detailed discussion of these issues see, for example, LAWRENCE P R *and* LORSCH J W. *Organization and environment*. Harvard Business School, 1967

8   PETERS *and* WATERMAN *op cit*

9   CHILD John. *Organizations – a guide to problems and practice*. Harper and Row, 1984

10 A study carried out by the IPM's National Committee for Organization and Human Resource Planning in 1985 concluded that

> most personnel executives in British organizations may be described as having a 'team' rather than a 'leadership' role in the field of organization restructuring. By this we would imply that they are not in most cases initiators of major organization change nor do they generally have a major role in advising on the forms that new structures might take.

(EVANS Alastair *and* COWLING Alan. 'Personnel's part in organization restructuring'. *Personnel Management.* January 1985).

See also COWLING Alan *and* EVANS Alastair, 'Organization planning and the role of the personnel department'. *Personnel Review.* Vol 4, No 4, 1985
11 DEAL Terrence E. 'Cultural change: opportunity, silent killer or metamorphosis?' in KILMANN Ralph H, SAXTON Mary J, SERPA Roy *et al. Gaining control of the corporate culture.* Jossey-Bass, 1985
12 DEAL T E *and* KENNEDY A A *op cit*

Part IV

Change in Action

In Part IV we include detailed accounts of the case studies that have formed the heart of our examination of organizational culture change. The preceding five chapters draw heavily on the practical experiences recounted in the following pages. In addition, we also carried out a number of other case studies which, for a variety of reasons, we have not included in full. Nevertheless these also added to our ideas and influenced our views.

We hope that the case studies, far from being an appendix, will bring to life the concepts and issues examined elsewhere in the book. We hope that they will illustrate vividly the practical importance of culture change. We also hope that our analysis will have provided readers with a framework for evaluating the effectiveness of the techniques and approaches described.

We would add two brief comments. First, the following accounts are based, in each case, on interviews with comparatively senior managers, both from personnel and from line functions. We have not attempted formally to corroborate the views expressed by interviewing staff at other levels in the organizations concerned. Readers should therefore bear in mind that the accounts almost invariably constitute a senior management – and in most cases a head office – perspective on the events described.

Secondly, we have not been able to measure whether, in the final analysis, a 'culture change' really has taken place in these organizations. We have attempted to view each case with an objective – and occasionally slightly sceptical – eye. We have our own views on whether or not a genuine culture change has occurred in each case, but we have chosen not to prejudice the reader. Instead, having outlined our criteria for culture change in the preceding chapters, we simply present a detailed and straightforward account of each case study. Beyond that, readers must judge for themselves.

Abbey National Building Society

Background

Abbey National Building Society is a permanent building society incorporated under the Building Societies Act 1874. It was formed in 1944 with the merger of two long-established London-based societies, the National Building Society founded in 1849, and the Abbey Road Building Society founded in 1874. Following the merger, Abbey National became the second largest building society in the UK. It has maintained its ranking and today has assets in excess of £26 billion. In 1985 Abbey National had a market share of approximately 17 per cent of the total assets of all building societies and operated through 677 high street branches and 3250 agents. Abbey National's income is derived principally from interest charged on mortgage loans, income from liquid assets and fees received in connection with loans. Abbey National's major items of expense are the interest paid on its shares, deposits and other borrowings together with management expenses. In the last year, following the Building Societies Act 1986, the society has expanded its activities.

It is important to point out that Abbey National was, prior to the changes that have taken place, a successful organization by virtually any standard that could be applied. Change was not driven by impending disaster or by imminent failure, but rather by the clear belief that in order to fulfil its strategic aims of continuing as a successful provider of an ever-widening range of personal financial services it had to make some radical changes.

Building societies

Building societies were formed in the first half of the last century, generally by small groups of people who had a desire to own their own house, particularly as property ownership was the key to enfranchisement. The chosen mechanism was that all members of the group put their money into a common fund until there was sufficient accumulated to purchase or build a house. A ballot was then held to determine which of the members had the house allocated to them. This process was repeated until all of the members owned their houses, at which point the building society was wound up. These were called 'terminating societies'.

It was a fairly logical progression from this to the formulation of building societies which provided a home for people's savings, giving a reasonable rate of return and lending the money so raised to those who wished to purchase a house. These societies, called 'permanent building societies', were the foundation of what has become a major part of the UK financial services industry. It is worth noting that, if the top two societies were capitalized at seven times earnings, they would sit in the league table at numbers three and four behind National Westminster and Barclays but ahead of Lloyds and Midland Banks.

Building societies have operated for most of their history in a single, captive market. For most of that time they had a simple product range consisting of a savings account (the traditional share account) and repayment mortgages.

In the late nineteenth century legislation was passed which defined the role, purpose and powers of building societies. This was consolidated, but largely unchanged, by the 1962 Building Societies Act and remained the legal basis for their operations until the Building Societies Act 1986 was passed by Parliament.

Coupled with this, during the latter part of their history, the societies operated an interest rates agreement, one of the few legal cartel agreements. It has recently been terminated.

The Building Societies Association (BSA) is an association of practically all of the UK societies and one of its high profile roles used to be the determination, through its council of members, of the interest rate to be applied to share accounts and that to be charged on mortgage loans.

Abbey National's culture prior to 1980

Three factors were important in shaping the culture of Abbey National for the one hundred or so years prior to 1980. These were: the legislative framework within which building societies had to operate, the Building Societies Association, which ran a legal cartel, and the marketplace.

The legislative framework pre-1986

The Act under which the building societies operated was very precise in its definition of the purpose for which societies could operate. The relevant extract from the 1962 Building Societies Act reads:

> The purpose for which a Society may be established under this Act is that of raising, by the subscriptions of members, a stock or fund for making advances to members out of the funds of the Society upon security by way of mortgage of freehold or leasehold estate.

It was also precise in its statements about the responsibilities of directors for ensuring that each property taken into mortgage represented adequate security for the loan in terms of its state of structural repair and its value in relation to the loan required.

Clearly, this meant that, when societies were small, each and every mortgage application went before the Board for approval. As societies grew and the volume of business increased, Boards had to delegate their powers to some extent and generally this was done by creating large central departments to agree all but the very largest mortgages. This centralization process of all key functions was prevalent in Abbey National until the early 1980s.

Power and authority were concentrated in very few hands. This formed the basis of the paternalistic and patronage-based culture that developed.

Cartel

The existence of a price-fixing mechanism for the rates of interest to be paid on investments or charged on mortgage loans also had an impact on the type of culture that emerged.

The reason for this was that it removed the need for any concept of profit in the organization. Providing that expenses were held at a level which allowed for a 'surplus' to be transferred to reserves, no questions arose as to overall profitability which would be highlighted for commercial organizations by looking at 'Return on Assets' or 'Return on Capital'.

The cartel fixed the rates and, as the rates determined margins, in doing so it effectively determined the profitability of the entire sector. Consequently, only top management needed to have any view on profit and, as a result, there was a marked lack of commercial realism among the managerial population. Margins were established and expense ratios kept broadly in line with competitor building societies.

The marketplace

For most of their history the marketplace in which societies operated was basically very simple. The products on offer were simple propositions consisting of simple savings accounts and basic mortgage loans.

There was little or no competition in either of these areas as banks were concentrating their resources in the more profitable areas such as corporate and sovereign debt. National savings and trustee savings banks offered some competition but not enough to be serious. Individuals were not encouraged to enter the equities markets and, indeed, they were not particularly accessible or worthwhile unless the persons concerned had a 'high net worth' and could afford to take risks with their capital.

On the mortgage side, there was a similar lack of competition. Building societies with wide access to retail savings and fixed common rates offered mortgages at rates well below those on the money markets, making this market unprofitable for banks and insurance companies without access to the cheap source of funding. The latter tended to restrict themselves to the relatively small market of top-up loans, where reasonable rates of interest could be obtained. Demand for mortgage finance exceeded supply and the building societies operated a queueing system in response. All the societies had to do was to open a branch in the High Street, administer the mortgage quota quickly and efficiently and the operating surpluses rolled in. As a result building societies grew very quickly, compounding in excess of 15 per cent year after year.

The resulting culture

The centralization of power and authority coupled with the image of staid, sound and secure institutions bred and reinforced a culture which was based on patronage and discouraged any risk-taking activity. Taking decisions at a low level in the organization was positively discouraged and low-profile, sound administrative management encouraged.

This lack of commercialism was reinforced by the activities of the BSA in fixing interest rates and by the simplicity of the marketplace. No entrepreneurialism was needed to develop the business and there was little need to market actively either investment or loan products. Competition was largely between building societies and even that was at a comparatively low level.

The patronage system extended to promotion, thus removing any need for any active participation in career development by individuals. It also ensured that many of the mobility problems which surround moves of a geographic, as well as promotional, nature remained hidden from the organization. It took a brave man or woman to say no to a promotion on this basis and as a result few ever did, as it was a high-risk career strategy and could lead to being permanently sidelined.

The changing nature of markets

In the late 1970s and early 1980s the marketplace in which Abbey National operated began to change. The first pressure came from the industry itself and was on the investment side of the book. Success came to be measured in terms of asset growth and inevitably Chief Executives wanted to be seen to be at the top of the league table. Thus, in order to grow more, societies had to lend more and in order to do that they had to raise more money on the retail savings market. (One should bear in mind that societies could lend all that they had available as mortgage queues were prevalent.) This led to interest rate competition on investment business which imposed severe strains on the cartel interest rates agreement.

There was a proliferation of savings plans and increased competition amongst the societies for personal funds. The cartel came under pressure in the early 1980s when small societies, having agreed to a particular interest rate, rushed out and topped the rate by a quarter of a per cent or so. The larger societies felt obliged to honour the rates agreed. However, they became increasingly irritated by this behaviour and in the early 1980s Abbey National withdrew from the interest rates agreement precipitating its breakdown in the middle 1980s.

In the early 1980s corporate demand for finance was at a lower level and sovereign debt had proved disastrous for the clearing banks. In addition, interest rates were at an all-time high, making the mortgage markets more attractive financially.

The clearers made an entry into the mortgage market. In two and a half months they captured around 30 per cent of the market. Fortunately for the societies the banks had earmarked limited funds for this activity and they partially withdrew allowing building societies time to regroup. Also around this time there was a spate of privatization issues also competing for personal funds.

The building societies reacted by changing their policy from one of rationing supply, to one of meeting as far as possible market demands. This drove both investment and mortgage rates to nearer money market rates. In addition, they began to find ways and means of using the wholesale money markets as a source of funds to top up that available from retail sources.

Paradoxically, the move upwards in interest rates made the market more attractive to other lenders and, as a result of this strategy and general deregulation (such as the removal of the 'corset' provisions on bank domestic lending), the mortgage market during the course of the 1980s has become much more competitive. A number of new entrants now operate in the market, such as Merrill Lynch and Saloman Brothers, the Bank of Kuwait and Sumitomo Bank. Building societies now need to market their loan products, develop other innovative new products and price competitively.

Changing culture

The break-up of the cartel and the entry of the banks had introduced competition into the marketplace. Initially the response of Abbey National was not particularly planned nor systematic. Clive Thornton, the then Chief Executive, sponsored the introduction of internal advertising and use of an assessment centre for staff appointments. With the line manager making only a partial input this disbanded 'at a stroke' the patronage system as well as attempting to promote more suitable applicants.

Decision-making began to be decentralized with big central departments reduced in size and branch managers given the authority to make lending decisions within guidelines. Largely manual systems of accounting began to be replaced by new technology.

In 1984 a new Chief Executive was recruited from outside the industry as well as a new Personnel Director. In 1984 the new Executive held a series of meetings to consider the fundamental questions of the business such as, 'Where are we going?' and 'How are we going to get there?' The outcome of this review was the realization that the Society was operating in a competitive environment and that it needed to strengthen its capital base through increased profitability. It was clear that, although many things had changed since 1979, in that a degree of decentralization of authority had occurred and that the patronage-based system of promotion had been removed, the existing culture was inappropriate for the years ahead. Increased competition in all the traditional markets, coupled with diversification opportunities demanded a change of some significance.

In particular managers, including senior management, needed to become more profit-orientated, innovative, commercially aware and professional. It was also recognized that this radical change in culture would have to be top-led and the change in orientation cascaded down the organization. A professional commercialism had to be developed and also a profit consciousness among employees, if the Society was to compete successfully in a competitive market place. It was clear that the last vestiges of autocratic paternalism had to be cleared out and replaced with a more participative and motivational style of management. At the same time, the primary need was to improve the general reserve ratio (the ratio of total reserves to total assets) which involved looking at the overhead expenditure with a very jaundiced eye and to consider all the opportunities of reducing it . . . including head count reductions.

A number of steps were initiated to move the Society from an amateur administrative, low-risk organization to one which could compete and seize the opportunities likely to be offered by the Building Societies Act 1986 – including the possibility of relinquishing the Society's neutral status and going for a stock market flotation. The steps taken to change culture were:

- development of a professional and trained management conversant with effective business practice
- customer service training
- recruitment of graduate management talent
- redundancy of 150 managers
- clarification of business objectives
- dissemination of objectives cascaded down the organization
- pay related to attainment of objectives
- introduction of a new appraisal system
- introduction of a profit-sharing scheme for all employees
- use of improved communications to emphasize business orientation and to portray senior managers as role models

Training in business

It was decided that the most effective way of introducing a culture change of the magnitude required was to use training as the vehicle. It was also clear that this training should be applied from the top of the organization and work its way downwards.

The programmes that were chosen, after an extensive review of what was offered, were those being offered by the Presidents Division of Management Centre Europe (MCE). The first two layers of top management were sent on the 'Presidents Programme' and the 'Top Management Briefing' respectively. Thereafter MCE was contracted to run a customized programme for the senior management. Subsequently, when MCE closed down its Presidents Division, the consultants Miller–Ginsberg were contracted to run the programmes which they are still doing with the Branch and Estate Agency managers.

The programme sets out to define 'professional management' as involving Planning, Control, Organization, Climate Setting and Leadership. Against these headings are packaged a number of well-tried and trusted management principles in a coherent and integrated form. Instruments are also suggested with which to implement these principles, such as a planning matrix. The instruments for ensuring that planning took place on a top down, bottom up, basis and the financial basics provided a platform on which further to build commercial skills. For Abbey National the programme addressed the primary concerns: to change the style and behaviours of managers at all levels.

The valuable thing about cascading the same programme down the organization is that subordinates often question why their bosses' behaviour has not changed. When fed back up the line these observations re-emphasize and reinforce earlier training and have frequently resulted in further change.

Having decided on the type of commercially aware, performance-based and participative management culture that was required and the medium through which it was to be achieved, it was also clear that there was a need to review a number of existing policies, especially on the human resource side. This was necessary so as to ensure that human resource policies did not inhibit or punish the behaviour that was being introduced. Thus there have been far-reaching changes to planning, budgeting and communications methodology. This process was started at the same time as the first few managers were going on the training programme.

Customer service

Training in interpersonal skills and customer service is also currently being carried out by Life Skills. The emphasis here is that everybody has a customer. Training has underlain most of the changes that have taken place over the last three years, namely, training in business, appraisal and customer service. Since 1984 the amount of training received per employee has increased from 0.3 to 10.2 days per annum.

Recruitment

Prior to 1984 the Society recruited school leavers who joined as clerical assistants and slowly progressed up the organization. The majority of senior managers have followed this career path. Given the need for a more professional and perhaps more able manager, the Society started to recruit graduate trainees in 1984. Twenty trainees were recruited in that year and the numbers have steadily increased since. One hundred graduate trainees were recruited in 1987.

Redundancy

Some of the older, longer-serving managers were unhappy with the new approach to running the business. These were approached with generous early retirement packages and the offer of outplacement counselling. In all about 150 – approximately 25 per cent of management – left under such arrangements. With one or two exceptions they left feeling good about the organization. (This was important because the Society needed the support and goodwill of those who remained.) The exercise of removing from positions of influence those who had negative reactions to the changes also provided the opportunity to rationalize Regional and Head Office departments and further to allow the promotion of some of the Society's high flyers to key positions.

Placement

The decision was made to move managers around more frequently. Those who had been in their post for more than seven years were, with their agreement, moved to fresh pastures. Normally this involved moving a branch manager to an adjacent branch. In practically all cases there were marked improvements in performance – both in the branch left behind and in the one to which they have moved.

Performance-based pay

Management objectives were cascaded down the organization partly by linking goal setting to pay. Initially a performance-based pay system was introduced for senior management in 1986 and this served as the pilot. Performance-based pay was introduced for the rest of the employees in 1987.

A key factor was the overhaul of the appraisal system. For most of the staff, performance appraisal had either consisted of a tick in the box system based on subjective assessments of behaviour against one-word factors, or alternatively an impossibly complex format of measurement of business results from which it was difficult to draw any firm conclusions.

These systems were replaced by a method based upon agreed objectives. Objectives are used which are measurable in either quantified or time-scale terms. Standards of performance are also agreed. At the end of the review period a discussion takes place on progress made in achieving these objectives. The result is an overall rating which determines the pay rise. Part of the appraisal is devoted to career aspirations and developmental activities. Any training needs identified are followed up by the Manpower Development Department – this follow-up is part of the appraisal contract. Communication and consultation on a widespread basis were key factors in the implementation of this change. The use of a video programme, leaflets, consultations with the staff union and the training of everybody affected, both appraiser and appraisee, were critical to its success.

Profit sharing

In 1986 a profit-sharing scheme for all but the most senior managers was introduced to recognize group contribution to business success. This works on the simple basis that until the profit budget for the year is hit nothing is paid out; when the budget is reached, 1 per cent of the total profits is paid into the pool; thereafter 10 per cent of the excess is paid into the pool. Most of the Society's staff are employed in retail outlets and in some way or other can have a direct impact on the profit figure. The implementation of this scheme was once again supported by the use of videos.

A cash-based system has also been introduced for senior management in which up to 25 per cent of salary is available if certain targets are met.

Communications

Improved communications have also supported the change in culture. *Abbey View* is a monthly video shown to branch managers regarding business objectives, performance and future developments. This is a professional product which uses TV presenters. Senior management have been trained in communication skills and TV presentation. An annual conference was held in 1987, the purpose of which was to communicate the strategic thinking of the top management team, to show the top team in operation and as being professional and united.

The Directors and General Managers have each been allocated an area of the country which they visit. Every branch should be visited once every fifteen months by senior personnel. This provides an opportunity to reaffirm management policy and to gain first-hand reactions to the difficulties of implementation.

All of the above changes have required new infrastructure support systems. The changes have enabled the Society, in an integrated way, to relate personal objectives to corporate objectives by the cascade system used and to monitor and control corporate and individual performance.

Product of change?

Pre-tax profits increased from £118 million in 1984 to £353 million in 1987, an increase of approximately 200 per cent. The total assets of the Society increased from approximately £17 billion in 1984 to £26.5 billion in 1987, an increase of approximately 55 per cent. This has taken place in a period of greatly increased competition.

Source: Terry Murphy, formerly General Manager Personnel, Abbey National Building Society

Jaguar Cars Ltd

Background

The history of Jaguar dates back to 1922 when Sir William Lyons founded the Swallow Side Car Company in Blackpool to produce motor-cycle side cars. After five years the business started to produce aluminium car bodies and in 1928 moved to Coventry, with the car and side-car manufacturing companies being split into separate concerns. In 1931 the Swallow Coach Building Company launched its first complete car; three years later it became a public company, introducing its first 'Jaguar' car in 1935.

During 1939–45 the company switched to military production and at the end of the war the name of the company was changed to Jaguar Cars Ltd. With output expanding, the company moved to its present factory in Brown's Lane, Coventry in 1951–2. Production grew during the 1950s, exceeding 20,000 cars for the first time in 1959. Meanwhile it was achieving notable success in the racing sphere. Jaguar Cars won Le Mans five times in the 1950s.

In 1960 the Daimler Motor Company was acquired and Jaguar machine and engine production was subsequently transferred to the Daimler factory at Radford, Coventry. During the 1950s and early 1960s Jaguar was a profitable company, with a reputation for high quality luxury cars. Industrial relations were excellent.

In 1966 Jaguar merged with British Motor Corporation Ltd. Two years later the new holding company, British Motor Holdings Ltd, merged with Leyland Motor Corporation to form British Leyland Motor Corporation. In the same year Jaguar launched the XJ6 which won the European Car of the Year Award, as did the XJ12 in 1972.

In 1975 the Government-commissioned Ryder Report recommended that Jaguar Cars should not continue as a separate entity and the Brown's Lane and Radford factories came under the control of a new company, BL Cars. This strategy was changed three years later when Jaguar became part of the specialist car division, Jaguar Rover Triumph.

Separate accounts for Jaguar are not available during the period 1975–9, though it is probable that heavy losses were being made by the end of this period. 1980 was the nadir for the company with 900,000 man hours lost to industrial disputes, productivity at 1.4 cars per employee per annum and losses approaching £1 million per week.

Within BL Cars Ltd Jaguar was stripped of most of its management support functions. Thus finance, sales and marketing, purchasing, etc were centrally based. Communication and coordination was bad. The company had six new Chief Executives in eight years. As a consequence there was a lack of leadership at the top. Business plans, if they existed, were not known by local management, nor was company performance; it took six months to sort out the Jaguar accounts when the company was reborn in the 1980s. There were no plans for replacements to the XJ6, XJ12 and XJS sports car range. When the Series III XJ6 was launched, it was only available in white, yellow or red.

The Coventry workforce perceived a lack of commitment by BL to Jaguar's future. Steps were also being taken to reduce marque loyalty: the telephonists were instructed to respond to callers with 'BL Large Car Assembly Plant No. 2'. Despite being a highly paid workforce, morale was poor and industrial relations suffered. The quality and reliability for which the products had held an unrivalled reputation, began to decline seriously. In 1980 only 3000 cars were sold in the USA, a demanding market but the largest in the world for luxury cars. Sales were not helped by Jaguar cars being sold through the BL dealer networks. Too many dealers selling too few cars resulted in under-investment by the dealers, which was inconsistent with the luxury car market. Also, overvalued sterling did not help overseas sales. The combination of low productivity, bad workmanship and overvalued sterling resulted in a performance which threatened the entire future of the company.

Changing culture

In 1980 Sir Michael Edwardes decided to unscramble BL and
Jaguar management was given responsibility for the operations
of Brown's Lane and Radford. Jaguar was given its own
board and Mr (later Sir) John Egan appointed as Chairman
and Chief Executive. Much of the turnaround of Jaguar's
fortunes has been attributed to the leadership of Sir John
Egan.

To increase the confidence of employees in the new
management and of its commitment to the company, the
workforce was informed of the true financial position of the
company. Confidence was also boosted among the City
analysts and the motoring press with a similar 'It's not going
to be easy, but we are getting there' message.

The new management had to clarify the business objectives –
essentially to improve customer satisfaction, increase productivity and introduce appropriate structures and systems.

The layers of management were reduced and accountability
increased. In addition, the company was divided into clear
operational units. For example, the whole of the Daimler
Limousine side was split off, a manager appointed and given
sink or swim profit targets.

In 1983 a system of team briefing was introduced, which is
still in existence today. The company objectives and
performance are cascaded down the organization from
the Executive Committee and Functional Management
Committees to all employees by a series of briefing groups.
The Plant Directors meet all supervisory staff and supervisors
meet hourly graded and staff employees on a weekly basis.
Supervisors have been trained in holding briefing meetings,
which may include competitor-sensitive information, in order
that employees are kept informed of business plans and
progress.

There are also bi-monthly management conferences which
involve all levels of management. Themes vary, but include
key company items; company objectives and performance;

explanation of roles and functions; establishing management working parties to find solutions to company problems.

Productivity

The manufacturing workforce was reduced by 30 per cent in 1981. However, as Jaguar was at the same time recruiting functional specialists, particularly engineers, the actual reduction was nearer 40 per cent. It was recognized that employee commitment was essential to the long-term survival of the company and it was considered that one big cut was preferable to a series of smaller ones. Who was to be made redundant was decided by each department submitting lists of essential and expendable jobs. In recent years the workforce has increased from a low of 7873 in 1981 to 12,438 in 1988 – 2000 more than Jaguar employed in 1980. Selection tests have been introduced for hourly paid job applicants. The company now operates a partial double-shift system as opposed to a single shift in 1980.

A bonus scheme was introduced in 1982 which is linked to manufacturing efficiency and revenue/employment costs:

- an hourly graded bonus linked to efficiency improvements
- staff bonus linked to efficiency improvements and revenue/salaried employment costs

With the bonus, which can represent as much as 25 per cent of basic pay, hourly graded employees are currently the highest paid in the UK car industry. The bonus scheme is a group bonus and is not paid on an individual basis. An audited plant scheme has been introduced in which agreement is reached on plant target levels of productivity and quality. All three plants have now accepted performance targets for the immediate years ahead.

Quality

In 1980 11 per cent of the workforce were engaged on inspection. Individual employees were not responsible for the quality of their work and consequently poor quality work was passed on and re-work hours were high. In 1981 the number of inspectors was dramatically reduced and employees made responsible for the quality of their own work through a programme of 'Getting it Right First Time'. The number of re-work hours is used to adjust bonus payments.

Initially, task forces were set up to deal with quality and production problems. These had led to the development of quality circles of which there are now 179 operating across the three sites. Supervisors have been trained to lead quality circles. Quality circle suggestions which lead to improvements in quality or productivity may receive financial rewards via the Company Suggestion Scheme.

Initial analysis of the quality faults revealed that about two-thirds were attributable to suppliers. Thus, suppliers were made to sign contracts which resulted in stringent penalties if the component quality did not reach specified levels. Suppliers were also made aware that if they were responsible for disrupting production they would be deprived of business. The company runs a series of awards for suppliers. There is a 'Supplier of the Year' trophy and a number of 'Pursuit of Excellence' awards. Progress has also been made in developing a network of solus dealerships. The number of dealers has been reduced and investment by dealers increased to provide premises and service more compatible with the luxury car market.

Quality is controlled by a number of mechanisms. At the individual plant level the products are audited on a sample basis and the Quality Index for the week is determined by this method. Statistical Process Control has also been introduced. A follow-up of customers is also undertaken on a regular basis; this provides feedback on product quality and customer service.

Employee commitment

Thus far, what has been discussed largely represents the changes that Jaguar has made to management structure and systems. A sustained improvement in quality and productivity also requires a change in employee attitudes. Jaguar has attempted to develop the commitment of employees to company objectives by improving communications, increasing employee involvement and developing a positive company image.

Improved communications

A Communications Manager was appointed in 1982 to provide communications support services. Initial communications were one way, top down; but within 12 months efforts were made to extend in two other directions: bottom up and lateral communications. A company magazine is circulated to all employees on a bi-monthly basis. There is a monthly management bulletin to managers and supervisors which details performance against objectives information. Noticeboards are used to display company information, production and quality performance, bonus achievements and union items. Poster campaigns for product quality and sports and social events are also used. Information for individual employees is circulated via supervisors or mail. A more direct form of communication is the team briefings led by managers and supervisors, though these are essentially one-way meetings. In 1987 a 'Speak Up' scheme was introduced whereby employees can write to the Communications Manager to raise a concern, opinion or question. After the writer's identity has been removed, a written reply is obtained from a Director.

Video programmes are shown to all employees approximately on a quarterly basis. These conferences include a question/answer session with the senior managers. The questions are recorded and any not dealt with satisfactorily at the time are followed up. Themes vary but have included annual results and objectives, a preview of new models, pension schemes, share schemes, technology, implications for employees of privatization of Jaguar, etc. Many videos have been used to increase employee – and manager – awareness of quality problems.

Employee involvement

One form of employee involvement within Jaguar is through Quality Circles which have now been established throughout the company. In the main, Quality Circles are controlled by supervisors.

Quality manufacturers also have to be quality employers. Since 1982 Jaguar has introduced an extensive Sport and Social programme for employees and their families. This is outlined below:

Hearts & Minds/Jaguar sporting & social programme for Jaguar employees and their families

1982
62 family evenings attended by 15,000 people
Open Day attended by 36,000 people
History of Jaguar Cars – free hardback for employees
Information brochures
Improvements to all aspects of internal communications
Uprated employee induction programmes

1983
Jaguar Fun Run (280 runners plus spectators)
Bonfire night celebrations (17,000 attended)
Subsidized excursions to Jaguar XJS racing meetings (1000 attended)
Inter-departmental sporting competitions (1700 employees participated – 225 teams)
Christmas pantomine excursions for employees' children (6200 attended)

Summer and Christmas raffles
Uprated pre-retirement programmes
Increased employee support services
Employees' children's painting competition

1984

Inter-departmental sporting competitions (2200 employees – 314 teams)
Subsidized excursions to Jaguar XJS racing meetings (1500 attended)
Jaguar Fun Run (709 runners plus spectators)
Summer and Christmas raffles
Children's poster-colouring competition
Bonfire night celebrations
Improved pre-retirement programmes
Increased employee support services
New Social Club (Brown's Lane)
Christmas pantomine excursions for employee's children (6200 attended)

1985

Inter-departmental sporting competitions (over 3000 employees, 388 teams)
Jaguar Fun Run and Summer Fayre (800 runners and over 5000 spectators – both employees and local residents)
Jaguar/Warwickshire Cricket Club challenge match (1700 spectators)
Summer and Christmas raffles (first prizes were Austin Rover cars – ticket sales for each event £14,000)
Children's poster-colouring competition (500 entries)
Jaguar hillwalking competition (140 employees – 30 teams)
Bonfire night celebrations (over 19,000 attended)
Christmas pantomine excursions for employees' children (8 shows – 6800 children)

1986

'J Days' exhibition at NEC for employees and families to celebrate the launch of the new XJ6 saloon range attended by over 28,000 people
Inter-departmental sporting competitions (over 3000 employees – 392 teams)
Jaguar Fun Run and Summer Fayre (820 runners – over 6000 spectators)

Summer & Christmas raffles (first prizes Austin Rover cars –
ticket sales for each event £17,000+)
Children's poster-colouring competition (750 entries)
Jaguar hillwalking competition (235 employees – 47 teams)
Subsidized racing tickets – WSCC – Brands Hatch & Silverstone
Bonfire night celebrations (over 22,000 attended)
Christmas pantomine excursions for 6500 employees' children

1987 and 1988 programmes similar to 1986 but no 'J Days'.

Jaguar provides in-company evening open-learning facilities
for employees who wish to study for a formal qualification,
to enhance their job skills or broaden their knowledge on a
variety of topics. Currently 35 per cent of the workforce have
attended or are attending at least one course.

Jaguar employees were allocated shares worth £450 when
the company was privatized in 1984. Each year since then
further shares have been issued to all employees with more
than one year's service so that in mid-1988 an employee with
the maximum holding has 761 shares held in trust on his/her
behalf. In addition, employees have had opportunities to join
a savings-related share option scheme. Employees own
approximately 6 per cent of the company's authorized share
capital.

Company image

Jaguar is a company with an illustrious past based on the
qualities of 'grace, pace and space', and associated with sports
car racing at Le Mans. By 1980 this image had become
tarnished. An inferior product undermined the image;
consequently part of the redevelopment of the Jaguar image
has been the improvement in the quality of suppliers,
components, dealers, employees and products.

Jaguar has opened new facilities at all three plants where
products past and present are displayed 'to establish pride in
the company'. A book of the *History of Jaguar Cars* was

given free to all employees in 1982 at the family evenings. Jaguar has re-entered sports car racing and has been very successful, having achieved victory at Le Mans in June of this year and won the World Sportscar Championship outright in 1987 and 1988. Advertising and promotion support the quality image.

Product of change?

Jaguar has attempted to improve productivity and quality of its products through leadership, accountability, control, more open and improved communications, employee involvement and the development of a positively valued company image. Jaguar must be judged by its prime objectives, quality and productivity. Both have improved quite dramatically since 1981. In 1981 productivity was 1.9 cars per annum per employee; in 1987 it was 3.9 and up to June 1988 it was 4.5.

Cars per employee	
1981	1.9
1983	3.4
1984	3.6
1987	3.9

It would appear that most of the improvements in productivity occurred between the years 1981 and 1983, although the new XJ6, launched in 1986, now accounts for two-thirds of the production of Jaguar and also has two-thirds of the build time of the old XJ6.

Quality has also shown considerable improvement and Jaguar in the USA now offer a three-year warranty for cars. The fact that the quality has improved is also indicated by customer tracking surveys. There has also been a considerable improvement in industrial relations. Labour turnover runs between three and four per cent per annum. Improvements in profitability have shown a consistent upward trend which continued until 1987 when pre-tax profits were hit by a weakening dollar.

Sources: Alan Hepburn, Manager, Personnel Planning & Policies
Jose Freedman, Manager, Communications
GOLDSMITH W *and* CLUTTERBUCK D. *The winning streak.* Penguin, 1985

Toshiba Consumer Products

Background

Toshiba's first UK operation was Toshiba UK Ltd, a marketing company which was set up at Frimley in Surrey in 1973. Regulations restricted the company to the import of 20,000 television sets per annum. A joint venture with Rank began in November 1978 when Rank Toshiba Ltd (RTL) was set up. Toshiba had a minority shareholding in the venture and the view of the then Managing Director was that the management of the company was the responsibility of Rank. As a consequence RTL failed to make use of Toshiba's engineering and organizational expertise. It employed 2700 people in 4 factories in South and West England. There were 7 unions in all in these factories, with the Electrical, Electronic, Telecommunications and Plumbing Union (EETPU) having 80 per cent of the union members. The factories produced 62 different models of television sets and many of the sub-assemblies such as transformers and printed circuit boards. In September 1980, having sustained heavy losses, Rank decided to terminate the joint venture. There was considerable doubt locally whether Toshiba would take over. However, in late 1980 Geoffrey Deith and David Smith the Managing and Personnel Directors elect were appointed. RTL continued to trade until March 1981 when there was a clean break until the start-up in May 1981.

By the end of January 1981 all management, supervisory and support staff of the new company (Toshiba Consumer Products UK Ltd) had been appointed. Indeed, with only one exception, all of Toshiba Consumer Product (TCP)'s employees were selected from RTL. The foundations for the style and organization of the company were laid during this period and the influence of the beliefs of the principal actors is very noticeable.

Management values and attitudes

Geoffrey Deith was on loan for one year from Rank. He is described as being charismatic, entrepreneurial and a visionary. As a student at Bradford Management College he had been impressed by the Glacier Metal case study where Wilfred (later Lord) Brown introduced an enlightened form of works council. At an earlier company Deith had instituted a similar form of participative forum and thus had experience of the strengths and weaknesses of such a consultative mechanism. He believed that, while workers perceived managerial authority as arbitrary and absolute, only marginal participation in the operation of the company could be expected from employees. Deith believed involvement in the affairs of the company was necessary if employees were to be cooperative and flexible in their behaviour. This required openness in the dissemination of information. One needed simple, easily understood information. Similarly, the 'them and us' attitudes were compounded by differentials in status, conditions of employment and privilege. There was a need to get away from the golf club image of management and let employees see managers working.

Deith also believed that business required a task orientation, that optimum organization should be derived from the analysis of the work to be done and the techniques and resources available. Deith believed that a unified management team was required with integrated departments – the aim being to produce a smooth 'clockwork' manufacturing operation in which design, industrial engineering, production engineering and manufacturing engineering would be closely linked. There should be few units or managerial levels and a cooperative management team who work for the company rather than their functional specialism. Personnel responsibility was to be given to individual managers and a personnel specialist selected who would act as a catalyst.

Roy Sanderson, National Officer of the EETPU, wrote to Geoffrey Deith on 10 December 1980 outlining what he considered as essential to include in any future agreement:

1 EETPU to have exclusive bargaining rights
2 annual agreement on salary and conditions
3 single-status employment for everyone
4 salary structure based on job evaluation
5 positive rights of the union members and encouragement
   to join the union
6 check-off for union dues
7 procedure for grievance agreements and disciplinary
   matters – 'pendulum' arbitration as final stage
8 a sophisticated method of consultation and communication
   with shop stewards for each department or work unit,
   who are elected as representatives by secret ballot.
   'Smaller committee' for industrial relations consultations
   and communication matters
9 system of consultation based on company presentation of
   future business plans
10 regular communication involving supervisor and shop
   steward of each department with all departmental
   employees
11 no industrial action to be taken for, say, 3 years, when
   this principle to be reviewed

Many of these points were ultimately incorporated into the
new policy. Point 8 above was modified so that representatives
may or may not be stewards; and the three-year time limit
was dropped from point 11.

Based upon his analysis of strikes between 1970 and 1980,
Sanderson believed that they had made economic nonsense.
The majority of those who had gone back, especially after
the long strikes, were not able to make up lost earnings. He
believed that the adversarial IR system did not give workers
a chance to influence management. The adversary's objective
was to defeat the opposition, not to create an efficient
company. It was in the members' interest to find a better
industrial relations system that would give them more stake
in the company and better prospects. He considered that the
adversarial system was responsible for the UK's industrial

decline because it separated the people who were doing the job every day on the shopfloor from management. The latter were concerned with status, while for the workers 'that's a management problem' was the normal attitude. In Sanderson's view, this splitting of the company by the adversarial system was not the way to make it efficient, which in the end was the only way in which the jobs of union members could be secured.

Sanderson saw what he termed 'class' as a major problem: meaning blue and white collar sections, different conditions, different canteens and fringe benefits. They were destructive because they were a major cause of even subconscious distrust. People never felt that they were part of the same team.

> Rank had a pretty traditional view of industrial relations and experience has taught me that in British industry most workers do not feel that they want to be part of the company. They want to know how to buck the system and it is the company's attitude that invariably creates that sort of feeling. Rank certainly did not hide the fact that certain grades of employee were very privileged and there is no prospect – not even the remotest chance – of there being genuine cooperation with that sort of division created by the company (from Trevor 1988).

> To change from the 'traditional' system, where workers have no say in company management, to a system of employee involvement requires a deeper commitment than the formal establishment of some types of consultative schemes. So many consultative schemes are phoney; they just involve the company communicating a decision that has been made. Information needs to be communicated before a decision has been made (from Trevor 1988).

Toshiba Consumer Products is owned by the Toshiba Corporation of Japan. There was one Japanese member of the Executive at TCP, the Engineering Director. The company has been allowed to develop its own style, drawing on Japanese expertise – particularly in engineering and production planning – as required.

The heads of many Japanese manufacturing companies are technically trained. The President of the Toshiba Corporation was an engineer, not an accountant, lawyer or other non-industrialist. However, it would be wrong to assume that 'the Japanese approach' is purely technical. Graduate engineers are considered to be only theoretically trained and it is not uncommon for graduates to start on the shopfloor in order to learn the practical side of the business. (Of course, long-term employment with the company promotes this career-development approach.) Japanese organizational philosophy is opposed to job descriptions, functional specializations and attitudes that restrict a manager's job to narrow exclusive preserves. British managers frequently complain about demarcation on the shopfloor, but rarely comment on a similar lack of flexibility among managers. Japanese managers are frequently surprised that British managers tend to be inflexible and unprepared to share information with colleagues. The 'Japanese approach' is therefore one of an integrated workforce, cooperation and joint problem-solving. Consequently, Japanese companies frequently select employees as much upon attitude as upon technical expertise.

The development of the new organization

In late 1980 and early 1981 Geoffrey Deith started as he meant to go on. He circulated a list of issues that he wanted the management team to discuss together. He included in the final paragraph of his circular:

Success will be dependent on our joint ability to identify the business priorities and then utilize our small but growing team of managers to best advantage. Even now it is clear that we will have to assist each other as the pressure moves from function to function and this is no bad thing – for it gives us practice at the critical skill needed for TCP in the future – that is, a well-coordinated, committed, flexible team (from Trevor 1988).

Deith circulated a list of 26 items to the projected Board members who were asked for written comments. Meetings were then held to explore the issues. The decisions made are given below. They are notable for their consistency with the espoused values of the team – namely cooperation, flexibility through single status and an involved workforce.

Wages   All employees are paid monthly by bank transfer.

Grades   Four grades were identified, linked to proficiency in a range of job skills and the flexibility of their contribution to the company.

Hours of work   All employees have the same hours of work.

Overtime   Only Directors and Managers are not paid overtime. Their performance including extra hours of work is rewarded through salary increases.

Clocking   All employees eligible for overtime are required to clock.

Overalls   All employees, including managers, wear blue company 'coats' with their name on.

Dining room   Rank had had six different dining rooms. They were: the hourly paid canteen, staff canteen, supervisory dining room, management dining room, senior management dining room and Directors' dining room. TCP opted for a single-status restaurant in the refurbished hourly paid canteen.

Social club   Rather than support the social club which tended to be run by the few for the few, the company tends to organize events for all the workforce.

Communication   TCP introduced 5-minute briefing sessions at the beginning of the day, when performance could be discussed and workers told what particular points to look out for. Weekly departmental meetings for staff were introduced, but they have now tended to be changed to daily morning meetings.

Sick pay   There is a uniform sick-pay scheme for all members. The scheme is self-certified for up to 3 days. The company retains the right to investigate absence and to seek the advice of a medical advisor. Managers or supervisors visit sick employees and every employee returning from sickness is interviewed.

Holiday pay   All employees have a 25-day holiday entitlement per annum.

Company Advisory Board (COAB)

David Smith, the Personnel Director, viewed the proposed Advisory Board as an essential body for the dissemination of company information and for the involvement of all employees in the company business. He considered that the system must be given management support and commitment and be able to discuss all aspects of the company performance. He felt that the trade union structure should be integrated into the process rather than exist as a challenge to it − thereby avoiding the traditional 'them and us' conflict and the mutual suspicion it fosters.

> Companies where management support and commitment are inadequate, or which attempt to graft participative structures like COAB on to a basically traditional top-down and non-participative organization, are unlikely to succeed (from Trevor 1988).

The Company Advisory Board was charged with the responsibility of reviewing the performance and plans of the company and with recommending to the company policies, procedures and practices which would be to the mutual benefit of the company and its employees. In making any recommendations, COAB also had to recognize that the company must meet its commercial obligations and objectives at the same time as fulfilling its responsibilities to employees, its customers and society at large. COAB's 'rules' include:

- representatives elected by secret ballot
- meetings in company time and on company premises
- extraordinary meetings, in addition to the regular monthly meetings, to be convened if requested by any two COAB members
- all members required to report back to the constituencies after meetings and to be given appropriate facilities
- members themselves to decide the rules for the conduct of meetings
- no pre-meetings for any group of members

COAB members are elected by the constituencies. Initially there were eleven members, but with the increase in the number of employees it is now fifteen. The senior shop steward is automatically a member, if not already elected, and the Managing Director takes the Chair. COAB is entitled to full disclosure of information and raises the question of the annual salary review three to four months before it is due to take place. A sub-committee collects relevant information on going rates and general economic conditions and the company presents its plans for the coming year and puts forward its proposals for discussion. When pay is under discussion those shop stewards who were not elected as COAB representatives attend as observers in order to be fully briefed.

If the advice of COAB is not accepted, then the trade union has the right for its full-time official to negotiate directly with the Managing Director. Should this negotiation fail, then the matter goes to 'pendulum' arbitration.

At its monthly meetings COAB is supplied with company accounts and business information on the performance and plans of the company. The union, through COAB, has much more information than is usual in a traditional company. In return, the members are expected to respect the necessary confidentiality needs of the business. Feedback to all employees was originally provided by video tape. However, as there was some dissatisfaction with this form of one-way communication, feedback is now presented face to face.

COAB representatives are expected to represent all staff in their particular constituency and not to be mandated or to represent any fixed line. Observers are encouraged to attend COAB meetings.

The start up

The management team decided that they needed to start on 4 May 1981 as they wished to continue:

> To assume that you can start at a low base may not be a good option. People settle into a habit and they do not like changing afterwards (from Trevor 1988).

TCP opened up at the Plymouth factory. The technology was the same, though a more logical layout was used. Batch production was utilized and sub-assembly operations given to suppliers. TCP was going to concentrate on the assembly of five models of colour television set. Japanese expertise was used in production planning.

> All the blue coats and strike-free agreements in the world would not have mattered one iota, if the production had been badly planned (from Trevor 1988).

Looking back at what had changed in production management in 1981, the management team identified five points:

1 a greater quality engineering emphasis on suppliers, who were now more carefully selected
2 less diversification
3 better use of Toshiba technical support
4 introduction of the 'work and check' principle, with operators responsible for their own quality checks
5 a more logical plant layout

Managers were conscious of the totality of the inter-locking systems and what the connections between the different parts were. They knew that there had to be an approach that would integrate the different parts in a way most likely to achieve the company's objectives.

The inter-locking systems referred to were: the selection and training of employees, designed to build in flexible working practices; the new production system, concentrating on making television sets; the new type of relationships with suppliers, designed to ensure the supply of parts and materials of the right quality and price and at the right times; the single-status employment conditions, to motivate employees and to create a more cohesive organization; the union agreement, with its provision for pendulum arbitration; and

the Company Advisory Board, to give employees a stake in
its running and to get the benefit of their ideas for policy
making.

The big problem facing management, with TCP in the same
factory, with the same workforce and largely the same
technology as the old RTL company, was how to get people
to see that they were working for a different company. Four
principles were used to guide the start-up:

1 to establish a high standard from day one
2 to recruit the right people
3 to develop employee attitudes
4 to develop supplier attitudes

The selection process

Recruitment advertisements referred to 'assembly operators'.
They did not quote the specific skills such as machinist or
whatever. 900 people applied for 300 jobs. The applicants
filled in a form, had their photograph taken and then were
shown 2 video tapes. One outlined the nature and role of
COAB, the other made quite explicit the type of company
TCP was to be and consequently the type of individual who
would be suitable. Geoffrey Deith presented the self-selection
video, entitled 'Toshiba the Commitment', which is quoted in
full on pages 80–83 above. Those who still felt that Toshiba
was for them were then interviewed by three managers.

The What's New Programme

Applicants who were selected were assembled into groups of
fifty to one hundred and the management team presented
'The What's New Programme'. The purpose of this
programme was to underline the fact that they were now
working for a different company, with different ways of doing
things. The management team took it in turn to outline the

changes that had been made in organization, method and working conditions.

What's New Programme 1981

Managing Director
Batch production
Materials management
Open management
Bottom up inter-locked departments

Engineering Director
Realism – 70,000 sets per annum
Single common design
Unification of engineering
Production-orientated engineering
Attention to detail

Buyer – Mechancial
Batch order and delivery
Firm orders
No delivery schedules
No progress chasing
Suppliers' conference
Payment on time
Strict cost control

Production Control Manager
Fixed production plan
New production control system
Daily production assembly plan
No buffer stocks

Industrial Engineering Manager
Logical production – material paths
Convenient stores
All machine operations in one area
Single dining area

Personnel Director
Single union
One set of terms and conditions
Wearing of coats
Company Advisory Board
Role of the personnel department
No smoking in manufacturing areas
No food in manufacturing areas
All responsible for good housekeeping
No bonus
Flexibility

Management Services and Systems Manager
Open-plan office
System integration
Job costing
Batch control
No data preparation

The following table produced by TCP summarizes
the steps taken by the company to develop 'positive
employee attitudes':

a   careful selection and induction
b   autonomy of local management
c   open-style management and consultation
d   5-minute morning meetings – monthly meetings –
    six-monthly business reviews
e   few levels of management
f   open-plan offices
e   development of team approach
h   all on monthly staff with common terms and
    conditions
i   single-status restaurant
j   wearing of coats
k   grade promotion opportunities
l   total flexibility

m   attendance and timekeeping disciplines
n   no smoking or food in production areas
o   individual responsibility for space cleaning
p   small-circle activities
q   annual formal performance review

Product of Change?

The new company arose out of the failure of the old.
Realizing that management could not go on in the same old
way, it committed itself to a new structure and style of work
organization, employee participation and relationship with
suppliers.

Toshiba succeeded in first putting its new system into
practice and then, in a competitive environment, increasing
its production, productivity and market share. It expanded
out of its original production area of television to include
video tape recorders and microwave ovens.

In 1981 three hundred employees produced 76,000 TVs
with eight models. In 1986 eleven hundred employees
produced 400,000 TVs with fifty models and, in addition,
100,000 VCRs and 170,000 microwave ovens. Toshiba's
market share has increased from $3\frac{1}{2}$ to 7 per cent and the
value of its output 7 times during this period.

Absenteeism is one quarter of that in the original RTL and
since 1981 the percentage of products 'right first time' has
risen from 60 to 93 per cent.

Source: Mike Oram, Company Secretary, Toshiba UK Ltd
TREVOR M. *Toshiba: the first of its kind.* Policies Studies Institute, 1988

Hampshire County Council

Background

Hampshire County Council is one of the three largest non-metropolitan local authorities in the country, providing a range of essential services to $1\frac{1}{2}$ million people living in the county. These services include education, transport, highways, police and fire services, waste disposal, trading standards, social services, libraries and recreational facilities. In 1987 the council had a net budget in excess of £650 million and employed nearly 37,000 staff.

Hampshire County Council receives two-thirds of its income from local ratepayers and from services for which a charge is levied. The remainder of its income comes from central Government, in the form of the Rate Support Grant, though the Government has significantly reduced this element in recent years.

Over the past few years many of the Council's operations have undergone a significant change in culture and approach. The perception of 'culture' as an important issue has developed against a background of major organizational and operational change, influenced by numerous political, legal, social and commercial factors. These include, for example:

- various legislative changes, such as the Local Government Planning and Land Act 1980

- increasing financial pressures arising from reductions in the Rate Support Grant and the avoidance of excessive rate increases

- the increasing trend towards competitive tendering for services, partly as a legal requirement and partly as a response to financial constraints

- the public expectation of an increasingly sophisticated range of services and facilities

- the growth of new technology

The Council's Annual Report for 1986/87 identified a general trend in its operations which illustrates the overall process of change which has been taking place in response to the above factors:

> . . . we do in fact 'put people first' and at all levels in the organization examine carefully how our services are delivered and how well they meet the needs and expectations of the recipients. The idea of putting the customer first is being applied vigorously within the County Council.

The trend in the Council is a move from a traditional 'public service' orientation towards a more precise and commercial focus on 'customer need'. This trend has been evident in a number of the Council's operations, but the following study concentrates on the clearest and most distinct example of such a change in culture, that of the Direct Labour Organization in the County Surveyor's Department.

County Surveyor's Department

Until 1985 the Maintenance and Works Division of the County Surveyor's office was responsible for the maintenance of all the County's highways. The department was run on a geographical basis, with six divisions each taking responsibility for a different geographical area. A headquarters section was responsible for the coordination of the policy and direction of these divisions. This section was also responsible for the administration of maintenance carried out on the County's behalf by District Councils. Each geographical division was headed by a Divisional Surveyor, who reported directly to the Assistant County Surveyor, but was the County Surveyor's 'representative in the field' (see figure 1).

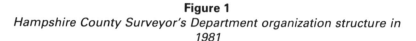

Figure 1
Hampshire County Surveyor's Department organization structure in 1981

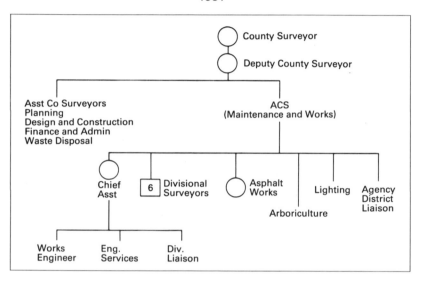

The divisions had traditionally been run on a 'public service' basis, with priority being given to providing effective levels of maintenance service. In this context, the Divisional Surveyor had generally been responsible both for determining what highway repairs were needed and for deciding how and when these repairs would be carried out. In other words, the Divisional Surveyor was required to take on the dual roles of 'client' and 'contractor', and had to determine priorities accordingly. This was logical in terms of providing an effective public service, but meant that financial accountability effectively rested solely in the hands of the Divisional Surveyor.

The Local Government Planning and Land Act 1980 introduced legislation which was intended to make direct labour organizations in local government more accountable.

In particular, the legislation required that a larger amount of local authority work was offered for competitive tenders. This prospect was not entirely new in Hampshire, because the County Surveyor's direct labour had in the past competitively tendered for major jobs on its own initiative. It was therefore felt that the department had a proven track record of success in the area, and the department management was not particularly disturbed by the prospect.

Nevertheless, there were difficulties. In particular, it was recognized that in the past there had been a tendency for the Divisional Surveyor, who was a powerful figure within the divisional structure to juggle resources to suit changing needs. As the Divisional Surveyor was both client and contractor, it was therefore possible for the requirements of the original contract to be changed significantly without recourse to any third party.

However, in a situation where work was subject to competitive tender, all tenders had to be seen to be treated equitably. The terms of the tender could not be changed once the contract had been issued. In other words, there had to be a formal internal split between the client (ie the Authority) and the direct labour which carried out the work. This would ensure that the direct labour was accountable to a third party just as an external contractor would be.

Initially, it was felt that it would not be possible to justify the extra staff costs involved in creating a complete split between client and the direct labour. In 1981 a partial separation was created within each division, with some staff taking on 'client' roles and others taking on 'contractor' roles. The Divisional Surveyor and some other members of staff remained 'two-hatted'.

At first, the new system operated reasonably effectively. The Authority was required to put 25 per cent of the DLO work out to tender, and in the first year of the new arrangement the DLO won eight out of ten jobs for which it had to tender. It also succeeded in achieving the 5 per cent rate of return on capital required under the legislation.

However, it rapidly became clear that the new arrangements, although valuable, were largely cosmetic and had had
no significant effect on the way the divisions operated. It was
still not uncommon for the Divisional Surveyor to change the
terms of contracts after they had been issued and the culture
of the department was still orientated towards a general
notion of 'public service' rather than to fulfilling the precise
requirements of a particular contract or the spirit of the
legislation regarding public accountability. Because of the
department's success in the past, there was a degree of
complacency about its ability to cope with the changing
business requirements imposed by the legislation.

Nevertheless, because of their refusal to change, the
divisions were, in the words of one manager, 'stumbling from
minor crisis to minor crisis', unable to provide the level of
accountability and customer orientation required. Furthermore, in the years between 1981 and 1984 the regulations of
competition were gradually being tightened to the point
where there was a significant doubt that the direct labour
force could continue to win sufficient tenders to achieve the
required return on capital.

During this period a number of attempts were made to
improve management systems with the aim of encouraging
efficiency. However, these were largely ineffective because,
although they improved the efficiency of the DLO on its own
terms, they made no difference to the fundamental culture of
the department.

In 1983 there was an attempt to revise the organization's
incentive bonus scheme, which was perceived as ineffective.
A report on the scheme notes that ' . . . management staff
take only minimal interest in the scheme and it has tended to
become a payment system administered by work-study
officers'. The report also noted that the scheme was 'post-
evaluated'. Significantly, this meant that 'the work claimed is
subject to inaccuracies and may not relate totally to what
management initially directed to be undertaken'. Because of
this it was difficult to evaluate the work efficiency of the DLO

with any consistency, which in turn made it difficult to compare internal and external tenders for a given contract.

The report therefore proposed an incentive scheme which would be pre-evaluated and which would provide a common information base to help the DLO and client prepare and evaluate estimates and quotations. The report commented that, to achieve this, 'managers at all levels and on both sides of the client/DLO split are required to change their approach towards managing and controlling work'. The report concluded that 'under present arrangements, it is difficult to see how accountability can be demonstrated', and that a genuinely accountable culture could only be created if there was a complete reorganization to create a clear distinction between client and contractor. Until then, the current 'public service' culture, dominated by the powerful Divisional Surveyor, would prevail.

Culture change

The first steps towards significant culture change were taken in 1983/84. At this stage, a new incentive payments scheme was introduced, along the lines recommended in the report. This was used as an opportunity to attempt to initiate a new awareness of commercialism and accountability, with the ultimate aim of achieving a full-scale, formal split between 'client' and 'contractor'. Various techniques were applied. These included face-to-face meetings with manual workers at which the new systems were explained and week-long training courses in the systems for supervisors and shop stewards.

During this process, in addition to providing practical training in the new systems, attempts were also made to raise the staff's awareness of the issues of accountability, commercialism and the problematic relationship between client and contractor. It was felt that, if staff were fully appraised of these issues, they would become aware of the inherent contradiction of their dual role. It was hoped that they themselves would then begin to press for a more rationalized and distinct structure. In other words, training was used at this stage as a means of fostering a sense of commitment towards the concepts and motivations that would underpin the ultimate structure of the organization. The creation of the new 'culture' began, therefore, even before the restructuring took place.

These initial stages in the development of a new 'commercial' culture were followed, through 1984/85, by a major re-organization and restructuring of the department's work.

The first stage was the necessary division of the department clearly and unequivocally into 'client' and 'contractor'. The old geographical divisions of the organization were discontinued and the Direct Labour Organization (DLO) was set up as an entirely separate quasi-independent operation. The intention was that the organization should act effectively as a commercial concern, tendering for work from the Authority in the same way as any external contractor (see figure 2).

Figure 2

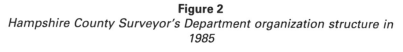

Hampshire County Surveyor's Department organization structure in 1985

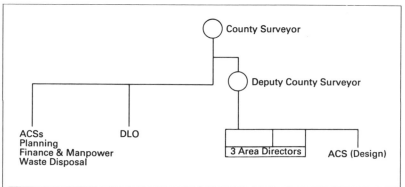

Immediate and strenuous efforts were needed to develop an appropriate culture and sense of purpose in the DLO. The problems in this respect were enormous. The organization was highly isolated and required a commercially based management style which, at the time, was virtually unique in the Authority. Furthermore, significant effort was required simply to enable the organization's employees to overcome the negative connotations associated with the hiving off of the DLO.

Interestingly, no Divisional Surveyors applied for jobs in the new DLO, presumably because they saw its independent status as providing uncertain job security. In the eyes of the junior staff, this was in itself an ominous sign which severely affected morale. Many of the staff were also concerned about the suitability of the unfamiliar new managers who were replacing the Divisional Surveyors in the new organization.

The first priority, therefore, in the months before the DLO officially came into being was to build up the confidence of those who would be working in the new department. The management of the new organization began to work closely with the Authority's Manpower Services Department to develop an approach programme. Initial approaches were made through straightforward face-to-face communication. Staff meetings were set up, addressed by the County Surveyor, to explain the objectives of the new organization and to stress the interdependence of all staff working within it. Simultaneously, one-to-one meetings were also held with all the staff-level employees, again concentrating on the objectives of the new DLO and the need to operate on a commercial basis. Great emphasis was placed on the potentially liberating effect of the new organization, which aimed to avoid bureaucracy and encourage staff to perform at their full potential.

Next, the Manpower Services Department began to run formal training courses for managers in the department, partly to provide practical training in the revised systems but primarily to introduce new concepts of commercialism and competitiveness. Various workshop approaches were devised to encourage staff to give priority to commercial issues. Participants were, for example, encouraged to take part in business games, playing the respective roles of client and contractor with immediate and direct responsibility for profit and loss. Some of the learning experiences were comparatively straightforward but proved difficult initially to instil. Staff who were accustomed to operating on a 'public service' basis, for instance, would happily provide effort or resources additional to that specified in the original contract if this seemed necessary. Significant training was required to emphasize that the organization's profitability depended on strict adherence to the original contract unless the client requested otherwise.

Other training was more complex, encouraging staff to consider issues of business strategy, again in a business game context. This proved valuable even to those staff who were likely to have no direct responsibility for any strategic planning, in that it provided an understanding of the issues faced by management. Staff were therefore encouraged to give their own consideration to the business objectives of the organization (see figures 3 and 4).

In general terms, the new DLO was carefully structured to ensure that it resembled, as closely as possible, the Authority's perception of the structure of a commercial, private-sector operation. A Board of Management was set up, which comprised all the organization's managers and which took on the same functions as a Board of Directors in a private-sector company. All managers had equal voting rights and all were involved in any strategic decisions that were made, again stressing the concept of mutual responsibility. Efforts were also made to disseminate information as widely as possible to ensure that all staff understood the significance of particular actions or strategies and to minimize the parochialism that had tended to characterize the old divisions.

Some months before the DLO came formally into being, its new managers held a management seminar – an

Figure 3
Outline training programme

Venue – College of Maritime Studies, Warsash		
Wednesday 29 April	9 00	Registration
	9 15	Introduction by John Ekins
	9 45	Simulation Exercise – Part I
	10 30	COFFEE
	10 45	Group presentations
	11 15	Working in small groups – Part II
	11 50	Group Presentation
	12 30	LUNCH
	13 45	Simulation Exercise – Part III
	15 30	TEA
	16 00	'Relating to Reality'
	17 00	Discussion on priorities and blockages
	19 00	DINNER
	20 00	Talk by Alan Davies (Director of Technical Services Southampton CC)
Thursday 30 April	9 00	Summary of previous day
	10 00	Working in Groups
	10 30	COFFEE
	10 45	Group Work (continued)
	12 30	LUNCH
	13 45	Group Work (continued)
	15 30	TEA
	16 30	Summary and Action Points

unprecedented initiative in the department. The aim of the seminar was, in the words of its organizer, the Assistant County Surveyor (Works) 'to get to know one another better and to tackle some of the problems facing the DLO as we move towards April 1985 [the official start-date]'. Furthermore, it was pointed out explicitly that one of the major objectives should be to 'evolve a corporate philosophy on which we can base our operations in the months ahead'. Inevitably, much

Figure 4
Simulation Exercise

PART I

1 Identify the major changes that have happened to the Surveyor's Department of Erkshire County Council over the last 12 months – this should be based on your experience as a representative group of Erkshire's Surveyor's Department at 3rd and 4th tier level. Use your own real experience to identify the issues.

2 Assess the impact of the most significant changes on the staff working in the following functions:
    DLO
    Forward Planning
    Highway Management
    Finance and Manpower
    Materials and Information
    Design Services

Summarize your answers to these questions on flip chart paper and be prepared to present your findings to the rest of the course.

PART II

Your group has now been allocated the role of one of the categories of staff as described in PART I of the exercise. You should now individually adopt a realistic role within the category you have been allocated before proceeding with this part of the exercise.

1 Remind yourselves of the impact that the recent changes have had on you as a group and individually within the roles you have adopted.

2 What misunderstandings or conflict could arise between yourselves and any of the other groups?

3 What methods would you wish to adopt or see adopted to resolve the most significant problems or issues that your group has raised – short of any structural changes.

Summarize your answers to questions 2 and 3 on flip chart paper and be prepared to present your findings to the rest of the course. (It might be helpful in presenting your findings to draw a visual representation of your group's position in the structure of organization.)

PART III

Having developed a group perspective on the issues which now hinder the effectiveness of 'Erkshire', you should seek to resolve them by meeting with members of other groups.

You will have to manage your access to the other groups as they will also have competing needs. Use division of labour and develop an agreed meeting plan if appropriate.

In dealing with other groups try to ensure that your mutual differences are clearly stated and understood. Try to ensure that you don't agree or disagree on the basis of misunderstanding.

[In this part of the exercise some of you may occasionally feel distant from the role you are in – so give attention to trying to feel what it is like being the person whose role you have adopted in the group. Try to understand the way you would feel in that role. If you are unable to do this – ask yourself why? The whole purpose of the exercise is designed to let everyone experience the perspectives of others within this imaginary organization which has been created as a result of your own real experiences and attitudes.]

of the seminar was taken up with practical issues – organizational structure, working methods, technical matters – but the seminar also included explicit sections on 'corporate philosophy', 'morale', 'marketing strategy', 'what the client expects', etc (see figure 5).

Figure 5
DLO Management Seminar, Portsmouth Management Centre – 29/30 November 1984

Thursday 29 November 1984
09 00   Assemble
          Coffee
09 30   *Topic 1*   Basic Organization:
                           Management structure
                           Works Unit staff
                           Supervisors
                           Job description scale 1/5. 4/6
                           Appointments

10 45	Coffee	
11 00	*Topic 2*	Basic Organization:
		Depots
		Deployment of labour
		Minor Works Orders cyclic grass cutting
		Micheldever Asphalt Works
		Call-out
		Winter maintenance
12 30	Lunch	
14 00	*Topic 3*	Administrative & Financial Routines:
		Costing
		Overheads
		Profit centres
		Revenue
15 30	Tea	
15 45	*Topic 4*	Revenue
17 00	*Topic 5*	Plant & Equipment:
		Vehicles
		Plant
		Winter maintenance
		Computers/information technology
		Radio telephones
19 00	Dinner	
20 30	*Topic 6*	Corporate Philosophy

Friday 30 November 1984

09 00	*Topic 7*	Industrial Relations:
		Trade union liaison
		Role of personnel section
		Negotiations
		Training
		Incentive bonus scheme
		Health & safety
		Morale
10 45	Coffee	
11 00	*Topic 8*	Marketing Strategy
12 00		Conclusions So Far
12 30	Lunch	
14 00	County Surveyor's View	
14 30	What the Client Expects	The Area Engineer's View
15 30	Tea & Close	

TOPIC 1 – Headquarters Organization DLO Management Team

Role of Chief Assistant Works
Role of Works Support Manager
Works Manager (Valuation) – need to have measurement of
  curator
Remaining posts at Headquarters should they be all filled
Works Units, role of Works Unit Manager
Organization within Works Unit
Split Works Engineers construction/maintenance
Production Unit – materials procurement concept
Profit centre approach
Role of Admin Unit at Works Unit
Deployment of Supervisors
Technician support on site vis-à-vis supervisors
Mobile supervisors for maintenance
Site Clerks – do we need them?
Measurement – who should do this?
Scale 1/5 Supervisors Job Descriptions Role Flexibility
Remaining appointments

Objectives of Session 1

1 to define the role between Headquarters and Works Units
2 to establish a structure and organization for Works Units
3 to establish job descriptions and roles for Scale 1/5 posts
4 to confirm job descriptions and role for Scale 4/6 posts

TOPIC 2 – Depot Locations and Requirements

Main depots for Works Unit Headquarters – where?
What needs to be done to get Works Unit Headquarters ready
  for use?
What other operating bases – dumb depots?
What do we need? – what should we sell? – should we own
  anything at all?
Deployment of labour – where are the men? – how do we
  deploy them to the new Works Units?
How do we operate on the ground? – should all men report to
  depot or report to dumb depots? – what should happen to
  vehicles?
Stores – what stores do we need? – what do we need to issue
  from stores? – what inventory should we keep?
Deployment of labour to different operations: construction,
  minor works, cyclic and grass cutting

Role of Micheldever Asphalt Works

Dealing with emergencies, call out and standby – should we have duty crews?

Winter maintenance, salt routes, ploughing – should we readjust the focus of salt routes? – what supervisor involvement should there be in standby?

Objectives of Session 2

1 list of depot requirements
2 list of depot disposals
3 an operational plan for deployment of the labour force
4 terms of reference for standby
5 outline winter maintenance plan

TOPICS 3/4

How do we organize the administration? – how do we push the paper?

What work should be done in the Works Unit and what work at Headquarters?

How do we deploy the personnel we shall have? – can we simplify the systems and, if so, how?

The impact of the new general ledger system

Works Units ought to be separate profit centres – how do we split the overheads? – how do we deal with cost control?

What measures can we take to simplify paperwork by next April?

Revenue measurement of work – how do we shift from an emphasis on claims to an emphasis on measurement? – how do we get better at valuing variations?

Who do we deploy to do measurement?

Objectives of Session 3

1 establish a working plan for admin and finance functions
2 establish a plan of campaign to simplify paperwork for April 1985
3 plan of campaign for reinforcing the measurement role

TOPIC 5 – Mechanical Engineer's Section: Reading the Audit Commission Report

How should we proceed next April? – what repair facilities do we require?

What standard of service do we require?

How do we deal with the service to other departments?

Do we need mobile fitters? – where do we need workshops?

Review of plant and vehicle holding

What kit do we require?

How will we deploy this year's replacement funds?

Feedback from Public Works Exhibition

Specialist equipment for Winter Maintenance – to what extent does it hamper DLO? – should some be held by client and, if so, which?

Do we have too many lorries because of Winter Maintenance?

Computers and Information Technology – hardware aspects – should we move into micros?

Software developments – can we improve the interface with client systems for minor Works Orders? – should we go for office automation and electronic mail eg PROFS? – what further developments would help us?

Radio Telephones – what sort of system do we require? – can we enhance our present system of selective calling, remote paging etc? – how will we set ourselves up in April 1985 with call signs etc? – how will we deal with the interface with the client?

What future developments would we like to see?

Land Line Telephones to depots – should we provide a clearly identified telephone number for the works organization? – should we provide home telephones?

Objectives of Session 4

1 operating requirements from Mechnical Engineer's set-up
2 how do we implement Audit Commission Report
3 plant and vehicle requirements for 1984/85
4 details of computing requirements
5 details of radio telephone requirements

TOPIC 6 – Generation of a Corporate Philosophy

Discuss the Business Plan

Identify policies and strategies which require development – what additional policies do we need to address ourselves to eg plant and vehicle policy?

Morale and group identity – what can we do to lift morale? – should we do something about our livery? – should we have a new DLO title and other indicators of a corporate body?

Where might the future take us? – problems and risks and dangers ahead

MAW – how do we tackle and what input do we want into any disposal of the Micheldever Asphalt Works?

Objective of Session 5

To define a way ahead to success

TOPIC 7 – To Establish the Line Management Function

The Works Unit Manager is the boss

But open door policy to ACS (Works)

Future of consultative arrangements with Trade Unions, eg JLC/JCC

Need to have a forum at Works Unit level

Need to have an informal forum at Headquarters level and establish a new framework

Personnel function – Personnel Unit has advisory role

Comment on County Surveyor's remarks at JCC

Future of incentive bonus scheme

Do we perfect the one we have got?

Do we abandon it?

Do we move to a group bonus?

How to tackle the immediate problem of cyclic and sweeping?

Should we move to consolidation of profit sharing?

Where do we go with negotiations on the present set-up?

Matters to be negotiated with the Unions

New travelling arrangements – any other custom and practice arrangements which hamper our progress

Training – training requirements for men and management

The future of Sulhampstead – could we provide a more cost-effective alternative?

Health and Safety – what policies need to be revamped? – who has what role with respect to Health and Safety? – role of John Roberts

Morale – what can we do about it?

Should we have mass meetings to establish the new DLO?

Objectives of Session 6

1 define the approach to industrial relations
2 identify items to be negotiated with Trade Unions
3 proposals for future of the incentive bonus scheme
4 identify training needs
5 identify any modifications necessary to Health and Safety policy

TOPIC 8 – Marketing Strategy

Consider capacity to do the work – split between construction, surfacing, routine maintenance, surface dressing – how do we deal with our 30/70 split on tendered work? – what work should we be tendering for?

How do we deal with Schedule of Rates?

What should be in the Schedule of Rates and how should we approach it?

Differential pricing

Relationship with a client – what information do we require from the client? – how do we tackle the competition? – when should we be tendering below cost?

Objectives of Session 7

1 to define DLO marketing strategy in more detail
2 to define how we will operate on Schedule of Rates
3 to define what we require of the client

An attempt was also made at this seminar to set a distinctive tone in the organization's industrial relations. All developments in the new DLO were discussed openly with the appropriate unions and management encouraged a continuing process of informal discussion in addition to traditional formal negotiation in an effort to promote greater involvement. Similarly, informal quarterly liaison meetings were set up to exchange views and ideas on a consultative basis. Again, the aim of these is to promote a greater sense of commitment among staff to the aims of the enterprise.

Various other techniques were also adopted with the overall aim of promoting a simple and unified sense of identity. It was decided at an early stage that the term 'Direct Labour Organization' was too formal and bureaucratic to reflect the new business objectives of the organization. The name was therefore changed to the succinct (and punning!) 'Hampshire Works'. Furthermore, the traditional Hampshire coat-of-arms, which was used universally as the Authority's logo, was rejected in favour of a stylized rose. This logo has subsequently been taken over by the Authority as a whole and forms a significant part of its newly developed corporate image.

Finally, in these early stages, social events were used unashamedly in an attempt to knit the organization together. Such events enabled staff to get to know their new managers and forged close links between staff who were working together for the first time. These kinds of informal measures played an invaluable role in assisting staff to overcome the traumas of change and begin to gain a new confidence, a new sense of identity and, above all, a new sense of purpose.

Results

By the end of its first year of operation, a strong sense of culture and identity had been developed in the DLO. The employees now saw themselves primarily as part of 'Hampshire Works' rather than of the Authority in general.

After the initial process of cultural development, the DLO management have continued to develop management systems to reinforce their objectives. At Board level, considerable efforts have been expended in developing strategic business plans. Residential planning meetings have been organized by senior management – itself an almost unprecedented approach in the Authority at the time – to enable managers to debate and explore strategic issues.

Among all staff, training workshops and seminars have continued to be used to develop customer awareness. In particular, considerable efforts have been expended to stress the sanctity of the customer specification, as well as to provide the skills necessary for clarification of customer requirements. The incentive bonus scheme has been further tightened up along the lines recommended in the 1983 report to ensure that it is post-evaluated and that employees are rewarded strictly on the basis of having fulfilled customer requirements.

These developments have not been without their problems,

not least because of the implicit challenge presented to the prevailing culture of the Authority. Like most local authorities, Hampshire has traditionally responded to change only comparatively slowly. It is an extremely large organization and furthermore, like all authorities, is conditioned significantly by its political control at any given time. These factors tend to discourage any kind of rapid change. In particular the overall culture of the authority tends to prevent a dynamic 'enterprise culture' – such as that developed by the DLO – from moving as rapidly as it would like.

It is not surprising that dramatic change in a small part of the Authority should conflict with the comparative conservatism of the organization as a whole. Some of this tension was straightforwardly practical. It was, for example, impossible for an organization operating as a competitive commercial organization, with the attendant risks and cash-flow problems, to operate under the bureaucratic cost-control procedures that were necessary elsewhere. As a result, the DLO sought, and ultimately obtained, a level of financial control unprecedented in the Authority at the time. Such developments inevitably inspired resentment in other departments, which were still constrained by local government controls.

Some of these tensions came to a head at the end of the DLO's first year of independent operations, at the first residential planning meeting. It had been decided that, rather than holding a formal Board meeting, the managers would spend a residential week in Bournemouth. In addition to planning discussions, the managers also invited guest speakers, from the public and private sectors, to discuss innovative management concepts, particularly in the area of organization culture. The week was highly successful and fostered a strong sense of common purpose among the management team. However, at the end of the meeting, the County Surveyor – although personally strongly committed to the management style of the DLO – felt obliged to reflect to its managers the feeling prevalent elsewhere in the Authority, that perhaps the DLO's efforts had 'gone too far'. The organization was perceived from outside as too aggressive and insular, operating to objectives which were not in accord with the culture of the Authority in general.

These criticisms may have had some validity. Certainly they indicated that the stated aims of the DLO managers had been achieved – and spectacularly so, in their own terms. Similar evidence of this is given by the fact that, in the words of one manager, the instinctive response of the DLO's management to this criticism was to be 'highly company protective' (and the use of the word 'company' is significant). In retrospect, the feeling of both the DLO and the Authority's personnel function is that problems arose, not because the DLO had gone too far but because insufficient efforts had been expended in other areas to achieve similar results. The DLO had to take the steps it did in order initially to survive and then to achieve full competitiveness. Nevertheless, the training input into the DLO was four times greater than that into the client organization and the growing tension was probably primarily the result of this inequity. The Manpower Services Department has subsequently begun a similar programme of training and development in the client department.

The general feeling within the Authority seems to be that the development of a distinct culture within the DLO has been remarkably successful. The Manpower Services Department believes that, in terms of training, the DLO has now developed to the point where it can operate by itself, running its own training workshops, seminars and planning meetings. These are continuing, developing the process of cultural reinforcement. The organization now possesses a remarkable level of self-confidence and is operating with a significant degree of independence. Work for the County Surveyor, which previously comprised some 85 per cent of the DLO's business, now contributes less than 50 per cent. This reflects, not a reduction in Authority work, but an increase in the DLO's other business, to the point where its turnover has grown from £12 million to £20 million in the last few years. Furthermore, the DLO's return on capital has increased well beyond the 5 per cent required under the legislation to a level of some 19 per cent in 1987–8.

Source: Bob Lisney, Assistant County Manpower Services Officer, Hampshire County Council
Tony Hawkins, Chief Assistant, County Surveyor's Department, Hampshire County Council

I. Johnson Matthey plc

Background

Johnson Matthey plc is a specialist in advanced materials and precious metals technology. Principal activities include: the manufacture of catalyst and pollution control systems; speciality chemicals; pharmaceutical compounds and intermediates; electronic materials, components and equipment; the refining, marketing and fabrication of precious metals; and the production of pigments, ceramic colours and transfers. The Johnson Matthey group has just over 7000 employees in 24 countries.

The company has over the hundred or so years of its existence expanded from its original activity of precious metal refining into the scientific and technological application of precious metals and into metal banking. During the 1970s it moved further downstream into the jewellery business and consumer spending. During this period there were a number of acquisitions and a proliferation of activities. The group included some forty or so companies. It was very decentralized and loosely controlled. While there were many centres of excellence within the group there was not really any strategic planning or internal decision-making procedure. Consequently, a number of bad investment decisions were made. There was a lot of unplanned and under-researched diversification. In the early 1980s Johnson Matthey Bankers became involved in commercial lending unsecured by metal; and heavy losses were incurred in the United States in the jewellery and refining business. Johnson Matthey found itself under severe financial pressure.

Changing culture

In 1984 the Bank of England intervened and, with the agreement of the major shareholders – the largest of which was Charter Consolidated – Johnson Matthey Bankers was sold for £1. Charter Consolidated put a new Chairman and a number of non-executive directors onto the Johnson Matthey board and head-hunted for a new Chief Executive. Eugene Anderson, previously President of Celanese International Company, was appointed as Chief Executive in May 1985. With the benefit of hindsight it is clear that the original board should have been more aware of what was happening throughout the group, but they never commissioned an external consultancy report. There was a major financial crisis for the first six or nine months and the company barely survived.

The new executive team took a number of actions in order to effect a turnaround: namely, changing people, business rationalization, re-organization, the introduction of internal planning processes and the introduction of a total quality improvement programme.

Changing people

Clearly the introduction of a new Chairman and non-executive members of the board resulted in a major change in the organization. These acted as new role-models for the rest of the management. At the same time there was an executive compensation review and a clarification of responsibilities among managers. Objective setting linked to an appraisal system was introduced as well as the introduction of a linked incentive scheme. Nowadays a hundred and fifty of the most senior managers are centrally reviewed and the intention is to move the company to the multi-national standard of, say, Digital or Esso. The rationalization in organization resulted in the workforce being reduced by approximately 40 per cent, from 11,600 in 1984 to 7500 presently.

Business rationalization and re-organization

A number of companies were disposed of and the portfolio rationalized. Four divisions were introduced with clear reporting structures and new accounting and control systems. These four divisions were: catalytic systems, materials technology, precious metals, colours and printing.

Internal planning processes

New internal planning processes were introduced in order to improve strategic decision-making of the group as a whole which hitherto had been weak and had resulted in a number of poor decisions.

Total quality improvement programme

A more or less standard Crosby QIP was started in May 1986. David Kitchen, the new Personnel Director recruited from Amersham International, was charged with getting it off the ground and he attended the Crosby Executive College for two months. The Chief Executive, Eugene Anderson, had been involved with QIP at Celanese. Johnson Matthey is an advanced tech company that needs to find specialist niches in the market. It needs to work closely with manufacturers and respond to their requirements. Companies such as Fords undertake annual suppliers' audits. As one of Johnson Matthey's major markets is in catalytic converters for the motor industry it is essential that the company can respond to their demands. The introduction of QIP within Johnson Matthey has been promoted by its clients' awareness and use of concepts such as 'Zero Defects' and 'Just in Time'. To a

large extent the quality concept was appropriate for Johnson
Matthey's business and it acted as a rallying cry for a new
planned direction. In short it was strategically relevant.
During 1986, 150 senior and 50 key middle managers were
sent on a one-week management course at Crosby's Quality
College. The course content revolved around the Absolutes
of Quality Management, the strategy of quality improvement,
the fourteen-step Quality Improvement Process, the education
system and corrective action. The commitment of the senior
management to this process was essential. The Johnson
Matthey quality policy is 'to set and strive to achieve
standards of quality which ensure defect-free operations and
administration to the satisfaction of the customer, shareholders
and the company's employees' (Johnson Matthey Annual
Report 1987). Quality goals are included in the annual
operating plan.

Quality Improvement Teams were set up in each of the
four divisions headed by senior line managers. The purpose
of the teams is to take on the task of 'improving things
around here' by developing a strategy with the aid of a
Crosby consultant. Fifty-five instructors were identified
throughout the four divisions and they attended the two-week
Crosby Instructors' Course. The instructors have run a quality
education course for all the 3500 employees up to the level of
supervisor and a modified shortened four-hour programme
was undertaken for the remaining 3500 members of the
workforce. The quality education course is a fifteen-week
course of two hours a week. The sessions have followed the
Crosby fifteen-step quality education process and have used
the supporting documentation and videos. The titles of the
sessions and brief descriptions of their content are as follows:

1 *The Need for Quality Improvement.* This session helps
  people realize that many customers are disappointed by
  the lack of conformance in products or services they
  receive. The company commitment is also shown by a
  brief videotape of the Chief Executive.

2 *The Concepts of Quality Improvement.* This is a presentation of the Absolutes of Quality Management in a way that everybody can understand.

3 *Identification of Requirements.* By means of an input/output analysis of any job, the student is shown that it is possible to identify the requirement components.

4 *Measurement of Conformance.* Taking some of the requirements from session three the students learn how to measure how well they are being met. One purpose of this session is to show that the measurement is merely a form of communication.

5 *Prevention of Non-conformance.* Having identified the requirement and then measured conformance or lack of it, the prevention of non-conformance is discussed.

6 *The Need for a Performance Standard.* This session emphasizes the necessity for a performance standard that cannot be misunderstood. The workshop in this particular module helps the student learn how to explain Zero Defects to other people.

7 *The Price of Non-conformance.* All the content that goes into non-conformance and conformance is given in a manner that the student can use to see what it costs in his or her own area not to conform to the requirements that were identified in session three.

8 *Quality Briefcase Company.* The executives of the company are interviewed and give their feelings on why problems of quality arise and what needs to be done about them.

9/10 *Elimination of Non-conformance* (Parts one and two). These sessions show how the Quality Briefcase Company, having got its attitude straight, approaches the problems of non-conformance and their elimination.

11 *Team Approach to Problem Elimination.* The field service team of the Quality Briefcase Company is used to show that examining the problems together produces more practical solutions.

12 *The Company's Role in Causing Quality Improvement.* The Presidents of the two participating companies discuss the

differences in their companies and the problems they have in causing quality to happen.

13 *The Managers' Role in Causing Quality Improvement.* This includes a discussion with an operating manager who is having problems with housekeeping, with getting material into his area and with getting it out in time. There is a self test after this so that all those participating can determine whether they are having a positive influence on their areas.

14 *Supplier's Role in Causing Quality Improvements.* Here the emphasis is not only on the supplier who brings things in from outside, but also on the internal supplier. Most of us receive material we work on from someone else in the organization. A conversation with some of the participants in the first fourteen sessions follows and a statement is made by each participant on what he or she is going to do differently having attended this course.

15 *Summary.*

The product of change?

The quality improvement process represents a major commitment and investment. Over £1 million has already been spent. It is expensive, but has the ability to change people's thinking and behaviour. Quality goals have become business goals – they are no longer training goals. Error-corrective action has resulted in measurable change. For example, one of the divisions has reviewed and updated its financial and accounting system. The management at the Wembley plant has become aware that something can be done about late dispatches. The quality improvement process has been used to change the design of the plant, reduce production costs and improve sales ordering in the refinery in New Jersey.

Five-year summarized accounts are given below. They

indicate a substantial recovery in the fortunes of Johnson
Matthey since 1984/85.

Figure 1
Summarized accounts – five years review

	1987 £ million	1986 £ million	1985 £ million	1984 £ million	1983 £ million
Profits					
Profit before taxation					
excluding JMB	50.5	30.1	20.1	27.1	15.7
JMB	—	—	—	9.5	24.8
Profit on ordinary activities					
before taxation	50.5	30.1	20.1	36.6	40.0
Taxation	(14.5)	(8.5)	(8.0)	(15.9)	(5.4)
Profit after taxation	36.0	21.6	12.1	20.7	34.6
Extraordinary items	(10.3)	(8.2)	(176.3)	(26.1)	—
Dividends	(10.9)	(5.4)	(0.7)	(13.3)	(13.3)
Profit/(loss) retained	14.8	8.0	(164.9)	(18.7)	21.3
	Pence	Pence	Pence	Pence	Pence
Basic earnings per ordinary					
share	25.2	14.7	8.6	15.6	26.0
	£ million	£ million	£ million	£ million	£ million
Assets employed (see note)					
Fixed assets					
Tangible assets	162.6	164.5	202.5	202.4	227.3
Investment in JMB	—	—	—	99.7	94.8
Investments	5.7	35.2	40.5	10.6	32.7
	168.8	199.7	243.0	312.7	354.8
Current assets	364.0	340.5	446.4	567.8	320.7
Less:Current liabilities	212.7	189.9	308.4	431.9	232.2
Net current assets	151.3	150.6	138.0	135.9	88.5
Total assets less current					
liabilities	319.6	350.3	381.0	448.6	443.3
Borrowings repayable after					
one year	60.3	120.1	167.1	90.5	106.2
Creditors over one year and					
provisions	32.5	15.4	8.5	6.7	5.8
Net assets	226.8	214.8	205.4	351.4	331.3

	£ million	£ million	£ million	£ million	£million
Financed by					
Called up share capital	160.1	158.9	158.8	133.5	133.5
Share premium account	19.3	20.5	20.7	21.8	21.8
Reserves	47.4	35.4	25.9	196.1	176.0
	226.8	214.8	205.4	351.4	331.3
	1987	1986	1985	1984	1983
Average number of employees	7454	8598	9271	11,335	11,680

Note: the summarized accounts for 1983 have not been restated to include borrowed metal.

Source: Johnson Matthey Annual Report 1987

Source: David Kitchen, Personnel Director, Johnson Matthey plc
CROSBY P B. *Quality without tears*. McGraw-Hill, 1987

II. BP Chemicals International

Background

The British Petroleum plc is the parent company of one of the world's largest international oil and natural resources groups. BP Chemicals International has worldwide responsibility for the company's chemicals and plastics interests. It operates partly or wholly owned manufacturing interests in the UK, Belgium, France, West Germany and Holland, as well as research laboratories in the UK, Belgium and France. The company has an annual turnover of nearly £2 billion and employs some 15,000 staff around the world.

BP moved into chemicals initially by way of joint ventures. Its initial aim was to 'balance the barrel', that is, to find a profitable means of utilizing the surplus naphtha produced when crude oil is refined. In fact, the business proved highly successful and grew rapidly throughout the 1950s and the 1960s, particularly with the development of polymers. During those decades, BP formed partnerships with chemicals companies in the UK, France and Germany.

During the next twenty years, as BP's chemicals business continued to develop, efforts were made to rationalize operations. However, the company has continued to grow by a process of acquisition. In 1977/78, BP acquired most of Union Carbide's European chemicals and plastics operations and, more recently, the company has acquired the chemical operations of Standard Oil, as well as taking over responsibility for BP Detergents.

Culture change

For much of its history the company has experienced rapid, if rather piecemeal, growth, as a result both of acquisition and of market expansion. In the early years of the company development was dramatic, with the market growing at a rate of 15 per cent or more per annum. However, because the company had grown partly through acquisitions, there tended to be a lack of common culture and identity. Employees, particularly those outside the UK, tended to think of themselves as belonging to a local operation rather than to the BP Group. It was felt that the company needed to develop a stronger sense of international identity and a clearer understanding of its strategic and cultural objectives.

Quality

The concept of 'quality' initially became a significant issue in the company's production areas. Production staff found that there was an increasing demand for 'quality' from their customers and that quality in production techniques was a growing area of discussion. As a result, investigations were carried out into precisely what was meant by 'quality' in this context and what, if anything, the concept might have to offer BP Chemicals.

It rapidly became clear that the concept offered significant potential for the company's operations. In September 1986 a conference was held for all the company's senior managers which incorporated presentations on the theory of quality, as well as presentations from companies already making use of quality techniques. The conference excited considerable interest and a manager was given the task of facilitating a similar approach within BP Chemicals.

Efforts were then made to identify commercially available quality programmes. A number were identified and the company selected the approach developed by Philip Crosby. Crosby's method was selected for a number of reasons. First, it had a proven and well-documented track record. Secondly, it was not a system imposed on the company by, for example, a team of consultants. The Crosby approach provides the

training, knowledge and skills but allows the company itself
to implement the system. It was felt that this 'ownership'
would inspire a higher level of commitment. Thirdly, the fact
that Crosby is US rather than UK based was itself felt to be
an advantage. There had been a tendency in the past for BP
Chemicals' UK headquarters to dominate the company's
operations. It was felt that a US approach was more likely to
be perceived as 'neutral'.

Initial training was provided on a cascade basis. First,
senior managers were provided with an appropriate level of
education and awareness. Subsequent groups were then
provided with training designed to enable them to train others
in quality techniques. In total, some 300 staff went through
this week-long training programme. After this, training was
carried out on a site-by-site basis, using local staff and
facilities. Again, it was felt that this local 'ownership' would
encourage a strong sense of commitment to the aims of the
programme. To provide coordination and to prevent
parochialism, a corporate quality steering committee was set
up, which included representation from each of the sites.

Quality was defined as *conformance to customer requirements*. Individuals were encouraged to consider their work in
terms of its contribution to fulfilling customer needs
(customers could be internal or external). Crosby stresses the
high cost of non-conformance to customer requirements and
suggests that products that do not fulfil customer needs –
whatever their apparent intrinsic merit – are, by definition, of
low quality.

The system operates through a series of work groups,
involving all staff. The aim is to identify precise customer
requirements and then determine how these can be most
accurately and easily achieved. The system is participative,
with those who actually carry out the work being encouraged
to suggest how the processes may be improved. Within BP
Chemicals such work groups operate from senior executive
level downwards, covering all the company.

The process of identifying conformance to customer needs

is necessarily a continuing one. In the words of one manager, 'We became cleverer and cleverer at spotting non-conformance.' As improvements are made in those areas where there have been obvious compromises with ideal customer requirements, then other, less obvious incidents of non-conformance become evident.

There is a strong belief within BP Chemicals that the Crosby system is most valuable if accepted absolutely without dilution or compromise. The aims of the Crosby approach are uncompromising and it was felt that any qualifications would swiftly undermine the integrity of the whole method.

Benefits

It is probably too early to estimate the contribution made by 'total quality management' to the effectiveness or profitability of BP Chemicals. Nevertheless, the company has continued to be highly profitable over the past two years, with annual operating profits in excess of £200 million. Within the company, there certainly appears to be a strong feeling that Crosby's notion of quality has made an important contribution and has enormous potential for the future.

Perhaps most importantly, in the longer term, total quality has given a focus to the company's continuing efforts to create a unified culture and identity. The company was reorganized in January 1988, with the specific aim of providing a consistent international identity. This reorganization was matched by conscious changes in image, designed to reinforce corporate identity. For the first time, for example, the aim of a consistent house style for all documents and literature throughout the company was established.

These efforts have been strongly reinforced by the presentation of BP Chemicals as a 'quality' company. This emphasis on quality is reiterated again and again in the company's literature, in its in-house publications and even on plaques in offices and in the foyer of its headquarters. Internal magazines have been used to promote the quality approach, reporting on the success of work groups, developments in training, etc. Those who have undergone training are encouraged to wear 'quality' badges.

Quality has become a common, international theme in the company, providing a consistent objective for staff in all jobs and all parts of the world. This has facilitated the development of a culture which is both more unified and more autonomous than previously. Employees now have much greater influence on work methods and practices, but, at the same time, there is a more coherent sense of purpose to the company as a whole.

In the longer term, there is considerable scope for developing the concept of quality to influence other management systems and processes. It would be appropriate, for example, to produce new job descriptions which defined jobs in quality terms, that is, in terms of their contribution to the fulfilment of customer needs. Similarly, it would be appropriate to appraise staff in terms of quality objectives.

Source: P Worden, Organization Development, BP Chemicals International

III. Rank Xerox UK Ltd

Background

Xerox is a multinational organization employing some 100,000 staff worldwide. The parent company, based in the USA, is responsible for all financial services, for the development and manufacture of most products and for the marketing and servicing of products in the USA. Rank Xerox is a joint venture between Xerox and the Rank Organization and is responsible for the marketing and servicing of Xerox products in Europe, Australia, New Zealand, Africa and the Middle East. Rank Xerox UK Ltd is responsible for the marketing and servicing of products in the UK. Fuji Xerox and Modi Xerox are joint-venture companies in Japan and India respectively.

From the early 1960s Xerox enjoyed a virtual monopoly of the copier market. However, in the mid-1970s the copier patents ran out and the Japanese entered the field, rapidly reducing Xerox's market-share. Xerox's previous profitability and monopoly had led both to a fat middle-management structure and to a degree of arrogance towards customers. Responsibilities were duplicated, communications poor and products were becoming outdated. By the early 1980s Xerox was experiencing fairly significant financial problems.

Xerox quality philosophy

In 1980 Fuji Xerox was awarded the Deming prize for quality. David Keans, the Xerox CEO, impressed by the Japanese quality and commitment, became determined to effect similar cultural changes in Xerox. A team of senior managers created the Xerox quality philosophy:

> Xerox is a quality company. Quality is the basic business principle for Xerox. Quality means providing our external and internal customers with innovative products and services that fully satisfy their requirements. Quality improvement is the job of every employee.

Quality offices were established at Xerox headquarters and around the world. The unit heads formed a Quality Implementation Team which, after consultation with quality gurus such as Philip Crosby and David Nadler, and visits to other organizations, put together a detailed strategy and plan. Hal Tragesh, Xerox's Director of Human Resource Development and Systems, played a key role and Xerox sees a clear link between its Leadership through Quality programmes and human resource management.

The company literature describes 'Leadership through Quality' as first a goal, second a strategy and third a process:

> It is a goal because we have to attain it. It is a strategy because we will achieve a competitive edge and attain leadership in our chosen business through continuous pursuit of quality improvements. It is a process because in Xerox quality is the fundamental business principle upon which our management and work processes will be based.

The mechanisms for achieving quality are:

– adherence to a set of quality principles
– the use of a variety of quality tools and measures
– a set of management practices which ensure that managers
  orchestrate the change and walk like they talk

An overview of the mechanisms for achieving Leadership through Quality are given in figure 1.

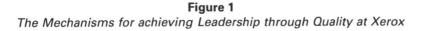

Figure 1

The Mechanisms for achieving Leadership through Quality at Xerox

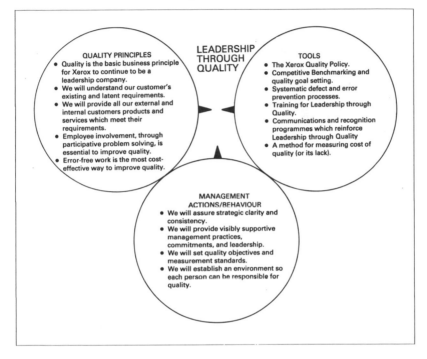

The Xerox view of quality is that:

– it refers to conformance to customer requirements, giving the customer no more and no less than he/she requires
– the customer is defined as anyone who receives a service, either inside or outside the organization
– acceptable performance is measured in terms of satisfying customer requirements, not in terms of percentage of defects
– the emphasis is on error prevention not error detection
– quality is measured in terms of the costs incurred by failing to satisfy customer requirements (eg costs of design changes, lost opportunities, etc)

Five mechanisms were used to assist culture change:

1 standards and measurements – training was provided in techniques such as rational problem-solving, competitive bench-marking and quality measurement
2 recognition and reward – incentives were related to 'quality' behaviour
3 communications – using magazines, films and meetings to communicate company objectives
4 training – cascaded through the whole organization
5 management behaviour and actions – management from the Chief Executive Officer down used quality process as part of their daily work, promoting quality behaviour as the norm

Leadership through Quality is intended to be a clear, consistent and long-term strategy, which influences the whole of the company's business approach. It is top-led, but must involve every employee:

> We clearly identify which executives are with us and which are not with us. We are patient with those that have to make the change, but in the end, if they do not adapt, they have to leave. Quite simply, if you do not want to be quality performer, you do not work here.

Change in Rank Xerox UK

In the early 1980s Rank Xerox, like the rest of the organization, faced financial crisis. It endeavoured to respond to this both by staff reductions and rationalizations, and by the introduction of Leadership through Quality. Initially, however, there was a lack of support among senior managers and the concept of conforming to customer requirements was felt to conflict with the traditional company approach.

In 1986 David O'Brien from Burroughs took over as Managing Director at Rank Xerox UK, with the objective of developing the company's involvement in the office systems market. Given that the company was traditionally divided on strongly functional lines and internally focused, this required significant organizational development. In addition, David O'Brien sought the help of Cambridge Associates consultants in introducing a process of 'Business Development Planning' to determine key strategies and objectives. A similar process was then used at functional level to identify the rules, system requirements, management processes and resources required to achieve these objectives. A renovated Leadership through Quality programme, along with consensus management and across functional terms, was used to implement the strategic requirements.

The Integrated Planning Process is given in figures 2 and 3.

Figure 2

The Framework for the Integrated Planning Process

Level of Responsibility within the Organization	Definition of Role	Methodology	Outputs
Direction	What are we going to do?	Business Development Planning	• Mission • Strategy • Responsibilities
Function Management	What do we need to do it?	Business Systems Requirements	• Management Process • Systems and Rules • Resources
Operational Management	How are we going to do it?	Leadership Through Quality	• Quality Improvement Projects • Operational Improvements • Team Commitment
Operations	Doing it	Teamwork	

Figure 3
Stages in the Integrated Planning Process

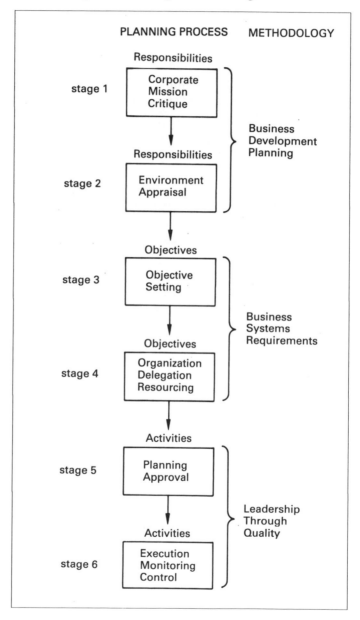

The UK Quality Office, including ten full-time trainers and two staff concerned with strategy and planning, was responsible for devising the programme. Quality training – in identifying customer requirements and measuring non-conformance costs – has been cascaded through all 4500 employees. Further training, one-to-one counselling, support and follow-up have been used to modify behaviour, with the assumption that changing behaviour leads to changes in attitude. Emphasis has also been on error prevention and 'right first time'. The programme has also been supported by reward and appraisal systems, induction training and monitoring mechanisms such as attitude surveys, to ensure that quality is not perceived as a separate entity. The next stage is the handing over of quality responsibility to line managers.

Source: Mike Williams, Quality Manager, Rank Xerox UK Ltd
CHAPMAN P. 'Changing the corporate culture of Rank Xerox'. *Long Range Planning*, 21, 1988. pp 22–8
GILES E. 'Leadership through Quality at Xerox – a case study of organizational change', paper presented at the Occupational Psychology Conference, British Psychological Society, University of Manchester, 1988

Unisys Ltd

Unisys was formed in the summer of 1986, resulting from the acquisition of Sperry by Burroughs. The acquisition process commenced in May and was agreed in June of that year, with the legalities completed by September. The combination of the two companies produced an international organization with a turnover of over £10 billion, employing nearly 100,000 staff worldwide.

The company provides advanced computer-based information systems, networks and services to industrial, commercial and financial markets, as well as to the Government and the public sector. It is also a major supplier in the defence electronics market. Unisys has some 60,000 customers in more than 100 countries.

Unisys is based in the United States and the process of change that followed the merging of the two companies has been an international experience. For the purposes of clarity, the following study concentrates on the experiences of the company in the UK, although clearly reference is made to the international dimension where appropriate.

Unisys in the UK and Ireland now employs over 4000 staff, the majority being professional and technical employees. Of these, some 2250 are employed by the UK marketing subsidiary. Business turnover in the UK is currently over £300 million, produced by four major business divisions:

- financial: providing computer systems for banks, building societies, insurance companies, Stock Exchange brokers and other financial institutions
- public sector: providing systems in central and local government, public utilities, the police and other legal authorities and education
- commercial/manufacturing: providing systems for the manu-facturing sector, construction industry, engineering, oil, airlines, retail and distribution

– indirect markets: responsible for the sales of Unisys computers through the company's distributor/dealer network and by value-added resellers

In the UK subsidiary, the company is primarily concerned with sales, marketing and customer support. It maintains, in addition to its UK headquarters in London, support facilities and an education centre in Milton Keynes and sales branches at fifteen sites in the UK and Ireland. The company also has a manufacturing plant at Livingston in Scotland, employing over 750 staff. The headquarters for the company's Europe/Africa operations is based at Uxbridge.

Background to change

Prior to amalgamation the two companies, Burroughs and Sperry, had a similar image and reputation. Both were well-established. Burroughs was over a hundred years old, having its roots in mechanical business machines, and Sperry had a history which, although complex, was long by the standards of the computer industry. Both companies had been strong in the provision of systems for the finance, commercial/manufacturing and public sectors. The two companies had been part of what was known as the BUNCH (Burroughs, Univac (Sperry), NCR, Control Data and Honeywell), a group of broadly comparable companies operating in the computer field. The similarity of the two companies was also evident in the UK, where both were primarily sales and marketing operations. Burroughs employed some 1800 staff in the UK, whereas Sperry employed about 1000.

Although both companies had been successful, there was a general feeling that neither company was achieving its full potential. The companies were felt to be undermanaged, under-performing and not developing or growing as fast as might have been expected. Internally, both companies were felt to have excessively hierarchical structures, designed to prevent failure rather than to promote success. Among individual employees, competence rather than excellence seemed to be the expectation and both companies seemed more interested in controlling than in facilitating performance.

Nevertheless, the two companies had extremely well-established user bases and both had generally good reputations in their field of operation.

The process of change

Burroughs had made an unsuccessful attempt to acquire Sperry in the summer of 1985. A second attempt, in the following year, was successful and by September 1986 the acquisition was complete. A new Chairman and Chief Executive, Michael Blumenthal – formerly the Chairman of Burroughs – had been appointed in July of that year. He immediately set about determining clear objectives for the change process. Blumenthal described the amalgamation as 'a launching, not an arrival' and made it evident from the start that the action had been taken for 'long-term strategic stakes'. In other words, his aim was not merely to survive the traumas of merging the two companies – as Blumenthal pointed out 'most mergers, even those sound in concept, fail' – but to use this as a springboard to launch a new, much more dynamic culture in the combined organization. In the company's first Annual Report Blumenthal admits: ' . . . no doubt this was a bold and risky experiment, but its potential rewards were sufficiently large . . . to justify the risks'.

It was evident from the start that, if Blumenthal's objectives were to be realized, the company needed to gain a strong sense of identity very quickly. This process went beyond the practical difficulties of combining two well-established companies, complex as these undoubtedly were. It was necessary for the new company quickly to overcome the psychological problems arising from the general experience of change, so as to create a new sense of company loyalty and unity. There were no doubt many – particularly those who had worked for one of the companies for many years – who resented even the prospect of change, let alone the alterations in duties and responsibilities and even job losses that accompanied it. The first task, therefore, was to ensure that this resentment and understandable trepidation about the implications of the amalgamation did not obscure the potential benefits.

To achieve this, Blumenthal identified four major principles – partnership, merit, unity and dispatch – which guided the company's actions in developing its new operations and culture.

Partnership

In reality, the amalgamation had resulted from the acquisition of Sperry by Burroughs. It was realized immediately, however, that the cultural implications of this could be extremely damaging. A conscious decision was taken that, from the top downwards, the amalgamation should be treated as a merger between two equals. Blumenthal commented:

> Partnership meant that Sperry and Burroughs were treated as equals. This principle goes to the core of our business strategy: we are equally committed to both customer bases; therefore, we are equally and fully dedicated to maintaining the established systems facilities of the two companies.

The concept of 'partnership' was essential to the success of the new company, both for its customers and its employees. If the new company was to develop a strong culture and a strong sense of staff loyalty, it was essential that the change was not seen as an imposition of alien values and that both partners felt able to contribute on an equal basis. There was a particular problem in that, in creating the new company, there was an inevitable necessity to lose staff, particularly in those areas where there was duplication between the two companies. The decision was made, again at a very early stage, that the selection both of staff and all policies and procedures in the new organization should be made solely on the basis of merit.

Merit

The selection of all staff and of the policies and procedures in the new company was carried out on the basis of 'who and what is best for Unisys'. It was decided, for example, that no one could be sure of an automatic post in the new company. Similarly, it was decided that, in developing management procedures, neither of the former companies' policies would take precedence. All inherited customs would be carefully scrutinized to ensure that they were in the best interests of the company. This inevitably caused problems in those areas where policies or procedures diverged. In Sperry, for example, all staff in the UK worked $36\frac{1}{4}$ hours per week, whereas in Burroughs staff worked 35, $37\frac{1}{2}$ or 40 hours, dependent on their duties. It was decided that in the new company all staff would work $37\frac{1}{2}$ hours and the change was quickly accepted. A similar process was undertaken with the company's UK company car policy. The car policies of the two companies diverged considerably and there was a danger that any changes would offend some staff in some way. As it turned out, the new policy was drawn up with considerable care so that all the staff involved benefited to some degree from the changes – if, for example, the new allowance was for a car with a smaller engine size, then this was offset by making it a higher range model. In consequence, the new policy proved acceptable to virtually all concerned. This approach was tried again and again in developing procedures for the new company.

Unity

The primary concern of the company was to create a new sense of identity for the company as soon as possible. This involved, in Blumenthal's words, 'rapidly transferring all allegiance from the old companies to the new enterprise'. The choice of a name was crucial. Clearly, if the new company was really to be a partnership, it was important that neither of the old names was retained. The new name 'Unisys' was actually selected through a worldwide competition among employees, attracting some 30,000 entries. This process again encouraged a sense that employees themselves were participating in the development of the new organization.

Dispatch

It was believed that, if the company was to overcome the traumas of merger, the process had to be completed quickly. The speed with which the legal aspects of the merger were completed has already been referred to. The practical implications had been handled equally quickly. In the UK, there was no formal contact between the two companies, except at Manager Director level, until September 1986. However, once the legal formalities had been completed, management teams were drawn from the senior management of both companies to establish the terms of the new organization. In the period from October to December 1986 the teams set about defining the new company's mission statement, structure and objectives.

The creation of Unisys

As Blumenthal's comments suggest, the creation of Unisys was almost the creation of a 'greenfield' organization. Every effort was made to define the culture of the organization from first principles. An organizational structure was developed which was different from that of the two former companies, based on the new company's 'lines of business' (finance, public sector, commercial/manufacturing and indirect markets). The structure of the new organization was made as flat as possible, with every effort being made to avoid layers of management which could not contribute directly to decision-making. The overall aim was to ensure that the customer was as close as possible to the highest levels in the organization and to promote a more direct sense of accountability.

At the start of 1987 Unisys began to develop its new employment and management policies. A new employee handbook was published immediately and the process began of developing new terms and conditions for the new organization. The human resource function had been involved, at director level, in the original project team and now became heavily involved in the formulation and execution of policy.

In creating the policy of the new company, a conscious decision was taken that, as far as possible, there should be no reference to the old companies. This was adhered to very strictly – and with some difficulty – in all areas except the pension handbook, which had to refer to the still existing pension schemes of the old companies. A new Unisys pension scheme was set up in due course.

This refusal even to mention the names of the old companies was a recurrent theme in the development of the new organization, often handled humorously. At an early stage, for example, conferences were held for sales staff as part of the process of communicating the objectives of the organization. At these, staff were forbidden to use the names 'Burroughs' or 'Sperry' on pain of forfeit! Similar efforts were made to ensure that, as far as possible, all company buildings, documentation, etc, were inscribed with the name 'Unisys' at the earliest opportunity.

This initial process of obliterating the old cultures was succeeded by an enormous effort to communicate the values and objectives of the new organization. These values were spelled out explicitly in documents circulated to all staff, with key messages emphasized in short, memorable slogans:

– the customer comes first
– we work as a team
– we back the innovator
– we honour high ethical standards
– quality in everything we do

In the words of one manager, the company 'communicated like mad', issuing information bulletins, audio tapes and magazines, as well as using internal computer communications systems. One particular technique which proved highly successful was the organization of 'kick-off meetings' in specific departments. These were launch meetings, designed to provide a consistent and positive message about the company's policies and objectives. In particular, these meetings demonstrated a consistent theme of customer orientation, reiterated again and again in the company's published documents and briefings. A typical edition of Unisys' quarterly news briefing, for instance, contains articles titled 'Protecting Customer Investment', 'Putting the Customer First' and 'Responding to Changing Demand'. The new company also made significant efforts to promote its immediate business successes in these magazines, with the intention of encouraging employee commitment and support. At the same time, the company also made major use of its 'external' corporate advertising on television and in the media to promote the values of the new company among staff as well as customers.

Not surprisingly, training in the organization became a major priority. Much of the training was highly practical, teaching ex-Sperry staff about Burroughs systems solutions and vice versa. In addition, training was used as a mechanism for disseminating the company's mission and to build up an understanding of how this could be related to particular jobs or departments. This was carried out through group exercises and team building, in which the human resource function acted as facilitator.

There was also a significant process of management development, aimed particularly at strengthening the manager's skill as leader and coach. This was carried out through a video-based scheme, developed through the company on a cascade basis. Each manager was also given a written 'management creed' to be posted in his or her office which identified the key themes that were seen as central to the manager's role as a leader.

At the same time efforts were made to strengthen the company's reward and remuneration procedures. The aim was to promote a higher and more pro-active level of performance. A full 'management by objectives' process was introduced, related directly to the objectives set for the organization as a whole. Salary increases were totally merit-related, with individuals obtaining salary increases of between 0 and 20 per cent dependent on performance. This was not entirely new, as both former companies had operated some form of merit-related systems, but it acted as a reinforcer of the new corporate philosophy.

Not all the changes were positive. The company had to shed some 400 staff in the merger process. Unisys endeavoured to treat staff as well as possible and, wherever possible, job losses were achieved through early retirements. In addition, outplacement consultancy and counselling was made available to these staff to ease their transition period. Interestingly, this process may itself have contributed to the speed with which change was achieved. Many of the longer-serving staff who found it hard to come to terms with the new organization chose to leave. At retirement dinners, for example, it was not uncommon to hear retiring staff say 'It will always be Burroughs [or Sperry] to me . . . I will never use the name "Unisys".'

Conclusion

The speed with which change has been achieved in Unisys is very impressive and the company seems quickly to have overcome the problems and traumas of merger. It is now in a position fully to take advantage of the potential of its new culture and organization. It is perhaps too early to identify the effect of the changes on the company's profitability, but there is little doubt that the company is highly buoyant and optimistic about its future. The company's results in its first year of operation were extremely impressive. Profitability had increased by over 100 per cent and productivity had increased by 60 per cent. There is a general feeling that the company has managed to create a culture of enterprise, accountability and high performance which has significantly affected the behaviour of all staff. In effect, Unisys has used the amalgamation of two well-established companies to create in Michael Blumenthal's words 'a new thing under the sun' – that is, a new organization with a new culture which has been developed from first principles. Unisys has effectively turned the potentially destructive trauma of merger into a positive means of overcoming strongly reinforced traditional culture.

Source: M B Smaje, Director of Human Resources, Unisys Ltd

Marley plc

Marley plc is one of the largest producers of building and related products in the UK. The Marley Group's products include Marley roof tiles, bricks, blocks, flooring, rainwater and drainage systems, and moulded foam car interiors. The Group has a widespread international presence.

The company was founded in 1924 by Owen Aisher. His sons, Sir Owen and Jack Aisher, were subsequent Chairmen, and the family's involvement continues to the present day. From its foundation, the company developed very swiftly, both within the roof tile business and by diversifying into other fields. In 1965 the company also moved into retailing, opening Marley Retail Ltd, which ultimately became Payless DIY.

This process of diversification was highly successful and the company became both a market and a technology leader in its field. Under the Chairmanship of Owen and Jack Aisher, the company built up a market share of 30–50 per cent in most of its primary areas of operation and became recognized as a household name.

The company's culture during this period was strongly conditioned by the Aishers, who inspired a high level of respect, loyalty and affection amongst their employees. The culture was strongly rooted in the company's tradition and public reputation, but was also forward-looking and adventurous. The company maintained its reputation for quality and value, but was not afraid to experiment with markets or products, usually with considerable success.

Despite its remarkable growth, the company endeavoured to sustain a 'small company' ethos, encouraging close links between the influential founders and the 'ordinary employee'. This is demonstrated, for example, by a booklet published to commemorate the company's diamond jubilee in 1984. The booklet emphasizes the company's traditions and the durability of its products, and includes photographs of employees who have completed a 'magnificent 50 years' service' with the company.

Not surprisingly, this highly centralized, personality-dominated culture was reflected in the company's management style and systems. Pay and remuneration were centrally administered and management tended to depend on personal contact and communication rather than the more formalized systems perhaps appropriate to a large, complex organization.

This culture served the company very well until the early 1980s. At this point, however, a number of strategic problems arose which challenged the company culture and approach. Although Marley continued to be successful, its profits were under threat and there was a possibility of takeover. The major problem was that, despite its unified image, the company had become over-diversified, with some forty subsidiaries over a wide geographical area. In particular, the phenomenal growth of the Payless DIY chain, although highly profitable, was swallowing a disproportionate amount of the company's resources. There was a widespread feeling that the company needed a new sense of direction, both strategically and culturally.

Jack Aisher retired in May 1985 and the company was then led initially by Sir Robert Clark, the non-executive Chairman, and subsequently by a new Chief Executive, George Russell. Under their leadership in 1986 Marley produced a Group Corporate Plan, with the aim of redefining the company's long-term strategic objectives. The plan identified specific areas for growth and the company decided to withdraw from operations seen as peripheral. This period was characterized by a series of major divestments and acquisitions, with the intention of clarifying the company's strategic direction.

This was accompanied by a process of structural rationalization. The business was divided on operational lines and Head Office was transformed from a controlling to an enabling function. To facilitate the decentralization of management functions, more formal systems were introduced. Formal staff appraisal was introduced, based on 'management by objectives'. A full job evaluation exercise was carried out and a management succession plan was developed. These mechanisms were seen as essential to the creation of a new culture of independence. The company's values and philosophies, rather than emanating directly from the Chairman's office, would be inculcated in formal systems which could be operated consistently by all managers.

Efforts were then made to encourage managers and staff to move away from the constraints of paternalism to a more pro-active approach. This process is continuing, but a number of initiatives have begun to exert influence. At the simplest level, the new Chief Executive sent out personally addressed 'Dear Colleague' letters to all staff, introducing the overall objectives for the Group and requesting comments or suggestions. Responses ran into hundreds, helping to build up commitment to the objectives, as well as creating a strong sense of community.

Appraisal has been used, not only to improve employee development but also as a means of encouraging communication. The process of communication has also been encouraged by training, conferences and publications, detailing group developments. Efforts have also been made to encourage a greater sense of company unity through inter-divisional meetings. Stronger connections between the interspersed parts of the Group have developed, reflected not only in formal issues like the sharing of resources, but also in greater informal links, such as inter-divisional social events.

The changes in Marley in the last three years have been enormous, although the process is continuing. The company has achieved a significant financial turnaround. Its pre-tax profits, for example, increased from £28.2 million in 1983 to £55.2 million in 1987. The return on capital employed increased from 14.8 per cent in 1983 to 22.4 per cent in 1987. Perhaps more significantly, there is also a much greater sense of identity and unity in the company as a whole. These changes have been promoted through corporate literature aiming to promote the new culture among employees, customers and shareholders. This theme is brought out strongly in the company's 1987 Annual Report which carries the slogan, 'You Know the Name. You'd Never Recognize the Company.'

Source: J A Salt, Head of Personnel and K Howell, Corporate Planning Manager, Marley plc

Three Further Views

I. James Cropper plc

Background

James Cropper plc is a major manufacturer of coloured and specialist paper and paper-related products, based in Burneside near Kendal. The company has manufactured paper and board at Burneside Mill since 1845, and has been a limited company for over 100 years. It is very much a family business. James Cropper, the current Chairman, is a great-grandson of the company's founder, and other members of the Board are also closely related to the family. The company has a high reputation in the industry as a manufacturer of high-quality products, as well as a strong reputation as an employer among its local community.

Throughout its long history, James Cropper plc has continued to grow, invest and innovate with a considerable degree of success. However, in the late 1970s, there was a recognition that the company was approaching a period of potential crisis. Much of its equipment was old and rapidly becoming obsolescent. Even some of its recently purchased machines were becoming outdated, and were certainly not world-class. Overall, there was a recognition that the company would need to invest substantially over the next decade, if it were to maintain its competitive edge.

As a result, throughout the 1980s, the primary focus of the company's business strategy was investment in new plant. In the words of Nick Willink, the Managing Director of the Papermaking Division, 'You might say that, during that period, management *was* re-equipment.' The impact of this re-equipment was dramatic, resulting in major increases in the company's production capacity, significant increases in efficiency and quality, and the development of a range of new products. During this period, all the major production machines were either rebuilt or replaced, and the majority of

258

the preparatory and finishing equipment was replaced. In addition to production plant, the company also invested in support equipment, most notably a gas turbine enabling the company to generate its own electricity. Also in this period, the company set up its first subsidiary, Technical Fibre Products Ltd, designed to sell a wide range of products made from synthetic and man-made fibres. This also involved substantial investment in new production facilities and the creation of new manufacturing methods.

Throughout this challenging period – the largest investment project in the company's history – James Cropper plc continued to be very successful. The investment project was completed in 1990, with one of the most significant projects to date – the replacement of the company's No. 3 MG machine with a highly advanced Fourdrinier machine.

With the completion of this project, the company recognized that there was little further potential for developing a competitive edge from investment in plant and equipment. The company had improved its technology to world-class levels, and believed that at least in the medium term it would have to seek further improvements in other areas.

The investment programme had also been completed at a point when economic recession, in the UK and worldwide, was beginning to influence the company's performance. Although the company remained profitable, there was an awareness that lack of demand in the UK market and excess paper machine capacity worldwide were beginning to have a severe effect on prices and margins. In this context, with costs under significant pressure, the company realized that it would need to match its technological investment with a focus on maximizing the potential and performance of its employees. And this in turn required the company to address its long-established and very powerful organizational culture.

The James Cropper culture

Not surprisingly, during its long history, the company had
developed a strong sense of its own identity and values. Much
of this culture can probably be traced back to the founder,
and it has been maintained by the subsequent family
involvement. The first James Cropper, who came from a
Quaker background, was a progressive and philanthropic
employer, and from its early days the company invested
substantially in the education of its workers and the
development of the local community. James Cropper and
subsequent members of the family have also been active in
the social and political life of the region. As an indication of
the powerful interrelationship between the company and the
community, as late as 1940 the company's turbines were used
to provide electricity to the village of Burneside. The company
has always been strongly aware of its responsibilities as
local employer and manufacturer. Even today, the majority
of its employees live in the immediate area. Many employees
are also shareholders and all employees share a proportion of
the company's profits. From a different perspective, the
company has placed an increasing emphasis on environmental
protection. In 1990, it established an Environmental Audit
Group and developed an Environmental Policy Statement,
providing substantial investment to promote continuous
improvement in the company's environmental practices and
policies.

As this background suggests, the company has developed a
very powerful, and largely positive, set of values and beliefs
which are widely accepted and owned by the workforce.
There is a high degree of loyalty and commitment to the
company and its objectives, such that employees are willing
to invest substantial efforts in meeting the company's needs
and expectations. There is a powerful sense of teamwork and
mutual support. There is common acceptance that the
company will take care of its employees to the best of its
ability. Above all, there is a belief that the company's

aspirations are closely aligned with those of the workforce and indeed the local community. Although, as in all organizations, some tensions and disputes may arise, James Cropper plc has come close to being a genuinely *unitary* company – a company where all members are pulling in the same direction.

As this suggests, the established culture of the company has many significant strengths – and indeed displays many of the characteristics that supposed 'leading edge' employers have tried to develop over the last decade. In setting out to change and develop the company's culture, management were very keen to ensure that these strengths were not undermined in the process.

At the same time, there was an awareness that, for all its strengths, the existing culture was capable of inhibiting individual and corporate performance. Because of the dominance of both the company and the Cropper family in the community, the culture inevitably tended towards the patriarchal – almost, in the words of one manager, to the point of being 'benign feudalism'. The result of this was a strong – albeit generally non-confrontational – sense of 'us and them' between employees and management, and employees saw themselves as having little responsibility for the management of the company or its operations. One manager commented that: 'The prevailing tone was "our job is to do what you tell us".'

The result of this was that employees, including many first-line managers, did not feel empowered to deal with problems they might encounter in the course of their work or to identify means of improving or developing their activities. Similarly, many employees, although feeling a high degree of commitment to the company, felt little personal ownership of the jobs or processes in which they were involved. Commitment to quality and performance, although generally high, tended to be abstract, reflecting overall loyalty to the company rather than a personal sense of mission or direction. Faced with operational difficulties or challenges, there was a tendency to duck the issue or to pass the buck to senior management.

In a straightforward mass production environment, this kind of culture might have been less problematic. However, for many years, James Cropper plc had been providing services which – particularly by the standards of the industry – were becoming increasingly bespoke. The company was capable of producing literally thousands of colours, and any weight of paper from 60 to 450 g/m^2. Product runs were becoming increasingly short. The company had always focused on the production of high added value products, and the expectation was that this would continue over the coming decade. In short, the ability to deal with continuous change, to overcome production and managerial challenges, and to maintain the highest quality of product and service would become increasingly critical to the achievement of its business objectives.

For these reasons, James Cropper plc believed that significant benefits could accrue from the development of a more involving and responsive organizational culture. The challenge would be to build on the company's existing areas of cultural strength, while at the same time finding means of overcoming or reducing its perceived cultural weaknesses.

Starting the change process

With these broad aims in view, in the latter part of 1991 the company's senior management began exploring some of the means by which culture change might be achieved. In particular, it began exploring some potential approaches to quality improvement. The company had recently received BS 5750 accreditation. This had been a useful process for tightening and codifying its existing operational and management processes. Nevertheless, there had always been a recognition that accreditation should be the start, rather than the conclusion, of the journey towards quality improvement. One manager commented that: 'BS 5750 certainly improved what was already in place, but it didn't fundamentally challenge our culture, values or ways of working. We were aware that there was still considerable scope for further development.'

In exploring further potential for quality development, the company began to recognize that this could also be an effective focus for delivering a change in culture. In particular, there was a growing awareness that the key principles of total quality management, as defined by many of the key commentators in the field, reflected very closely the characteristics that would be required of the future organization.

As a catalyst to this process, two managers, Nick Willink and Alun Lewis, had attended a seminar at the Strathclyde Institute of Strategic Manufacturing Management which included contributions from experts in the field including Taguchi and Goldratt. Nick Willink also subsequently attended a further seminar in Newcastle which provided an introduction to the major quality gurus. On this basis, supplemented by further research and reading, the company began to develop an understanding of the kinds of approach that might be relevant to its needs. It became clear, for instance, that the company would be unlikely to benefit significantly from the more mechanistic aspect of total quality, such as Statistical Process Control and Advanced Product Testing. Although the application of these tools might produce benefits in the longer term, the more immediate objective was a general development of attitudes, values and beliefs, together with the creation of a clearer customer focus and more effective performance management.

With this in view, at the company's Senior Management Conference held in the autumn of 1991, Nick Willink and Alun Lewis were charged with developing a Total Quality Initiative to meet the company's needs. It rapidly became evident that the company did not possess the skills or resources to support the initiative internally, and that some external consultancy support would be required. At the same time, the company did not wish to buy an 'off the shelf' package. Given the strengths of its existing culture, the aim was to develop a customized approach that would take account of and build on these strengths, rather than risk undermining them through an inappropriate intervention. On this basis, the company explored a number of consultancy options, and eventually selected ER Consultants, who had extensive experience of developing bespoke total quality initiatives with organizations such as the Post Office and British Rail.

The process began in earnest in early 1992. In many ways, the start was less auspicious than might have been hoped. The effects of the recession, which had begun to be felt in the previous winter, combined with the recent heavy level of investment had begun to impose some significant cost pressures on the business. There was a recognition that these would need to be addressed alongside the drive to total quality. Although there was a strong belief in the company that quality and improved cost efficiency were not mutually exclusive – and indeed could be seen as opposite sides of the same coin – there was also a determination that the exercise should continue to be driven by quality and culture change objectives rather than merely a need to control costs.

The first step towards reconciling these factors was the Burneside Challenge, a partially bottom-up exercise in identifying cost reduction opportunities. The aim of the process was to achieve cost savings of £2 million, through a mixture of improved efficiency and controlling employee numbers. At the same time, the intention was to avoid redundancies and to achieve staff reduction through natural wastage and controls on recruitment. Although the exercise was ultimately successful, and has been reinforced by the total quality exercise, at the time it engendered some predictable negative feeling. In particular, there was some concern that, if the company failed to achieve its cost reduction targets, this would inevitably imperil the more ambitious quality targets and intentions.

In the event, these problems did not arise, although there is little doubt that they affected initial employee attitudes, particularly during the opening phase of data collection. This process began with a survey of some 15 per cent of the company's workforce, designed to assess the existing organizational culture and climate. This survey, conducted through a series of focus groups supported by detailed interviews with managers and employee representatives, produced a number of overall conclusions. In broad terms, it was clear that the workforce felt a very high level of commitment to the company's products and to the success of the business. There was also a strong desire for the company to develop and grow. It was clear, therefore, that the company had a significant positive basis on which the culture change exercise could build. At the same time, the research also identified a number of significant opportunities for organization improvement, including:

- the need for a clearer understanding and articulation of the purpose and direction of the business
- the need for a more explicit focus on the customer. Although there was undoubtedly a strong commitment to the concept of customer satisfaction, this had not yet been translated into explicit goals or performance measures
- scope for a better and more detailed understanding of the market, supported by a less reactive approach to identifying and responding to market needs
- potential for greater clarity in the organizational structure and in operational and business processes, reinforced by a more precise focus on key supply chains
- the need to improve and develop internal information systems, and the processes of performance management
- the need to build on individual commitment and capability by promoting greater employee empowerment and accountability

- in general, the need to engender a culture of continuous improvement in the business, supported by a rigorous framework of tools and approaches for analysis and development

On this basis, therefore, it was decided that the Burneside Challenge should be supported and continued to achieve the desired short-term benefits, but that the process should be formally linked to a longer-term process of development, to be known as the Quality Performance Challenge.

The Quality Performance Challenge

The Quality Performance Challenge began with a series of workshops with the Board, aimed at distilling a clear vision of the company's intended direction and values. From this process, the company defined its Vision:

> Our Vision is to be THE company which excels in coloured and other specialist papers and paper related products for a worldwide market.

Underpinning this Vision, the company identified a number of key purposes, defined as follows:

- to work in partnership with our customers
- to design effective solutions for particular customer requirements
- to build upon our well-developed skills and capabilities
- to develop our flexible, well-trained and highly motivated workforce
- to continue our commitment to improving the environment and our responsibility to the local community
- to improve the goodwill of shareholders through increased shareholder values
- to grow and remain an independent company

Alongside these purposes, the company also defined the key values by which it intended to operate:

- to be a caring employer
- to have integrity in our dealings internally and externally
- to demonstrate environmental responsibility
- to remain independent
- to fulfil our responsibility to the local community
- to be customer focused externally and internally
- to demonstrate continuous improvement

The last two were seen as additional to the company's previous set of practised values.

Having defined these core objectives, the Quality Performance Challenge began to take shape. In developing its approach the company was mindful of the fact that, all too frequently, approaches directed exclusively to changing attitudes or behaviour have regularly proved unsuccessful. There was a recognition that, while it was critical to change the culture of the organization, this needed to be related to and reinforced by direct improvements in business processes and effectiveness. In other words, the approach needed to be based on *outputs* – a belief that, if the company could demonstrate significant business benefits accruing from quality development, this would provide a strong foundation for achieving a change in the culture.

To this end, the company adopted an approach which was partly top-down and partly bottom-up, with the two elements intended to be mutually reinforcing. From the top down, the Board established three key process improvement teams, focused respectively on commercial, operational and managerial process improvements. The aim of these teams, which were facilitated by the external consultants, was to identify practical ways in which policies, the process itself, and practices could be improved in line with the quality objectives. This included the development of core processes and tools which could be applied to deal with future business challenges.

The teams comprised Board members and senior managers across a range of functions, and their respective outputs were coordinated at Board level.

The operational team focused on direct improvements in operational processes and activities, using process analysis and redesign techniques. This has already produced both new ways of working and more effective measurement and management of processes. In particular, it has identified more effective cross-functional processes, which the company believes will result in improved product quality and improved delivery to the end customer.

The commercial team worked on means of improving the company's effectiveness in addressing market and customer issues. This has involved a revaluation and a realignment of the focus and objectives of the company's activities in these areas. Much greater emphasis is being placed on market research as a tool for guiding the business, and customer surveys are being conducted to provide feedback to the company. The team has also focused on the development of clearer goals, measures and review processes for the company's sales agents, who are scattered throughout the world. It is felt that this is already delivering business benefits and greater commitment from this previously rather detached group.

The managerial improvement team focused on developing the company's management and support processes in three broad areas:

- performance management
- resource allocation
- business planning

These three areas were seen as critical in supporting the overall direction of organizational change. Performance management focused on developing a number of key principles, confirming that:

- the performance of all employees and teams should be measured and managed in terms which are simple and meaningful
- the company should develop a culture which mixes high accountability with 'low blame'
- the focus should be on promoting teamworking and on effective delivery to internal and external customers
- there should be a strong emphasis on continuous improvement and problem resolution

In practice, these aims have gradually been realized by the team, although the definition of clear and acceptable performance measures is predictably a major challenge. The company is currently in the process of completing and implementing the performance management process. The remaining two objectives – resource allocation and business planning – have focused on developing rigorous and robust processes that can be applied at all levels in the organization. Again, the aim has been to ensure precise accountability, clarity and breadth of thinking and action linked to the core Vision and Purposes, and effective support for those involved in the process.

The outcomes of the three teams were formally presented to the workforce at a series of four Burneside Mill Conferences held early in 1993. This was the first time in the company's history that production had been stopped for such a purpose – an indication of the significance to the company of the Quality Performance Challenge. The outcomes were well received by the workforce, and the company is currently completing their implementation.

Alongside this top-down process of quality development, the company has also conducted an extensive programme of bottom-up skills and team development. This has included training in areas such as team-building and problem-solving, and the encouragement of staff at all levels in the organization to apply such skills in their day-to-day work, building on the experience of the Burneside Challenge. This process has been systematically expanded over the past year to the point where around 25 per cent of the workforce have now either been trained or are actively involved in problem-solving teams. Again, the aim has been to promote new attitudes and new ways of working by focusing on the achievement of performance improvement outputs. The perceived success of this process among individual workgroups is already building commitment and enthusiasm for the wider objectives of the Quality Performance Challenge.

The outcomes

The two elements of the Quality Performance Challenge are now coming together. The improved business, managerial and operational processes are being implemented, and are now being applied in practice in many parts of the organization. This is already leading to some significant improvements in effectiveness. In turn, this perceived success is igniting enthusiasm in the wider workforce, who are seeing the benefits of the exercise and are being encouraged to apply the skills they are gaining through training and development. Overall, the company believes that, in addition to the direct outputs of the process, the mix of disciplines represented by the teams has helped build a spirit of collective responsibility underpinned by a common set of goals and values. Although at one level the Quality Performance Challenge will be completed once all the resulting action plans have been implemented, the company believes that its managers have now developed the capacity both to analyse and improve their business processes on a continuous basis, leading to a continuous improvement in organizational performance and product quality. For example, the company has begun to experiment with benchmarking its activities against other, 'leading edge' organizations. This has provided a valuable source of ideas and, perhaps even more importantly, a sense of what is possible. In future, benchmarking will be included as a standard element of management responsibilities.

The company recognizes that it still has a long way to go before the transformation is effected, and that in any case the focus must be on continuing development and improvement. Nevertheless, there is a belief that the attitudes and behaviour of the company's senior management have begun to change, and that their skills have developed significantly in the course of the exercise. This is now beginning to permeate down into the management group generally. As an example of this, managers cite the company's growing willingness to seek continuing customer feedback and to respond quickly and effectively to customer needs. There is also a much clearer sense of purpose and accountability among the management group as a whole, and the first-line management team is becoming increasingly committed to the process.

Among the wider workforce, the changes are only just beginning to be apparent. Enthusiasm for team-building is growing, to the point where employees are actively volunteering to undertake training. Many are beginning to feel more involved and to accept growing accountability, and the expectation is that this will be significantly reinforced by the full implementation of the performance management process.

The culture change process will continue over the next year and beyond. Overall, the company believes that the great value of its approach is that it has combined a very hard focus on performance improvement with a softer emphasis on developing skills and changing attitudes. The company's performance improvement achievements have been delivered and supported, in part, by the development of new skills and ways of working. People are becoming clearer about their roles and responsibilities, and their activities are being supported by an expanding 'kit bag' of tools and approaches which can be applied to manage change in the longer term. This has been underpinned by the overt linkage of all activities and all parts of the organization to the company's explicit vision, values and goals. Above all, perhaps, the company has benefited from the experience of 'learning by doing', particularly in the improvement teams. Although external support has been sought where appropriate, the company has worked hard to develop its own solutions and strategies, building capability and commitment in the process.

At the same time, these new capabilities are reinforced by an awareness that the initiative has produced positive outputs even in the comparatively short term. The company has seen already that culture change and quality development can deliver substantial business benefits. Over the coming years, the company expects that the practical impact of business and performance improvement, supported by developing capabilities at all levels, will drive and sustain the process of culture change that has now begun.

Sources: Nick Wellink, Managing Director, Paper Making Division
Oliver Acland, Personnel Director
Alun Lewis, Finishing Manager

II. Royal Mail

Background

Royal Mail, in its current form, was founded in 1986, following the division of the Post Office into discrete businesses. Royal Mail comprises around 75 per cent of the overall group, alongside Post Office Counters Limited, Parcelforce, and a number of smaller businesses and centralized support operations in areas such as information technology and procurement.

Royal Mail currently employs some 170,000 staff across the UK and has a business turnover of £4 billion per annum. To give an indication of the size of its overall operations, Royal Mail has some 2,500 properties, a road transport fleet of around 30,000 vehicles, and handles over 60 million items of mail every day. In the course of a year, Royal Mail will deliver over 15 billion items to more than 24 million UK businesses and personal addresses. As these statistics indicate, the decision to undertake radical changes in the organization's structure, processes and culture was bound to be a bold and challenging step.

In the years following the initial restructuring into discrete businesses, Royal Mail's strategy has become increasingly clearly defined. In October 1988, it introduced the total quality management initiative, which was perceived as the first step on a seven- or eight-year-long journey towards total quality. At that stage, too, it began to formulate an ambitious business mission, along with the key goals and values needed to underpin this (figure 1).

At the time, these goals and values were seen as *aspirations*, and managers knew that Royal Mail was still some way short of achieving the required standards. Indeed, at that stage, the organization deliberately chose not to publish the mission and value statements, to avoid undermining their impact through employee cynicism. Nevertheless, there was an acute

273

Figure 1
The Royal Mail's mission and values

As Royal Mail our mission is to be recognised as the best organisation in the World distributing text and packages.

We shall achieve this:

- Excelling in our Collection, Processing, Distribution and Delivery Arrangements
- Establishing a partnership with our customers to understand, agree, and meet their changing requirements
- Operating profitably by efficient services which our customers consider to be value for money
- Creating a work environment which recognises and rewards the commitment of all employees to customer satisfaction
- Recognising our responsibilities as part of the social, industrial and commercial life of the country
- Being forward-looking and innovative

We each care about:

- Our Customers and their requirements for:

      Reliability
      Value for Money
      Accessibility
      Courtesy
      Integrity
      Security
      Prompt and Timely Response

- All our fellow employees and their needs for:

      Respect
      Training and Development
      Involvement
      Recognition and Reward

- The way we do our job and the way it affects our customers both inside and outside the Business
- Our role in the life of the community

We are proud to be part of Royal Mail.

awareness that, all too often, organizations produce high-flown mission statements which are never translated into action. Royal Mail was determined to make the mission and value statements work.

The road to change

The total quality initiative formed the first step on the path towards achieving these goals. This included the systematic development of an integrated Quality Network, comprising local Quality Support Managers and a Headquarters Quality Department. The intention was that the Quality Network should play a facilitatory role, providing the necessary support in all parts of the organization for managers to work effectively towards total quality. Following its formal commitment to total quality in 1988, Royal Mail then took a further significant step forward with the implementation of its Customer First programme, which began in January 1989. This included preliminary training and education, the promotion of an external customer focus, the development of the internal customer-supplier concept, the achievement through team contributions of improvements in business and operational processes, and the introduction of a formal process for benchmarking against external comparator organizations. These achievements were further underpinned by the application of significantly improved methods of measuring external customer satisfaction, including quantitative measures of performance and a qualitative measure of customer satisfaction – the Customer Perception Index.

In parallel with the development of the total quality initiative, Royal Mail also embarked on a major review of employee relations within Royal Mail, which led to significant changes in employee relations practices and policies. Employee satisfaction measures became a key part of Royal Mail's success criteria. Taken together, these various activities prepared the ground for the major step change that was to come.

The need for change

In many ways, the need for major change was not obvious. The employees of Royal Mail had undergone structural change comparatively recently, with the creation of the discrete businesses. Royal Mail itself was perceived as successful both internally and, to a considerable degree, by customers and the public at large. The business had been profitable for the previous 15 years. Quality standards, although not perfect, were improving significantly. According to independent measures, Royal Mail's image in the community was second to none among the major public and private sector utilities. There was no other immediate external impetus for change.

At the same time, there was an awareness that Royal Mail was some way from achieving its defined business goals. There was considerable scope for performance improvement in customer service, product development, operational processes, employee relations and leadership, quality and profitability. The business saw great merit in building on its strengths – in seeking to improve the business when times were good, rather than in the face of external pressures.

Nonetheless, this decision brought its own problems. It is never easy to change the structure of an organization, particularly an organization as large as Royal Mail. It is even harder to change the *culture* of such an organization – and there was no doubt that the achievement of the business goals would involve a significant shift in organizational attitudes and values as well as in operational methods. The business had to take its employees along a highly challenging road at a time when they would see no great imperative to change.

In short, Royal Mail faced a major challenge – to effect a

dramatic step change, not to save a struggling business, but to make a successful business even more successful. It was recognized that the defined business goals would involve major change across all aspects of its operations, including its culture, structure, business processes, the roles and jobs of individual employees, rules and regulations, and the overall climate of industrial relations. Specific goals included an increased customer focus, decentralization, reduction in management layers, widening of profit accountability, improvements in individual competence and capability, improvements in management systems and processes, and development of team skills.

At the same time, Royal Mail recognized that this level of change would involve a period of major insecurity for the workforce. There was a real risk that this insecurity would reduce employee morale and commitment, and would undermine the very goals and values the business was seeking to achieve. To minimize this risk, the business believed that it was important to make the transitional phase as short as possible. The business therefore set itself some demanding deadlines. The process of change was scheduled to begin in December 1990, and the intention was to have the new structure in place by the Spring of 1992.

Against the background described above, Royal Mail also felt that this focus on revolutionary, rather than evolutionary, change would bring additional benefits:

- First, it would help 'unfreeze' the highly durable culture that had inevitably developed in an organization as large, long-established and complex as Royal Mail. There was some concern that the traditional Royal Mail culture would otherwise be sufficiently resilient to accommodate, for example, the languages and systems of total quality without fundamentally changing employee attitudes or behaviour.
- Second, it would demonstrate the seriousness of Royal Mail's intention to change. There was concern that, without such an explicit declaration of intent, managers would

make minor alterations to their style or activities without
recognizing the genuinely radical changes that were implied
by the new business mission.

- Third, it was felt that Royal Mail's progress towards total
  quality would be accelerated by some comparatively rapid
  demonstration of achievement. If the organization could
  show that it had achieved real business benefits from
  radical change, this would underline the potential benefits
  of the total quality approach.
- Finally, there was a perception that rapid change would
  quickly become a way of life for Royal Mail, as for most
  other business organizations. Increasingly, the business
  would need the capability and the will to respond swiftly
  to volatile environmental and market pressures. The
  proposed changes would help the organization to develop
  the skills needed to adapt efficiency to future commercial
  demands.

These factors indicated the need for a process of revolutionary
change, not as an alternative to Royal Mail's long-term
objectives but as a further contributor and motivator towards
the achievement of those objectives.

The Business Development initiative

Against this background, the process of change, which Royal
Mail called 'Business Development', began to take shape. At
the very beginning, Royal Mail made what turned out to be
a critical decision. It was decided that, to achieve lasting
change, the change process had to embody the same methods
and values that Royal Mail wished to see operating in the
new organization. Several key themes emerged very quickly:

- *Involvement.* If Royal Mail were to achieve real and lasting
  change, it was necessary to involve employees as much as

possible in the development of the change process. It was essential to ensure that employees understood the organization's goals and objectives, and that the change process had taken full account of their views and concerns. Above all, Royal Mail needed to ensure that employees had 'bought in' to the ultimate outcomes of Business Development. At the same time, it was intended that the Business Development processes should serve as a role model for the kinds of involvement that would be central to the values and activities of the new organization.

- *Empowerment*. One of the key objectives was to increase the power and accountability of managers throughout the organization. It was felt that, as the business grew increasingly complex, diverse and customer-focused, it would be essential for managers to escape the confines of the traditional 'rule bound' culture and to exercise their own initiative in responding to internal and external customer needs. Similarly, at all levels and in all parts of the business, managers would need to develop an increasing awareness of and responsibility for profitability. It was essential, therefore, that the change process was seen to promote empowerment and accountability from the start.

- *Teamworking*. In the face of an increasingly volatile business environment, Royal Mail believed that traditional management hierarchies and reporting relationships would become increasingly irrelevant. In describing the goals and outputs of Business Development, Bill Cockburn, then Managing Director of Royal Mail and now Chief Executive of the Post Office, often referred to the new structure as an 'inverted pyramid'. At the top of the pyramid are all those employees – most obviously the postmen and postwomen – who deal directly with the customers. The structure below them, with the Board and senior management at the bottom, supports and services these 'front line' staff to ensure that they can effectively meet the needs of their customers. In practice, the ability to respond swiftly and appropriately to diverse customer

needs is likely to involve complex networks of supporting
relationships, overlaying the traditional functional and
geographical structures. Again, therefore, it was crucial
that the principles and techniques of networking and
teamworking should be embodied in the Business Development process.

The architecture of change

In the face of these various needs and objectives, the Business
Development process was an extremely delicate balancing
act. On the one hand, it was seen as critical to act in
accordance with the principles outlined above – involvement,
empowerment and networking. On the other hand, the whole
process was driven by tight deadlines and the need to ensure
that the business achieved its highly ambitious business goals.
It was also necessary to act in accordance with Royal Mail's
declared values in managing the people issues in particular.
Alongside this, there was also the need to ensure that day-to-
day performance standards did not slip while the change
process was going on – this itself was no mean feat given that
there was bound to be considerable disruption, both practical
and psychological, in the course of the exercise. To achieve
these goals, a Business Development Team was established,
led by Kevin Williams, now Royal Mail's Strategic Operations
Director. This team, which worked to the Royal Mail
Executive Committee, was carefully selected to include a
cross-section of high-quality skills, and was charged with
driving and managing the overall process.

Royal Mail began by analysing the strengths and weaknesses
of the current organization, with the aim of identifying the
strengths it should build on and the opportunities for doing
better. Over a very short period, workshops were conducted
with over 1,000 employees, including senior, middle and
front-line managers. On this basis, the Business Development

Team began to develop the strategy for achieving change. Although the very early stages of the project had inevitably been confidential to senior management, from this stage on every effort was made to communicate information and progress to employees, and to encourage reaction and involvement wherever possible.

Some key decisions were taken very quickly. First, nine new geographical Divisions were defined. These would cover the country, replacing the former structure of 64 Districts (figure 2). In developing this new structure, the intention was

Figure 2
Royal Mail's nine new Divisions

to ensure that all the Divisional Directors and General Managers could sit down at one table and operate easily as a team. Similarly, it was intended that the respective management teams within each Division could also operate effectively as a team.

Another early decision was to decentralize as many as

possible of the organization's functions and processes, in order to increase accountability and empowerment. Royal Mail Headquarters was ultimately reduced from a centralized support operation with 1,700 staff to a strategically focused leadership operation with only 162 staff.

On the basis of these initial decisions, the Business Development Team developed a complex pattern of inter-linked functional and geographical networks to develop and oversee the change process. At the top level, the project was driven and coordinated by the National Business Development Team. Each member of this team then chaired a Divisional Business Development Team (comprising appropriate regional level managers) and a National Functional Team (comprising managers from respective functions across the Divisions). These various teams interlinked, so that any given individual would have defined roles within several teams. Each team was then responsible for developing specific aspects of policy or practices, as delegated by the National Team. This kind of networking was then replicated at lower levels in the organization to provide the basis for involving staff in the development of the change process. A simplified picture of the structure is given in figure 3.

This network architecture was highly complex, but it produced a number of major benefits:

- it provided an efficient mechanism for developing and delivering strategy, policy and practice at appropriate levels in the organization
- it provided the basis for a major exercise of involvement and participation in the development of the change process, which ultimately involved literally thousands of Royal Mail employees
- it ensured that those involved in developing the change process had multiple accountabilities – for example, national, regional and functional. This helped to prevent factionalism, and ensured that the ultimate strategy took account of all relevant stakeholders

Figure 3
Business Development Planning Process

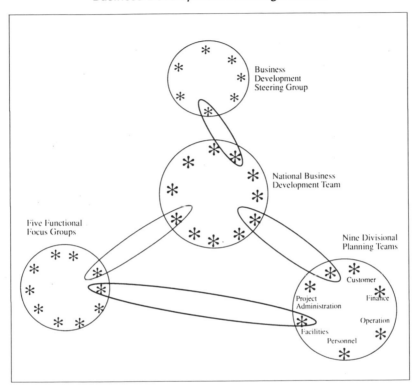

- it provided a foundation and a role model for the networking culture that would underpin the new organization

The network was used to develop detailed and comprehensive plans about all aspects of the proposed new organization. These included key national developments, including the evolution of the four new market-focused strategic business units – National, Streamline, International and Cashco – which were designed to provide a sharp focus for developing new markets and products. Other key national developments included the formation of the new Strategic Headquarters, the divisionalization of the sales function, the configuration of many of the former support functions as contractually driven Consultancy Support units, the establishment of processes to promote and support innovation and new product development, and the definition of the overall architecture of management processes to underpin the new organization.

Within this national framework, the network was then used to develop detailed policies, plans and processes for functional operations in the new organization and for the structures and activities of the new nine Divisions. This included, for example, developing the role, objectives and structures of each of the management functions in the new organization, developing the management structures of the new Divisions, and dealing with a range of practical issues.

Using this project architecture, Royal Mail believes that it succeeded in meeting the competing demands for speed on the one hand, and for sensitivity and professionalism on the other. At times, the process was undoubtedly nerve-wracking. Kevin Williams has subsequently commented that: 'There were times when you yearned for the "sealed room" project team method where a select group hid away and produced an overall final report on what everyone should do. Then you realized that that approach had failed again and again.'

Delivering results

On the basis of these detailed plans, implementation began towards the end of 1991. Initial stages included a massive selection process to identify all those managers who would be part of the new organization, with the intention of ensuring that appointments in the new structure were made on the best possible bank of information. By the end of the project, well over 10,000 managers had been through the process, which included extended assessment centre techniques to pinpoint areas for personal development. The appraisal process was accompanied by detailed job evaluation for all newly created posts, and the appointment of managers to the new organization. The appointments activity itself was highly complex, aimed at taking full account both of individual preferences and of suitability for the new posts.

Beyond this, the process of implementation was managed by a team of designated Project Managers, responsible for delivering implementation within each Division. The Divisional Planning Teams continued to exist, acting as advisory and focus groups, but the day-to-day implementation process was managed by a Project Implementation Team. Detailed implementation plans, at successive levels of detail, were developed within each Division, with defined processes for project reporting and closure. The overall aim, which seems in practice to have been achieved, was to ensure a seamless process of 'passing the batons' (to borrow Royal Mail's graphic terminology) between the old organization and the new.

The outcome

Using this approach, there is no doubt that Royal Mail succeeded in delivering major change against highly ambitious deadlines. The overall organization was restructured into the new nine Divisions, and Royal Mail planned and implemented the structure that would operate within each Division. It changed the focus of the Headquarters, and dramatically reduced its size. It shifted the focus of the organization from cost- to profit-centres. It created four market-focused strategic business development units (SBUs), designed to champion specific sections of the business's highly diverse market, working in partnership with the Divisions. In addition, five Business Centres were formed, whose prime role was to take a range of services off 'free issue' and 'sell' to the Divisions and SBUs. Overall – although Royal Mail stresses that this was by no means the primary objective – the exercise resulted in annual savings in the order of £65 million. All managers were taken through a formal assessment process designed to assess their suitability for taking up the roles required by the new organization. In transferring staff to the new organization, a total of nearly 12,000 appointments were made. By the beginning of April 1992, all these changes had been implemented, and the new organization was ready to begin operations.

During this period of intense change, there were inevitably some fluctuations in employee morale. Nevertheless, Royal Mail believes – and this has been confirmed through initial soundings from employee surveys and a subsequent evaluation review conducted by independent consultants – that it has avoided significant problems with morale or motivation. This reflects a number of factors. First, the high level of involvement meant that employees and trade unions were genuinely contributing to the process. Second, the sheer speed of the whole exercise helped to minimize uncertainty. Third, despite the major staff reductions that occurred, Royal Mail was able to avoid compulsory redundancies, through a combination of voluntary severance and a freeze on recruitment throughout the life of the project. And, fourth, the whole exercise was underpinned by a comprehensive communications strategy. This included: regular Business Development Updates, outlining progress and developments on a periodic basis; presentations and roadshows conducted by the managing director and senior managers; videos, including one which won an industry award; and a variety of training activities that were given a communications dimension.

Conclusions

Royal Mail believes that, to date, the change process has been remarkably successful and has provided a very effective foundation both for delivering the stated mission and values and for coping with whatever changes may emerge in the structure of the Post Office in the next decade. The business results for 1992/93 are expected to eclipse previous records across all fronts. Kevin Williams comments that: 'It proves in practice what we all know in theory: the time spent during planning, involving people whose behaviour has to alter as a result of the process of change, pays enormous dividends when it comes to implementation.'

Other immediate measures are also very encouraging. The financial year during which the exercise took place produced Royal Mail's best ever results, across all areas, financial and operational. This is seen as a fitting tribute to those who had been effectively performing two jobs during the period of transition. Subsequent to the exercise, as indicated above, Royal Mail commissioned a consultancy to conduct an independent review of the exercise, with the aim of producing an evaluation of the change process and highlighting key learning points, positive and negative, which could be applied to future change exercises. The overall conclusions were highly positive, suggesting that the majority of planning and change activities had been very effective. The few negative points identified reflected the speed with which the overall exercise was conducted – for example, the exercise's defined values had occasionally been compromised in the interests of achieving a satisfactory result within a tight timescale. Nevertheless, there was a widespread acceptance that the chosen route – rapid, revolutionary change – was both preferable and more effective.

The review also included an initial evaluation of the outcomes of the exercise, with the qualification that many aspects had not yet fully 'bedded down'. Again, conclusions were highly positive. The great majority of managers fully supported the aims and objectives of the exercise, and there was a widespread belief that these had been achieved. Although there was a recognition that some aspects of the new structure needed to be refined and further developed, there was a high level of confidence that the organization had built very effective foundations for future development.

Having achieved this dramatic change, Royal Mail feels that it is now well placed to move into the coming decade and the next millenium, regardless of potential changes in its operating environment and markets. Although Business Development was in many ways a highly radical exercise, it is seen as the beginning, rather than the end, of the change process – the foundations for a process of continuous improvement which will help Royal Mail achieve its ambitious business goals and maintain its declared business values.

Source: Kevin Williams, Operations Director

III. McVitie's

Background

The McVitie's Group is part of United Biscuits, one of the world's leading food manufacturers, with operations in 19 countries worldwide. McVitie's itself is Europe's second largest manufacturer of biscuits. The company operates in eight European countries, as well as the United States, and has leading market positions in the UK, the Netherlands, Hungary and the Nordic region. In recent years, the company has continued to strengthen its position as one of the dominant forces in European biscuits, in the face of an increasing intensification of competition and the difficulties of the economic climate in Europe.

Over the last few years, the company has expanded rapidly into Europe, through a mixture of acquisition, strategic alliances and organic growth. Key acquisitions include Verkade in the Netherlands, Oxford Biscuits in Denmark, and – the company's first venture into Central Europe – Györi Keksz in Hungary. These kinds of acquisitions, coupled with continuing growth in the company's existing operations, have enabled it to achieve significant increases in both profit and sales year on year. At the same time, the operational and cultural challenges of acquisition, coupled with the need to ensure maximum organizational effectiveness in a highly challenging and competitive environment, have required the company to focus with increasing precision on its organizational structure, management processes, strategic goals and corporate culture.

During the late 1970s and early 1980s, McVitie's focused primarily on consolidating its already strong position in the UK marketplace. During this period, the emphasis was very much on rationalization, particularly in the factory structure, with the aim of reducing costs and maximizing production volume. The company was highly profitable, but its management believed that there was still considerable scope for developing its potential. In particular, there was a recognition that the company needed to ensure that it was as well prepared as possible for the challenges of the 1990s – expected to be a time of rapid and volatile change in the market and competitive environment.

Preparing for change

Against this general background, McVitie's began to identify the organizational characteristics that would be needed to meet these prospective challenges. The drive towards change was facilitated by a number of factors, including the recent appointment of a new Managing Director and a number of other changes in the senior management team. This allowed the organization to revisit its current objectives, values and processes with a radicalism which might have been more difficult under a more established leadership. In retrospect, the company believes that this enabled it to challenge its previous ways of thinking and behaving, and to seize opportunities and exploit potential that might otherwise have been overlooked.

Apart from the general desire to improve further the company's organizational effectiveness, some specific change requirements were already becoming evident. For example, rationalization in the wider United Biscuit group in the late 1980s, particularly relating to the respective roles of McVitie's and KP, were compelling McVitie's to rethink its relationship with the marketplace. For the first time, McVitie's would be responsible for all biscuit production in the Group, including both 'branded' and 'retailer brand' (or 'own brand') products. The company therefore needed to assess how it could most effectively undertake this new corporate role.

In developing its strategy and values for the coming decade, the company was influenced by a number of broad market or competitive factors. First, there was an awareness of current and potential developments in consumer tastes and expectations, which in turn would influence potential markets. Major factors here included an overall increase in consumer sophistication; a population that was, in general terms, growing older and wealthier and was therefore looking for better value products; and changes in lifestyles that in turn were promoting a growing interest in snack foods. In addition to these consumer changes, there was a growing intensification and 'Europeanization' of competition – exemplified by, say, Nestlé's acquisition of Rowntree in 1988 – and the increasing emergence of Europe-wide purchasing groups, strengthening the influence of the customer. The impact of these various factors meant that, by the start of the 1990s, McVitie's needed to be in a strong position to:

- compete on a Europe-wide scale, with effective marketing, selling and distribution networks in all of the major markets
- secure and develop its core UK business in the face of growing competition from traditional and new competitors
- exploit changes in customer requirements and expectations as effectively and efficiently as possible

With these objectives in mind, it was recognized that there was considerable scope for development in the company's organizational structure and culture, in its capacity to respond to the external market, and in the efficiency and effectiveness of its internal processes and systems. Moreover, it was felt that, if the company was to be in a position fully to exploit the opportunities that lay ahead, this would require not merely incremental improvements in systems or structures, but a fundamental reappraisal of the whole organization.

At the same time, McVitie's was seeking to introduce these radical changes, not in response to some business or performance crisis, but to further improve an already highly successful business. The company was highly profitable, with an excellent range of products that were highly regarded both by domestic consumers and the wider marketplace. It was continuing to achieve year on year growth in sales and profits. It had already experienced some basic rationalization and restructuring to reduce costs and improve efficiency. In this context, some members of the company inevitably questioned whether further radical change was really needed, or whether the company could achieve its objectives through additional incremental development. The company's senior management, however, were in no doubt that McVitie's needed to take advantage of its current successes to prepare for the major challenges that would lie ahead.

In part, indeed, the company could be seen as a victim of its own success. There was a perception that, like many successful companies, it had in some places grown complacent and comfortable with its existing standards and achievements. There was a tendency to 'play safe' and to be satisfied with performance which, although good, was sometimes less than optimal. During the early phase of the change process, in 1990, for example, the company commissioned external reviews of the headquarters and manufacturing operations to identify scope for organizational improvement. In general terms, the reviews identified factors such as an excessive number of management layers, an excessive degree of 'double checking' or upward referrals, unclear accountabilities, and a focus on maintaining current systems and performance rather than on innovation or development. More specifically, the reviews identified an excessive emphasis on 'functionalization', with a tendency for activities to be driven by functional priorities, rather than by the needs of the wider market or the company as a whole. In support of this, the responses to an employee attitude survey conducted at around the same time, although highly positive in terms of job satisfaction and employee commitment, indicated a culture with a tendency to complacency and resistance to change. As a result, the company was failing to exploit many of its undoubted assets – such as the substantial reservoir of skills and talents and the high level of commitment to the company and its objectives.

Planning for change

With these aims in view, the company began to explore the potential for change and restructuring, using consultant-driven workshops and interviews with the senior management team to help crystallize the principal options for change. The process was underpinned by a number of specific objectives:

- the capacity to focus the company's resources as precisely and effectively as possible on its key marketplaces
- the ability to facilitate decision-making as closely as possible to the point of implementation, minimizing the need for upward referral
- the capacity to react efficiently and appropriately to market and other changes, while maintaining the required levels of volume output
- a focus on key businesses and markets rather than on functions, with an accompanying shift in the company's perceived 'power base'

Having explored a number of organizational options to achieve these objectives, the company rapidly decided that the new organization would need to be structured around Business Units, which themselves would be aligned to key markets. The intention was that the day-to-day business and its operations would be driven by these Units, which would provide a precise focus on their respective markets. The role of the McVitie's (UK) Board would then be redefined to provide a longer-term strategic focus separated from the operational activities and accountabilities of the Business Units. The Board would therefore be responsible for overall Group business strategy, for monitoring the collective performance of the Business Units, for developing acquisition and partnership strategy, and for identifying and optimizing cross-business synergies.

Over the succeeding months, the role and structure of the Business Units were clarified and refined. Three Business

Units were identified, to reflect the company's three distinct markets and product ranges – snacks, classics and variety. A further Business Unit was set up to deal with export issues. The intention was that the Units should be largely autonomous, each with the internal capacity to respond fully to the demands of its respective market. To this end, the Unit would incorporate not merely marketing resources, but also expertise in commercial issues, finance, quality assurance, new product development, planning and forecasting. In other words, the Unit would offer a comparatively high level of vertical integration, with responsibility for developing its own market strategy, managing a portfolio of products, developing new products, pricing issues, and the management of customer service.

The company's manufacturing capacity, however, would remain separate from the Business Units. Manufacturing had always been 'multidisciplinary', in the sense that each factory had serviced a wide variety of products. The intention was that this would continue, in order to provide the flexibility required to meet changing market needs. In effect, Manufacturing would become a service division, contracted to Business Units as appropriate, with Sales acting as an internal brokerage function. At the same time, in order to promote a stronger emphasis on the overall manufacturing process and to encourage cross-functional teamworking, the factories were restructured on an operational basis with day-to-day operational accountability resting with Operations Managers. These individuals would be responsible for production and maintenance activities, and would be supported by a range of support services ranging from Factory Services to Finance and Personnel.

From this basis, the new organization structure was developed, with considerable attention being paid to the interaction between the different parts of the business. Above all, it was seen as essential that relationships, particularly between the Board, the Business Units and Manufacturing, were as smooth as possible. The intention was that the new structure should provide the benefits of flexibility, market focus and an entrepreneurial culture, without losing the synergies of the overall organization.

Evaluating change

The new structure came into being in early 1991. In the months prior to this, there was substantial investment in the new systems and procedures that would be required to make the organization work. There was also investment in the human resource aspects of the new operation, including individual development in areas such as effective teamworking, designed to provide managers with the skills and commitment to meet the challenges of the new organization. At the same time, the company recognized that, in its highly competitive environment, there was no room for excessive delay. The intention was to ensure that the structure was as effective as possible prior to implementation, but then to introduce the changes as quickly as possible. The expectation was that a rapid implementation would minimize organizational uncertainty, enable managers quickly to grow accustomed to the new processes, and encourage employees to accept the challenges of the new organization rather than clinging to their old ways of behaving. Alongside this, however, the company recognized that it would be necessary subsequently to conduct a formal evaluation to ensure that the new structures and processes were refined and developed on the basis of experience.

To this end, therefore, in early 1992 – approximately a year after the introduction of the new organization – the company carried out a formal evaluation, incorporating a major written survey of some 200 individuals spread across the new organizational structure, including the Business Units, Sales, Manufacturing and Headquarters. In general, the findings of this evaluation were very positive. The great majority of respondents felt that both the role of the Business Units and their own personal accountabilities were clear in the new structure, and in general there was a perception that the new structure had brought significant business benefits. In particular, respondents felt that the structure had brought significantly greater clarity of accountability, a more precise customer and market focus, and more effective teamworking. At the same time, the evaluation also identified some areas of weakness, notably in respect of new product development and the marketing and sales of 'retailer' brands. It was felt that both of these areas needed to receive a higher level of priority than had initially been the case in the new structure. To reinforce this, specific new roles were created to manage these two areas, further reinforcing the effectiveness of the new structure.

In the longer term, the company believes that a significant change in its management culture is already evident. The focus of the company has moved from the management of functions to the management of the overall business, with an emphasis on proactively managing products and markets rather than on reactive 'firefighting'. There is now widespread commitment to the objectives and values of the company as a whole, rather than to the parochial needs of particular functions or departments. The overall structure is now seen as *enabling* rather than controlling – that is, it provides the clarity of accountability and the level of support needed to enable managers to maximize their contribution. It has reduced dysfunctional competition between different parts of the business, and replaced these with a greater clarity of relationships and a growing emphasis on cross-functional teamworking. Overall the company believes that – though it was undoubtedly successful prior to the changes – its new structure and the resulting culture have provided it with the competitive edge needed to grow and prosper even in times of significant economic difficulty.

Looking to the future

The new structure has also provided the company with the foundation needed to develop its wider role in Europe. In recent years, McVitie's European presence has increased dramatically through a process of rapid acquisition and organization growth. The company has aimed to ensure that this growth is tightly managed both in terms of operational performance, and in terms of ensuring a coherence of objectives and values across the McVitie's Group as a whole. To achieve this, the growth has been managed in line with the philosophy which underpins the UK structure – that is, to ensure clear accountability, a precise but creative focus on defined markets, and the combination of local ownership and commitment with the synergies of a large organization. The company has therefore created a zonal structure, covering respectively the UK, the Nordic countries, France and the Benelux countries, and central and southern Europe. Each of these zones has its own profit responsibility, but is also supported by central resources designed to reinforce cross-business synergy. In short, the aim has been to create 'the best of both worlds' – that is, a strong sense of local identity and culture underpinned by the overall values, objectives and disciplines of the McVitie's Group as a whole.

McVitie's believes that it now has in place a structure and a culture which will facilitate significant further growth across Europe, both through acquisition and organic growth. The company is now structured to accommodate further acquisitions efficiently and effectively if appropriate opportunities should arise. At the same time, all parts of the organization are now seen as capable of reacting swiftly and effectively to changes in their respective markets. The company believes that by introducing a radical structural change, with a clear focus on the effective delivery of *outputs* to customers and markets, it has effected changes in management values and attitudes which could not have been brought about by more gradual forms of organization

development. At the same time, the company believes that it
has significantly improved its management skills base, and
developed the effectiveness of its overall business processes
and systems. More directly, the company expects that, by
1994, it will have achieved a £20 million reduction in
overheads in the UK without factory closures. As a result of
these changes in structure, processes and culture, the company
has prospered even in the midst of a Europe-wide recession,
and believes that it is now well placed to ensure continuing
major growth in its European presence over the coming
decade.

Source: Paul Grant, Personnel Director

Conclusions

The main objectives of the research were to identify the methods and processes that have been used by organizations to change their culture and the role of the personnel function in culture change. In order to achieve these ends we undertook a literature review and case studies in fifteen widely differing organizations. The limitations of the research have been made clear in the Introduction.

The definition of organizational culture determines the nature of the entity and consequently what is to be changed, how it is changed and indeed whether or not it can be changed. From the outset we have rejected the approaches to culture that define it, in advance, as an invisible and unconscious entity which, by definition, is almost impossible to measure, change or investigate. Such approaches are intuitive and appealing but have virtually no objective evidence to support them. It is important to recognize that to define organizational culture in this way prevents it from being empirically investigated and impedes the development of our knowledge and understanding of the concept. We consider such approaches to be both premature and unhelpful, and – organizations beware – given to quackery.

It seems to us to be more sensible to define culture in such a way that it can be measured, changed, related to organizational performance and subjected to empirical investigation. This would appear to be more useful to organizations, practitioners and academics. Consequently, we have utilized a working definition, which is of practical value and theoretically defensible. We have defined organizational culture as 'the commonly held and relatively stable beliefs, attitudes and values that exist in the organization'.

There follows a brief outline of the major conclusions drawn from our research.

- Whilst organizational culture refers to common beliefs, attitudes and values, it is the beliefs, attitudes and values that *individuals* possess that must ultimately be changed if culture is to change.
- Beliefs underlie the formation of attitudes and values and consequently the target of culture change is the beliefs that individual employees hold. This acts as a yardstick against which to measure the likely success of change attempts, ie how likely is it that the methods employed have changed people's beliefs?
- People's behaviour is influenced by their beliefs about the rewards and costs associated with a particular behaviour, the probability of success or failure, their own capability, the resources available and the expectations of others. These beliefs largely result from their perceptions of the contingencies in the work environment. Behaviour has its roots as much in beliefs about the demands and constraints in the work environment as it does in the personal attitudes and values of the individual. If organizational culture change is to be linked to organizational performance then the beliefs that individuals hold about behaviour need to be addressed.
- Culture change can be imposed by changing these situational contingencies. In part, our case study organizations did do this but also recognized that a multi-method approach that included techniques designed to change individuals' values was required if significant costs were to be avoided. These costs may include: alienative involvement, dissatisfaction, lack of commitment, minimal effort, high labour turnover, absenteeism, demarcation, as well as the attendant costs of close supervision, excessive formalization of rules and procedures and lack of flexibility. Thus one can impose a change in common beliefs and behaviour by changing, for example, reward and control systems, but one is unlikely to change people's values in this way.
- A strong organizational culture results when individuals come to agree with – that is, internalize – the values of the

organization. This cannot be imposed but can be fostered by common and shared experience, involvement and persuasion. The benefits of a strong organizational culture are a commitment to the organization, effort above minimum, behaviour that is self-reinforced, spontaneity, cooperation, proaction and initiative in the service of organizational values, even in the absence of prescribed rules, supervision and external rewards.

- Typically, our case study organizations have attempted to change both the type and strength of an aspect of their culture. The methods they have employed have been a combination of: selection, re-deployment and redundancy, role modelling, group participation, role playing, management education, skills training, formal communications, one-to-one counselling, advertising and the development of the corporate image; as well as a realignment of the reward and control systems of the organization. Thus organizations have attempted to change their culture by changing people, changing places, changing beliefs, changing behaviour, changing the structures, systems and technology and by changing the corporate image. Individual organizations have used a wide variety of these methods; for example new people were recruited and others lost, people were moved around, training was cascaded, briefing groups were introduced, new skills were learnt, the reward and appraisal systems were realigned and a new shiny company image created.

- The process of change and the roles of the change agents are of critical importance in culture change. When one is trying to change the way people think on an organization-wide basis, the management of change demands special attention. 'Focused OD' would appear to be an appropriate term to use, for in all our case study organizations change has been strategy-led. The organizations have undertaken a strategic review early in the change process and, in this way, culture change has been linked to organizational effectiveness. Organizations need to recognize that strategic choice carries implications for the culture that will be appropriate and vice versa.

- Culture is both an input and an output: for instance senior managers are as much a product of the organization's culture as they are creators of it. Consequently, unfreezing the organization's culture is a significant issue. A number of factors appear to have enabled organizations to break out of this vicious circle: financial crisis; intervention by external stakeholders – for example, major shareholders, clients or, in the case of public bodies, Government constraints or initiatives; change at the top, in particular a new CEO from outside the organization; and an awareness of changes or impending changes in the organization's environment, for example changes in legislation, developments in IT, competitor activity, future privatization and so on. It would appear that the existence of clear criteria of success, the nature of the organization's political constitution and the extent to which the organization is externally focused are important factors underlying the ability of the organization to initiate culture change.
- Successful change requires leadership and, because of the nature of culture, this needs to come from within the organization. Outside consultants can play a supporting role when necessary, but relying on them is not enough. The CEO has a critical role to play. Culture change will not happen without clear leadership and commitment at the top of the organization. The line manager also has to be aware of his or her role, as a role model and an internal facilitator of change.
- Personnel has a number of roles to play in the management and implementation of the organization's culture and its change. First, it has a role in making the executive more aware of the cultural implications of strategic change. Secondly, it has a role to play as a process expert in the management of change. And lastly, its main role is the implementation of change through, for example, the selection, reward, induction and training systems of the organization.

As our case studies have shown, personnel can make an invaluable contribution to the management of culture change. However, in order to do so personnel practitioners need a greater strategic knowledge, vision and commercial awareness than is frequently the case. If personnel is to make an effective contribution to culture change, it requires a Board level presence in the organization and process expertise. The personnel function also needs to understand that most of its more traditional activities impinge upon the culture of the organization.

- The refreezing of the organization's culture results from the re-alignment of organizational systems, low turnover (particularly amongst the executive group), success and sustained and consistent effort. It takes a long time – three to five years seems to be the typical guess – for a new culture to develop where the organization's values have been internalized and become taken for granted.
- Culture change is costly. However, among our case study organizations there are some impressive financial turnarounds. We are not suggesting that we have provided any proof of the cost-effectiveness of cultural change. Nonetheless, it is difficult to see how a change in the very fabric of the organization, in how its members think and behave, could do anything other than impact upon the bottom line. The more important questions would appear to be how to change the culture of the organization and how to link such change to strategic requirements.

In reading the literature relating to organizational culture we were disappointed to find the ambiguities which exist in the use of key concepts and the relative lack of good quality research. Myths and stories abound! How can we develop our knowledge in this area? The most pressing need is for measures of culture that are empirically valid. Such instruments can be used diagnostically as a change tool to help organizations identify their existing culture and hence the cultural constraints, given current or future strategy. The instruments can also be used in research to clarify the nature of culture, to identify in a more rigorous way those methods and processes likely to change it, to identify the limits of cultural change for organizations operating in particular sectors and relatedly the cultural options open to a bank, car manufacturer, hi-tech company or whatever.

Index